# Community in Urban–Rural Systems

# STUDIES IN URBAN–RURAL DYNAMICS

## Series Editors

Gregory M. Fulkerson and Alexander R. Thomas, SUNY Oneonta

This series focuses attention on understanding theoretically and historically the development and maintenance of Urban–Rural Systems through a spatial, demographic, and ecological perspective. It seeks a blending or reintegration of the urban, rural, and environmental research literatures under a comprehensive theoretical paradigm. As such, we further specify Urban–Rural Dynamics as analysis of human population distribution on social variables, including politics, economics, and culture.

## Recent Titles in Series

*Community in Urban-Rural Systems: Theory, Planning, and Development,* by Gregory M. Fulkerson

*City and Country: The Historical Evolution of Urban-Rural Systems,* by Alexander R. Thomas and Gregory M. Fulkerson

*The Rural Primitive in American Popular Culture: All Too Familiar,* by Karen E. Hayden

*Urban Dependency: The Inescapable Reality of the Energy Economy,* by Gregory M. Fulkerson and Alexander R. Thomas

*Urbanormativity: Reality, Representation, and Everyday Life,* by Alexander R. Thomas and Gregory M. Fulkerson

*Rural Voices: Language, Identity and Social Change across Place,* edited by Elizabeth Seale and Christine Mallinson

*Reinventing Rural: New Realities in an Urbanizing World,* edited by Alexander R. Thomas and Gregory M. Fulkerson

*Reimagining Rural: Urbanormative Portrayals of Rural Life,* edited by Gregory M. Fulkerson and Alexander R. Thomas

# Community in Urban–Rural Systems

## Theory, Planning, and Development

Gregory M. Fulkerson

LEXINGTON BOOKS
*Lanham • Boulder • New York • London*

Published by Lexington Books
An imprint of The Rowman & Littlefield Publishing Group, Inc.
4501 Forbes Boulevard, Suite 200, Lanham, Maryland 20706
www.rowman.com

86-90 Paul Street, London EC2A 4NE

British Library Cataloguing in Publication Information Available

**Library of Congress Cataloging-in-Publication Data on File**

ISBN 978-1-66691-753-6 (cloth)
ISBN 978-1-66691-755-0 (pbk.)
ISBN 978-1-66691-754-3 (electronic)

# Contents

# Introduction

## *Defining and Studying Community*

Community has remained an elusive idea both for individuals searching for an ideal place to live and for social scientists attempting to understand community through concepts, theories, and empirical observations. This book offers a new entry into a long tradition of social science scholarship on the community with the hope of providing a better understanding of how they work, what they entail, how they are interconnected, and how we can improve them. We will take a unique approach by starting from the proposition that every community exists as a node within broader urban–rural systems (Thomas and Fulkerson 2021). Some communities participate from the rural end of the spectrum, engaging in the energy economy (e.g., farming, fishing, mining, forestry, etc.). In contrast, others participate in the industry and service of urban production (Fulkerson and Thomas 2021). Urban–rural systems can be organized within a local region, across a nation, and they can span the width of the globe. In any case, location within urban–rural systems has profound implications for nearly every aspect of community life. In order to understand community, one must look not only within them, but also between them. Before unpacking these ideas, we will reflect on why one should be interested in the subject of community from a personal standpoint.

## PERSONAL SIGNIFICANCE OF COMMUNITY

As individuals, we are embedded in the communities we call home—places where we live, work, and play. Our ties to and roles in communities can be highly complex, changing and evolving through different life cycle stages. Though often overlooked, the personal significance of community lies in the profound influence it has on nearly all aspects of life, including:

- whom we associate with and call friends
- whom we date, court, and marry
- what we do in our spare time for recreation and leisure
- where we work and what we do for a living
- what kind of structure we call home—apartment, townhouse, house, and so on
- how much time we spend commuting and on which types of transportation we rely
- how much money we make and spend (cost of living)
- the kind of values and beliefs we hold
- our levels of social and political engagement
- our sense of identity and belonging
- where (and if) we attend religious services
- our actual and perceived levels of safety and security
- the quality of education and health services at our disposal

This list could be expanded far beyond this beginning. In a nutshell, the community has a lot to do with who we are, our quality of life, and whether we feel attached or estranged. The power of community lies in how it organizes an array of privileges or obstacles that may either enable or constrain our choices and behaviors as individuals. For example, we do not get to decide the quality of schools serving the community into which we are born. However, the quality of schools can profoundly enable or inhibit our ability to achieve a desirable career and satisfying life. All the ambition, drive, and motivation in the world cannot help if we are born into an oppressive community that limits our growth.

Few people stop and think about the importance of community because, in the Western world (the United States, Canada, Europe), there is a greater focus on individuals than on the populations and communities to which we belong. We are raised to believe that success or failure, fulfillment or disappointment, and general happiness in life are decided by individual action alone with little concern for context. Visit a bookstore and note the size of the section devoted to self-help. Now, visit the section devoted to the community—if there is one—and note the difference. The culture and language of individualism can contradict community interests (Bellah et al. 1985), particularly when they emphasize a preference for individual privacy and anonymity over public engagement (Glynn 1981). Another reason we fail to consider the importance of community is the level of mobility we experience living in an urban society. While traditional rural communities tied humans to the land and local community for generations, the transition to urban life has created a population that, in many cases, has the power to choose where it wants to live. The typical American, for instance, will move 11.7 times in their lifetime (US Census 2021). However, most of that (9.1 times on average) happens between eighteen and forty-five. Living in multiple communities can bewilder individuals, as they experience new sets of norms, customs, and ways of life. Yet it may also expose them to a broader range of possibilities and experiences.

Mobility takes place when individuals are resigned to the idea that they will need to go wherever life takes them, forgetting the choice they have in the matter. Usually, the willingness to move is predicated on the notion that professional fulfillment will require it. There may be a sound reason for this since the geography of the economy does often demand mobility. Employment is a powerful determinant in molding migration decisions, but it is not the only factor. Broader concerns with the quality of life, social ties, or levels of community attachment can come into play (see Kasarda and Janowitz 1974; Brehm et al. 2004). It is essential to take a more nuanced and complex approach to the question of what drives us to either stay where we are or move to another community. Indeed, the values of the community we are born into may include expectations to stay or go. Youths in rural communities are sometimes encouraged to leave since the expectation for a better life is thought to lie somewhere outside the community. This expectation perpetuates the brain drain and hollows out rural communities across generations (Carr and Kefalas 2009). Others are pressured to stay put in order to carry on a legacy, such as maintaining a multigenerational family farm, which can limit professional growth. As individuals, we live in communities, but we also have connections to wider regions, nations, and the world. Our ties to these broader systems can create push-pull conflicts within us. If we opt to stay in a community that falls short of our ideals, there may be ways to create improvements.

Our desire to invest time and effort into our communities depends partly on whether we have developed a strong sense of community. McMillan and Chavis (1986) identify four key dimensions that are the foundation for a sense of community. The first is based on membership, which involves the feeling of belonging and of being an insider. The use of shared symbols can aid in promoting membership status. The next is influence, which is how much one feels they matter in their community. Mattering is a two-way street involving how the community matters to the individual and how the individual matters to the community. The third is the dimension of integration and the fulfillment of needs, which is based on the idea that the community is rewarding for the individual—they see value in their community membership because they receive positive reinforcement. The fourth and final dimension of the sense of community is the shared emotional connection, which has to do with a feeling of sharing history and experience with other members of the community. Those with a greater sense of community generally score high on all four dimensions—feeling like they belong and matter while deriving rewards and purpose from their community. These dimensions are more likely to emerge when we have community attachment, which usually takes time to develop.

Hopefully, reading this book will help to develop a deeper understanding, reflect on the most desirable qualities, and imagine ways to improve community. Part of this involves thinking about general issues that guide planning and development—ideas we will reflect upon as we go through each chapter. It is critical to learn about the process of community change before formulating strategies to optimize community agency and development. Before we are ready to elaborate on improvements, we need to understand what makes communities tick. How do they form, persist, and experience decline or collapse? We will therefore engage in a social science of community. To this end, sociology offers a valuable lens since it is a field that focuses on how the groups, communities, networks, and societies to which we belong function and shape our lives. In a culture heavily focused on individualism, sociology provides a valuable corrective. This book will apply a sociological perspective to the community question, drawing on classic and contemporary ideas while focusing on urban-rural system dynamics that explain how communities are connected. Before explaining this, let us consider the object of our study more carefully.

## WHAT IS COMMUNITY?

The word *community* is so widely spoken and written that it evokes an extensive range of images and ideas. For example, the community is often used interchangeably to describe an aggregate of people who share some trait or characteristic. As Kuhn (2012) did, we might speak of a community of scientists. Alternatively, the term *community* has been applied to describe intimate personal relationships. These usages are not helpful for what we want to investigate—essentially, the places where people live and work, engage politically, interact socially and culturally, and experience their environment. This community-of-place approach is an important distinction since a growing body of literature adopts a virtual community perspective, almost exclusively focused on social interaction without physical territory or space (e.g., Bruhn 2011). Such scholars might study the community of social media groups, for instance. As we will discuss, social interaction is central to community—that does not mean it should be the sole focus. Thus, while there is value in virtual community research, it is not the focus of this book. Everyone lives in a physical community of one form or another, and it is this physical settlement or community-of-place to which we will turn our attention. Even the community one experiences through a social media site such as Facebook involves a spatial consideration—social networks tend to map to specific geographic locations occupied at one time or another. Thus, it turns out that even in virtual communities, physical space plays a role.

The word *community* has long troubled sociologists and other social scientists who seek precision and valid measurement for their objects of investigation. Hillery (1955) found that there were over ninety-four different definitions in use among scholars. Nevertheless, some critical areas of agreement can be discerned. In short, these boil down to people residing in a physical territory and engaging in social interaction. Disagreement is on the additional layers of meaning. To this end, Keller (2003) offers a helpful discussion that identifies the following characteristics: 1) place/turf/territory, 2) shared ideals and expectations, 3) network of social ties and allegiances, and 4) a collective framework. These include the basics but also zero in on some of the most important secondary concepts.

The importance of shared ideals and expectations hinges on the cultural values of community members. Characteristics that community members find ideal vary wildly from place to place, with each community generating unique social norms, beliefs, values, and tastes. These may be stable, lasting years or decades, or fleeting and brief, creating uncertainty and some level of what Durkheim (2019) called anomie or normlessness. In some cases, community members hold opposing ideals and expectations, leading to conflict. The ability to resolve such conflicts will be a vital quality of communities striving for improvement. In short, culture is central to community.

Next, the network of ties and allegiances, noted by Keller, is also endemic. As we live in an increasingly digital world, some fear the decline of local social ties and networks could spell the end of community. Other research has found these claims to be exaggerated. According to field theory, the emergence of the community field (Wilkinson 1991) remains possible as long as there is some interaction about the community. There are likely to be urban–rural differences in the nature of social interaction. Living in larger places will typically result, for instance, in more weak ties (Granovetter 1973) relative to strong ties, while the opposite is the case for smaller communities. The nature of social networks and the extent of ties and allegiances can profoundly impact individuals' levels of social support and life opportunities. Thus, in addition to considering social interaction, we must also focus on social networks.

The collective framework referenced by Keller is also essential, as it points to the configuration of organizations and institutions that exist within the local community. This framework includes nongovernmental organizations, governmental organizations, private industrial organizations, educational institutions, health institutions, religious institutions, and voluntary associations. The collective framework encompasses much of the community's political, economic, and social structure. Small communities may not have much of a collective framework, and may have only a single building or organization, such as a school or church. There may be no local employers or health providers. Large cities, alternatively, will typically have a diverse array of associations, organizations, and institutions. However, even cities experience fluctuations due to deindustrialization processes that result in the simplification and reduction of organizations, associations, and institutions.

Returning to the dimension of turf or territory in the community, it is crucial to consider the built and natural environment. Within the natural environment, communities have control over resources that can be harnessed for local consumption, production, or trade purposes. Considering how to use natural resources should be weighed against the population's energy demands. Every community must find balance between what the population requires and what the environment can adequately provide (Fulkerson and Thomas 2021). While rural areas have the potential to remain somewhat self-sufficient, many become wholly reliant on trade with urban communities for their survival. This trade dependency is why some of the worst food deserts paradoxically exist in areas dominated by agriculture. Urban areas, including cities of all sizes, are dependent on resources that must necessarily originate in rural environments near and far since the urban environment is not well suited for work in the energy economy (i.e., the phenomena of urban dependency).

For example, the metropolitan area of Albany–Schenectady–Troy, New York, is home to about 875,000 people and encompasses 67 square miles (42,880 acres) of land. Using a caloric well approach, we (Fulkerson and Thomas 2021) estimate that a highly productive acre of land can feed about three people for a year, so for this metro area, roughly 128,640 people could be supported, or about one-seventh the actual population if the entire space was devoted to intensive agriculture. A tract of land needs to be under cultivation seven times larger than the metro area, revealing the depth of urban dependency. Rural food production is therefore crucial to support the food needs and basic survival of urban communities and metropolitan areas. The environmental demographic aspect of community does not always receive adequate consideration but lies at the heart of the urban–rural system dynamics approach.

## A Holistic Approach: The Community Capitals Framework

As should be clear, the complexity of community is difficult to capture in a single definition, hence we now turn to something familiar to most contemporary community scholars—the community capitals framework (see Emory and Flora 2006). This framework helps conceptualize the full extent of what community entails—the social, human, political, cultural, natural, built, and financial/economic dimensions of community. The term *capital* refers to assets that imply an investment of some kind with the goal of improvement and growth. Communities can make investments in each of these areas of community life.

Generally, community financial capital refers to locally owned and operated businesses and funding sources available to produce financial returns for the community. It is possible for a community to have no local financial capital but still have economic activity, as is the case when national or global connections dominate a community. Financial capital is the least metaphorical since the term *capital* usually has economic connotations. However, the other forms of capital may be less familiar or tangible, requiring some explanation.

Social capital is a concept that captured the imagination of social scientists in the 1990s when it was popularized by political scientist Robert Putnam (with Leonardi and Nanetti [1993]). Putnam borrowed the idea from James Coleman (1988) to describe it as collective norms of trust and reciprocity that enable communities to mobilize and act. Putnam applied the concept to understand varying levels of civic engagement at the local level. However, the French social theorist Pierre Bourdieu (2011[1986]) independently defined social capital as ownership of durable social networks that can provide individuals with various benefits—a slightly different interpretation. In this case, social capital refers to anything of value individuals can access through their social ties. From these two foundations, we can think of collective and individual social capital (Brehm and Rahn 1997). Combined, they imply value that emerges from social norms and social networks. In the context of community, social capital is usually consistent with the definition provided by Putnam and colleagues.

Human capital—also considered by Coleman (1988)—refers to the skills and knowledge held by individuals, which contributes to their productivity and improvement of the community. Coleman (1988) suggested that social capital was essential in creating human capital in his analysis of education. Human capital can benefit communities, as talented and educated people have a lot to offer. Communities with an educated and healthy workforce are attractive to potential employers, leading to gains in financial capital. Human capital also implies the presence of conditions that make learning possible. Among these are basic levels of security and safety. It is not easy to develop new skills and knowledge when one is constantly battling an illness, wondering about their next meal, or fearing violence and theft. For these reasons, human capital has come to encompass these additional considerations.

Cultural capital can refer to value derived from possessing a set of beliefs, values, and norms. Bourdieu (2011) was interested in how cultural capital was used to reproduce social class—how the wealthy remain wealthy across generations by training their children in cultural mores. Children learn to demonstrate their membership in the upper class by conveying elite understandings of abstract art, for instance, which is difficult to imitate or fake. If one epitomizes values, beliefs, and norms central to a particular culture, one will reap the benefits as an individual. Sociologists often refer to these as positive social sanctions. At a community level, cultural capital implies benefit from a well-developed historical legacy. As Keller (2003) notes, most communities have local lore complete with heroes that embody local ideals. When we examine the urban–rural system dynamics, rural people are often located at the bottom of the cultural hierarchy, subjected to urbanormative assumptions and actions. The cultural hierarchy attached to place leads entire communities becoming stigmatized (Hayden 2014).

Political capital generally refers to the benefits realized from having a high capacity for democratic governance, as indicated by community members' broad inclusion and participation in the collective decision-making process. Alternatively, communities may be run by a power elite, serving a narrow set of private interests. In sociology, we often contrast what Mills (1981[1956]) referred to as the power elite to the political idea of pluralism. These two extremes illustrate how power can be alternatively concentrated among a few individuals in the highest echelon or shared across a large number of stakeholders. Across communities, we can find the full array of these conditions. Community power studies by Floyd Hunter (2017) and colleagues in the 1950s successfully mapped the power structures of communities. However, this kind of research has largely been abandoned in favor of national or global power studies.

The remaining capitals have to do with the environment, including built and natural capital. In the case of natural capital, we refer to the natural world and the kinds of resources it provides a community and into which investments can be made. This view may imply a utilitarian approach to natural resources, as we see in farming, fishing, forestry, and so on. It may refer to more aesthetic approaches that seek to conserve or preserve natural ecosystems for the inherent value they provide. Communities approach the natural world with different sets of values and goals. Built capital refers to the human-created environment, including housing, commercial and retail space, and infrastructure. Communities invest differently in their built capital based on their varying sets of values and goals. For instance, if a high-amenity rural community wishes to capitalize on ecotourism, built capital investments will likely include hotels, campgrounds, restaurants, and shops. There will also be a need for supporting infrastructures such as a road system capable of accommodating high traffic, reliable water and sewage treatment, electricity transmission lines, and internet. Large urban areas typically have the most developed built capital to accommodate a diverse array of activities, while rural communities tend to have little infrastructure. Organizing and planning the built capital of a city is a complex undertaking and is often done in sub-optimal ways.

In sum, the community capitals' framework helps us understand communities holistically. One of the many pitfalls of community planning and development is too much focus on any one or two capitals, with the remaining capitals neglected or ignored. Investment in financial capital that ignores investment in human capital—the health, education, and safety of the population—can lead to disaster in an unreliable and unprepared workforce. So too can harmful consequences result from neglecting or ignoring the vitality of the natural environment, as communities may become polluted or even uninhabitable from unregulated economic activity. Suppose a powerful elite hoards political capital. In that case, this can lead to a community's eventual demise as residents come to feel alienated or apathetic or turn to crime and other forms of social disorder. The community capitals framework is highly compatible with sustainability principles—of balancing economic with social and environmental concerns. It is also compatible with social justice concerns—of ensuring equity, diversity, and inclusion through investments in cultural, social, human, and political capital. We will return to these principles in our concluding chapter. Next is a sketch of community scholarship to understand how the field of sociology has approached the community question historically.

## COMMUNITY SOCIOLOGY: ORIGIN AND TRAJECTORY

As Keller (2003) reminds us, the study of community long predates community sociology. Thousands of years ago, ancient philosophers such as Plato and Aristotle devoted attention to questions surrounding planning and developing the ideal human communities, making it one of the oldest lines of scholarly inquiry. Plato made recommendations about the Greek Polis, including precise prescriptions that would limit the population size to 5,040 persons. He noted the dual importance of mutual respect (*aidos*) and justice (*dike*) for establishing successful community life. Aristotle argued that a community should not be so large that individuals lose the ability to grasp what is happening throughout the community—only then could democratic decision-making be fully informed. Early Christian scholars, such as St. Augustine, argued that community was held together by a unity of faith. Thomas Aquinas suggested that communities are committed to the "common good" (Keller 2003, p. 39). One of the first sociologists, Ibn Khaldun, wrote extensively about social changes he observed in human communities within the Islamic world of the fourteenth century. Khaldun's insights continue to hold importance in human organization and settlement but, unfortunately, were overlooked until more recently, so his influence has been limited to contemporary studies (Abdullahi and Salawu 2012).

The history of community sociology in the United States is the history of sociology itself. American Sociology emerged at the turn of the nineteenth century, aided by Albion Small, who assembled an academic department that came to be known simply as the Chicago School (not to be confused with other disciplines, such as economics, which also have their versions of the Chicago School). The Chicago School included a collection of scholars who would develop the sociological perspectives of symbolic interactionism—the foundation of social psychology—and human ecology with its urban geographic focus. Both have had lasting impacts on sociology and other fields, including psychology and geography. Human ecology took inspiration from European sociology, and many towering figures within the Chicago School, including Robert Park and Albion Small, studied in Germany, where they encountered the ideas of Ferdinand Tönnies, Georg Simmel, and Max Weber. The sociological study of community is especially indebted to the foundational ideas of German sociologist Ferdinand Tönnies. They provided a way to understand the cultural and social changes unfolding due to European urbanization and industrialization. His classic, *Gemeinschaft und Gesellschaft*, would influence community scholars for decades. It may be regarded as the first theoretical framework in community sociology. Max Weber's notions of communal and associative relations drew upon Tönnies's theory to understand the bases of social interaction in the natural or rational will. Though the field of sociology does not always recognize Tönnies as a central figure, his influence on the classical canon is indisputable. The French sociologist, Emile Durkheim, offered the concepts of mechanical and organic solidarity that would challenge some of the ideas set forth by Tönnies, attaching an evolutionary framework that was viewed as progress in the shift away from rural mechanical toward modern urban organic solidarity. He understood this process as the result of the division of labor in society. By mid-century, the growing popularity of Durkheim in the field of sociology would eventually lead to a greater focus on society than community.

Several decades worth of community sociological research was conducted between the 1930s and 1970s, using a highly descriptive ethnographic methodology. Among its products are classic treatments—*Middletown* (Lynd and Lynd 1929), Yankee City (Warner and Lunt 1941), and *Small Town in Mass Society* (Vidich and Bensman 1958). We will not review this literature here, though a comprehensive review has been completed by Brook and Finn (1978) of both American and European contexts. A further insightful discussion is provided by Day (2006). This body of research provides a colorful snapshot of particular communities, focusing on culture, lifestyle, social relationships, and social class dynamics. By the late 1960s, critiques of these ethnographies began pouring into the point of becoming excessive (Cohen 2002). Bell and Newby (1971) were central to the final dismantling of the community ethnographic research project, criticizing it for being unsystematic, particularistic, and parochial. Pahl (1966, 328) concluded that the whole project of studying patterns of relationships in small towns and villages was a "fruitless exercise." Frazer (1999, 67) suggested that these studies were making some significant assumptions about communities that limited them to a traditional view: "a locality with settled denizens, a stable social structure consisting of dense networks of multiplex relations, and a relatively high boundary to the outside." These assumptions exclude communities with relatively fluid boundaries, those experiencing major migration events, or those undergoing sweeping social changes. Given these harsh criticisms, it is easy to see how scholars would want to change focus—regardless of the validity of these critiques.

## The Mass Society Focus

According to Ritzer (1996), the epicenter of American sociology in Chicago was joined and challenged by a competing institution that would also influence the development of early American Sociology: Harvard University. At Harvard, the focus of sociology was more broadly placed on "society" than on community and was influenced more by Durkheimian thought. The increasingly dominant work of Talcott Parsons, who was the creator of the structural-functionalist perspective, would later eclipse and even subsume the human ecology perspective at Chicago. Keller (2003) suggests that Parsons was partly influenced by Tönnies and Weber, incorporating their ideas into the "pattern variables," but he did not retain a community focus. In the Parsonian Era, community scholars began to feel that their object of study was obsolete, leading to a general sense of crisis and despair. Amos Hawley (1950) attempted the resurrection of human ecology based on an integration. Hawley incorporated many structural-functionalist concepts while abandoning concern with a physical organization that was central to classic human ecology. This neo-orthodox human ecology was primarily focused on the evolutionary functions of culture, which meant it was becoming Durkheimian.

Warren (1963) applied Parsonian systems theory to understand community as a subsystem dominated by the macrosystem of society—a process he described as the great change. This macrosystem dominance was due to the number of vertical relative to horizontal linkages in the community. Vertical linkages refer to extracommunity structural-functional patterns, while horizontal linkages are internal patterns. The significance of community thus depended on maintaining substantial horizontal linkages—though Warren suggested community significance was fading away. Within the macrosystem of society, the community is but a node within a network of far-reaching structural-functional linkages.

By the 1960s, American sociology began to withdraw from its Parsonian orientation, favoring an emerging conflict-based perspective with a Marxian foundation. While this offered a new way to understand power relations and the importance of the political economy, it maintained a focus on entire societies. It did not find much value in a community focus. Only a minority of Marxian scholars would apply the Marxian perspective at the community level, such as the philosopher Henri Lefebvre (1974) and the geographer David Harvey (1989). They would expound on a Marxian critique of human ecology. In sociology, Manuel Castells (1977) would contribute to these efforts, but only reluctantly, noting the overarching importance of societal patterns of class inequality, drawing insight from Pahl (1966). Castells would later abandon his community focus.

## The Resurgence of Community

The 1980s and '90s saw a resurgent interest, based partly on the work of Bellah et al. (1985, 1991), who restored hope that the local community could act as a critical mediator in a world of big government and corporations. In the 1990s, interest in the community further spread owing to the earlier mentioned research by Robert Putnam due to enthusiasm for his notions of social capital and civic engagement (Putnam, Leonardi, and Nanneti 1994; Putnam 1995, 1996, 2000). Study after study through the 2000s found empirical support for the proposition that community norms of trust and reciprocity—hallmarks of social capital—were decisive predictors for a range of desirable socio-economic outcomes. Putnam (2000) identified several such empirical findings in *Bowling Alone*.

A scholarly focus on social capital and community continues to flourish through the present. However, the community has never resumed the central place it held in the early twentieth century. Instead, it has proceeded as a subfield with an influence observed in a range of disciplines and subdisciplines. As a longstanding field of inquiry, it is surprising that there is not a dedicated journal of community sociology. Instead, much scholarship appears in either *Rural Sociology* or *City and Community*, in addition to the applied and multidisciplinary *Journal of Community Development.* Importantly, community scholars with urban and rural interests experienced a divergent trajectory that dates back to the pre-Parsonian era.

## The Divergent Study of Urban and Rural Sociology

Though interest in community sociology has ebbed and flowed, since the late 1930s, the study of urban and rural communities has been conducted as independent and divorced realities. The urban–rural rift in sociology dates to 1937, when rural scholars left the American Sociological Society (now Association) to form the Rural Sociological Society. Rural scholars were frustrated with the general disinterest in rural life expressed by ASA members—a tendency that holds through the present. From that point forward, the silos would grow more rigid. Today, urban sociologists continue to congregate at the American Sociological Association's section on Urban Sociology. They publish research in journals that emphasize urban life and settings, such as *City & Community*. Rural sociologists congregate at the Rural Sociological Society in the Community, Family, and Health Research and Interest Group (RIG) and publish research in journals that emphasize rural life, including *Rural Sociology*. Different conferences and publishing outlets have reinforced silos between these subfields and have hindered the cross-fertilization of ideas.

Prior to the 1920s and 1930s and before the rift, there was unified rural–urban sociology. The earliest examples of rural–urban comparative sociology were conducted by W. E. B. Du Bois, who examined the experiences of black farmers in the years following the Civil War in Farmville, Virginia (1899). He contrasted this with the urban experience of the black population living in Philadelphia (1899). Taken together the two studies provide a comparison that provides a fuller picture of life during Reconstruction. Later, Galpin's (1918) notion of "rurban" sought to integrate the study of urban and rural issues. Comparative rural–urban research did not necessarily look for or identify linkages between urban and rural communities, since the goal was mainly to draw contrasting pictures of urban and rural life. An impressive example of rural–urban comparative work may be found in the edited volume by Sorokin and Zimmerman (1929), though their later work would focus exclusively on rural communities, especially in the wake of the Great Depression's devastating impact on the countryside (Sorokin, Zimmerman, and Galpin 1930).

## COMMUNITIES IN URBAN–RURAL SYSTEMS

In 2011, with the publication of *Critical Rural Theory*, Thomas, Lowe, Fulkerson, and Smith began the project of restoring a focus on the intertwined experiences of urban and rural communities. This book became the seed for an evolving theoretical framework that sought to understand urban–rural system dynamics (note that "urban–rural" is used to distinguish it from the older "rural–urban" tradition mentioned earlier). These scholars emphasized how political economy intersected with sociocultural and environmental demographic systems within and between communities in urban–rural systems.

This work was further elaborated in three edited volumes: *Studies in Urbanormativity*, *Reimagining Rural*, and *Reinventing Rural*, contributing vital food for thought. The theoretical framework was outlined and elaborated in three co-authored books: *Urbanormativity* (Fulkerson and Thomas 2019), *Urban Dependency* (Fulkerson and Thomas 2021), and *City and Country* (Thomas and Fulkerson 2021). *Urbanormativity* focused on the cultural factors that led to the privileging of urban over rural life while concealing the reality of urban dependency. Related projects include *Rural Voices* (Seale and Mallinson 2018) and *The Rural Primitive in American Popular Culture* (Hayden 2021), which provided additional insights into the cultural implications of the emerging urban-rural system dynamics perspective by examining language and popular cultural representations of rural.

*Urban Dependency* (Fulkerson and Thomas 2021) developed the energy economy concept, noting the unsustainable fragility of urban settlements that grow to extreme sizes, while elaborating the caloric well approach. The environmental demographic perspective is fully unpacked in this volume as an integrative umbrella that incorporates ideas from multiple fields and subfields associated with the scholarship of urban and rural communities, the environment, population (demography), and physical space. The core urban dependency argument begins with a proposition of urban exploitation of rural resources. As urban settlements have larger populations than can be supported with locally available environmental resources, there is an inherent need to import resources from rural communities. As this urban dependency deepens, the extent of rural exploitation becomes more severe. The depletion of rural aquifers is one consequence of urban demand, threatening agricultural production's future, as shown in *Groundwater Citizenship*, by Ternes (2021). The following proposition suggests that this exploitation can be accomplished either through political coercion, as was the case in colonial times, or through cultural domination and ideological control, as is more common today. This is where urbanormativity comes into play. If cultures view rural populations as less important or valuable than their urban counterparts, societies may willingly condone rural exploitation. Rural cultural domination is accomplished through various forms of urbanormative cultural production, including art, literature, religion, music, film, and other media designed to convey rural inferiority. Since there is a high cost associated with political coercion, Fulkerson and Thomas suggest that the strategy of cultural domination is preferred, and this is why urbanormativity has become nearly universal among advanced nations. Thus, urban dependency is enabled by urbanormativity.

The last of the three theoretical books, *City and Country* (Thomas and Fulkerson 2021), unites the ideas of urbanormativity and urban dependency while providing a comprehensive history and discussions of urban-rural systems from ancient times to the present, concluding with a reimagined world-system concept. The historical analysis begins with the emergence of the first urban–rural system in the Fertile Crescent, roughly 4,000 BCE. At first, more localized systems involved an urban center trading with adjacent rural communities for food and other resources. Over time, these systems evolved into city-states that commanded an increasingly large geographic area. The emergence of empires, including the Uruk and Egyptians, were impressive examples of how powerful urban centers could become in the ancient world. The Greek and Roman Empires reached a size and scope previously unseen, dominating most of the Mediterranean world and subduing the mighty Egyptian empire. In the modern world system, the elaborate structure of urban–rural systems is poorly understood. Current ways of studying social change and development have not always centered urbanization as a primary force for change. More attention has been placed on industrialization and international capitalist trade among development scholars at the aggregated national or international levels. Finally, *City and Country* elaborated on the meaning of systems by applying the Complex Adaptive System (CAS) framework to explain urban–rural systems.

Because of this book's focus on urban–rural system dynamics, we will at times flip the view of the community from an inward to an outward-looking perspective, examining how communities fit within the broader networks and regions of urban–rural systems. In either case, it will remain essential to hold the view that communities are nodes within wider urban–rural systems. Community sociology has a long history of focusing exclusively on the internal organization—to a fault. However, no community exists as an island. Rural communities may achieve a degree of self-sufficiency but reliance on trade connects them to the outside urban world. Thus, each community is linked in unique ways, based on political, economic, human, social, environmental, and cultural networks (the capitals). The connections are hierarchical because each community occupies a different place of centrality or marginality. The largest and most well-known cities often provide a full suite of central place functions. Rural communities exist on the margins of urban–rural systems, as the source of natural resources that are transformed and shared with the rest of humanity through complex trade networks and urban industrial processing. In other words, rural is provides environmental services within urban–rural systems. Thus, we often find the most significant investment in rural communities are in natural capital.

Importantly, we must acknowledge at the outset that the entire world is urbanizing and that every nation places greater value on urban than on rural life. This means that communities on the rural end of the spectrum face unique challenges that threaten their very existence. However, since humanity cannot exist without rural resources, the challenges to rural communities should be viewed as challenges for everyone. Though often far-removed physically, socially, and culturally, urban communities remain entirely dependent on rural communities for the basic materials that make urban life possible (Thomas and Fulkerson 2019).

## THE OUTLINE OF THE BOOK

Before beginning our study of community, it may be helpful to preview a map of what lies ahead. Chapter 1 will delve into a baseline discussion of urban–rural systems since it is the book's central theme. This discussion will necessitate elaborating the meaning of urban and rural, drawing on different definitions and concepts. We review some of the latest iterations of official definitions set forth by various government agencies. We will then review the three-dimensional meanings of urban and rural, including the environmental demographic, political-economic, and sociocultural. We turn attention to how these three dimensions intersect to create urban–rural systems, examining the logic of how communities are intertwined. The urban–rural system concept can apply at a local and regional level but is scalable to national and global levels.

Chapter 2 will consider environmental demography, which addresses the relationship between population and the environment. Beginning with a review of carrying capacity, we will contemplate the many harmful social and environmental consequences of overpopulation. We will consider the foundational ideas of Malthus and Franklin, and we will review contemporary environmental theories proposed by Ehrlich and Catton. We will learn here about the concept of the energy economy (Fulkerson and Thomas 2021), which examines efforts to create an energy balance between what a population demands and environmental resources. The caloric well analysis is a valuable method for examining the mathematical relations of energy balance by accounting for calories produced and consumed. The limits of urban–rural systems will be evaluated on how successfully they have worked in the United States, where rampant hunger exists, indicating a lack of energy balance. Planning considerations will focus on how to create more resilient communities by investing in local environmental demography.

Since it is closely related to environmental demography, chapter 3 will consider political economy, which encompasses different strategies for administering resources. These strategies have varied based on type of environmental demographic system, from nomadic foraging to agrarian farming, pastoral nomadism, and urban–rural systems. To understand the political economy of urban–rural systems, we will begin with classic perspectives and early observations of Steuart and Smith on capitalism's social and economic consequences, followed by Marxian and later critiques that emphasized alienation and exploitation of workers. We will build on this to introduce contemporary ideas associated with the more contemporary Growth Machine theory. We will consider the way local political structures align with conditions that either support or resist the Growth Machine by embracing pluralism or a power elite. This chapter concludes with policy ideas directed toward strengthening the local political economy, informed by ideas from civic capitalism and pluralist political participation.

In chapter 4, concepts surrounding community culture will be discussed. We will review classic theories examining urban–rural cultural patterns from Tönnies, Simmel, Weber, and Wirth. We will then connect community culture to political economy and environmental demography. The concepts of identity, reputation, stigma, and representation in communities relative to the local lore are critical to this discussion. Contemporary scholars such as Flora and Flora (2015) offered key ideas that connected cultural capital—usually thought of as an individual quality—to entire communities and their legacies. Planning considerations will highlight the value and strategies for promoting a greater sense of place for communities by discovering, highlighting, and projecting the kind of historical legacy and image that community members want on display. Aligning political-economic decisions with careful cultural planning can result in better social and economic outcomes.

Chapter 5 will examine the importance of community social interaction, networks, and solidarity. This chapter will begin with a review of Wilkinson's theory of community as an interaction field. Ideas from Granovetter and Putnam contribute to a deeper understanding of strong/bonding and weak/bridging social ties—the basis of social networks. We then examine the classical ideas of Durkheim's organic and mechanical solidarity, which combine to give communities the capacity to act. Next, we will consider the consequences of a breakdown in social interaction and solidarity, taking the forms of anomie and social disorganization. These concepts were central to the study of community historically, and they continue to find relevance. When we examine social interaction from the urban–rural system dynamics perspective, we see how humans' social and physical separation into rural and urban communities has facilitated epistemic distance, creating barriers to social interaction. Policy considerations in this chapter will focus on strategies for creating the right balance of strong and weak, or bonding and bridging interaction networks that promote community agency while enhancing the capacity to act.

Chapter 6 will focus on the built environment and spatial organization of communities. Though relevant to environmental demographic concerns, the order of chapters is intentional, as both culture and social interaction have close relationships to the physical arrangements of communities internally and externally. The classical ideas of von Thünen will open the discussion, as he theorized a model of a local urban–rural system with various rings of rural land use surrounding a central urban village. This model provides a baseline regional understanding of spatial organization, showing how urban and rural can be connected. We then examine settlement patterns internal to urban and rural settings. We review the human ecological approach, including concentric zone theory and some of its rival theories of urban spatial organization. Theories of rural spatial organization are less developed, but relevant issues will be considered in terms of basic geographic patterns. The logic of spatial organization is explained by the theory of place-structuration, emphasizing how community character and tradition come to assume a physical form. The spatiality of community is understood, in this perspective, as an outgrowth of culture. Hence the connection to the two preceding chapters on culture and social interaction. From the urban–rural system perspective, we review the concepts of viable space, settlement space, and attractor points before shifting to an explicit focus on infrastructure. Balancing efficiency with need is part of the challenge of infrastructure.

Chapter 7 is outwardly focused, emphasizing how communities are linked regionally, nationally, and globally. The German scholar Walter Christaller's ideas identify central place functions as the mechanism connecting communities. However, this theory was developed with a regional focus—specifically, southern Germany. Nevertheless, central place functions remain the primary connections between communities, even though these connections now reach far beyond the local region to the national and global scales. This chapter will focus on the consequences of urban–rural systems becoming detached from a region. The process of urban coalescence, of urban areas growing into one another to form a mega-urban area, is one consequence. Now urban–rural systems span the entire world, connected primarily through market functions—global commodity chains organized by multinational corporations. The chapter ends with a consideration of a bioregional philosophy.

Chapter 8 takes an applied turn offering a discussion of community planning and development. The first part of the chapter discusses leadership styles and the concept of community agency. If a community has agency (the capacity to act), community development may not be needed. However, most communities benefit from the support offered by enlisting a community development specialist. Next, we will consider the three main community development approaches—technical assistance, self-help, and conflict. As we go through these approaches, we will consider relevant leadership styles and the historical context of how these approaches came to be. We end the chapter with a discussion on measuring progress of the community and in the community.

We will end with a conclusion that offers a dual focus on the principles of community sustainability and justice ethic. Hopefully, the conclusion will leave the reader with a sense of how the various concepts and theories discussed throughout the book can be put to good use while pointing the way to future research.

*Chapter 1*

# Urban–Rural Systems

Since it is this book's central theme, this chapter introduces the concept of urban–rural systems. The chapter begins with a critique of the contemporary meaning of urban and rural, comparing widely used government definitions provided by the US Census, Office of Management and Budgets, and Department of Agriculture. Next, the chapter will address the limitations of these definitions by introducing the meaning and logic of the three dimensions of urban–rural systems. We will consider the scale, complexity, and evolution of environmental demographic systems that preceded urban–rural systems, beginning with nomadic foraging, then moving into settled agrarian communities and pastoral nomadism. Finally, we will question the effectiveness of urban–rural systems, reviewing weaknesses and instances of system failure.

## GOVERNMENT DEFINITIONS OF URBAN AND RURAL

In the United States, community scholars usually adopt the definitions of urban and rural provided by various agencies in the federal government, including the US Census Bureau, the Office of Management and Budget (OMB), and the US Department of Agriculture (USDA). Reliance on government definitions is not unique to the United States, as other nations' scholars also rely on their respective federal agencies for comparable data, such as Statistics Canada for our northern neighbors. Scholars rely on the data produced by these agencies for their research, and using such data requires an implicit acceptance of the validity of the measures and corresponding definitions. We must acknowledge that we learn a great deal about urban and rural communities from government data sources and would be in the dark without such invaluable resources. At the same time, there is no reason we cannot challenge ourselves to think more broadly about the underlying multidimensional meaning of urban and rural. Doing so will reveal that government definitions capture only part of the rich meaning. This requirement is the primary justification for developing the urban–rural dynamics approach, and it will require exploring novel data collection and analysis approaches. Before elaborating, we will review how US governmental agencies define urban and rural.

## US Census

According to Ratcliffe, Burd, Holder, and Fields (2016), in their introduction, "The U.S. Census Bureau defines *rural as what is not urban*—that is, after defining individual urban areas, rural is what is left" (Ratcliffe et al. 2016, p.1; emphasis added). So, how then is urban defined by the Census? In the early part of the twentieth century, the Census defined urban areas to include all incorporated cities and towns of at least 2,500 persons. The definition of rural was left to include all unincorporated territory and all incorporated places with fewer than 2,500 persons. In 1950, the Census created a population density measure of *urban area*s due to increasing suburban development. No longer could we reliably expect the city proper to account for the full extent of an urban area, which now spills into adjacent political units. Census-defined urban areas have a threshold of at least 50,000 persons. However, these did not replace but rather coexisted with the earlier defined incorporated urban places with the 2,500-person minimum.

In 2000, the Census created the concept of *the urban cluster* to capture those urban places smaller than the 50,000-person upper-bound threshold and a higher (than 2,500) lower-bound threshold resulting in a range from 10,000–49,999 persons. Since urban areas and urban clusters are density-based, they require that each block within the core space have a density of at least 1,000 persons per square mile, while the secondary urban space must have a density of at least 500 persons per square mile. One limitation of the 2000 measures was that each block had to be continuously connected, which did not account for gaps in urban space that occur for several reasons, such as natural features of mountains and lakes or built features such as extensive parking lots or airports.

In 2010, the Census overcame this limitation and went beyond population density measures to incorporate land use criteria for delineating urban spaces that accommodate nonresidential features. The Census used the presence of impervious surfaces to make this determination, which captures airports, parking lots, commercial and retail space, and other nonresidential urban land uses. To be included as urban, nonresidential space must be within a quarter-mile of residential urban space. There are two exceptions to this rule that accommodate noncontiguous urban development patterns. These are 1) the *hop* criterion that includes areas within a half-mile along a road corridor and 2) the *jump* criterion that includes areas within up to 2.5 miles with only one jump along a road. In 2010, the area containing the hop or jump was included by the Census in the urban space.

In 2020, the US Census (2020) dropped the urban cluster and shifted its density measure from population to housing units, implementing a 385 housing units per square mile threshold for delineating urban areas. Since the average is 2.6 persons per household, 385 housing units approximates the older 1,000 person per square mile threshold. Part of the rationale for this is that housing is a better approximation of the built environment. Houses are counted whether occupied or not and therefore include urban spaces that may have experienced significant population gain, loss, or decay. This housing measure will likely create greater continuity as changes in housing stock are less volatile than population fluctuations. In place of population thresholds, urban areas are now defined as having at least 4,000 housing units or, when housing units are a poor proxy, falling back to the old rule of a population of 10,000 or more persons.

Further, the prior distinction between urban areas and clusters is being abandoned. The jump and hop criteria are maintained, but the intervening areas are now excluded from the urban area, allowing the corridor space to be considered rural. This change is vital for such areas to be eligible for programs that serve rural areas. Large urban agglomerations exceeding 2.5 million are broken into smaller urban areas based on commuting patterns that reflect varying levels of integration. Consistent with prior conceptions, "The term 'rural' encompasses all population, housing, and territory not included within an urban area" (US Census 2020). An incorporated place may be both inside and outside an urban area since being incorporated is no longer a requirement. Finally, to be included, at least one-third of a Census block must have impervious surfaces of at least 20 percent, and at least 40 percent of its boundary must be contiguous with a qualifying territory. Group quarters, such as college dorms, are now included in the urban space but are not considered housing units.

The Census measures are probably the most important since the other agencies addressing urban and rural issues rely on Census data, though at different levels and in different ways over the last century.

## Office of Management and Budget

Since 1950, the Office of Management and Budget has delineated Core-Based Statistical Areas (CBSAs) that include metropolitan and micropolitan statistical areas. CBSAs differ from Census-defined urban areas and clusters because they are based on counties. The goal of CBSAs is to identify a broad and integrated region of counties. A dense population center or nucleus is at the center, containing a county (or multiple counties) associated with the principal city. These central counties are surrounded by outlying counties integrated through significant commuting patterns. Counties not integrated with a central nucleus via commuting are considered outside the CBSA.

Metropolitan and micropolitan areas are similar in structure but have different thresholds for the size of the nucleus. In 2020, to qualify as a metro area, the nucleus must contain a population of at least 50,000, though there is increasing pressure to raise this threshold to 100,000. To qualify as a micro area, the nucleus must contain a population between 10,000 and 50,000. For 2020, the size distinction remains central to OMB classification, despite the Census's decision to abandon the urban area/cluster distinction. In addition, the OMB continues to focus on population density rather than shifting to housing units. Beyond the Metropolitan Area, the OMB also tracks Combined Statistical Areas (CSA) that address adjacent Metropolitan and Micropolitan Areas. The largest is the New York–Newark, NY–NJ–CT–PA CSA with 23,582,491 is 2020, up nearly 6 percent from 2010. Of the top 100 largest CSAs, only nine of them lost population between 2010 and 2020. The biggest loss among the largest CSAs was for the Charleston–Huntington–Ashland, WVA–OH–KY CSA, which shrank from 823,417 to 779,969.

Nonmetropolitan areas include those counties that are not included in any metro or micro areas and, as with rural, are defined by what they are not. It is important to note that counties may contain both urban and rural regions, thus complicating the correspondence between urban/rural and metro/non-metro. The OMB is careful to point out the limitations of assuming there is a direct correspondence. Part of the problem is the binary options of being either metro or nonmetro, or urban or rural. The USDA's continuum approach overcomes this limitation.

## US Department of Agriculture

The Economic Research Service of the USDA uses a system of rural–urban continuum codes derived from the OMB's method of identifying metropolitan and nonmetropolitan counties. The continuum creates nine levels between the most metro and most nonmetro counties. The last update to the codes was in 2013. It "distinguishes metropolitan counties by the population size of their metro area, and nonmetropolitan counties by degree of urbanization and adjacency to a metro area" (USDA 2020). Changes in the way the Census measures urban areas will influence the results of the continuum, and an update is expected soon.

The methodology for creating the continuum is offered in the available documentation (USDA 2013). It starts with the binary metropolitan and nonmetropolitan status. The metro counties are divided into three categories by size: 1) 1 million or more, 2) 250,000 to 1 million, and 3) smaller than

250,000. The nonmetro counties are divided by population into 20,000 or more, 2,500–20,000, and less than 2,500. After these size categories are created, the nonmetro counties are further categorized by whether they are adjacent to one or more metro areas. The result is a nine-category array that includes the three size categories of metro and the six combinations of size and adjacency for the nonmetro counties. The complexity involved with categorizing the nonmetropolitan counties reveals how much is concealed by the OMB category and why its direct correspondence to rural is haphazard.

Figure 1.1 shows the county map of the United States with the rural–urban continuum codes. The darker colors represent the more rural side of the spectrum. The most rural counties appear in the most significant number in the agricultural belt running from Texas northward through the Dakotas and Montana. However, rural pockets are scattered around many metropolitan counties found throughout the eastern half of the country and the West Coast.

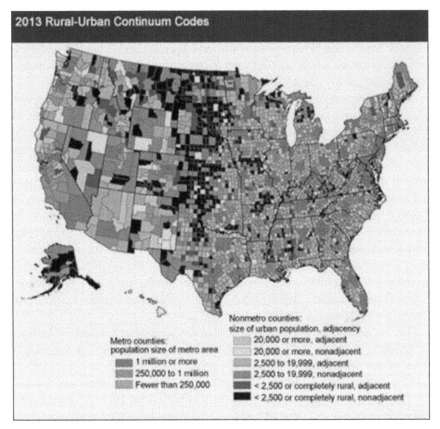

**Figure 1.1: Map of USDA 2013 Rural-Urban Continuum Codes.**
*Source*: (USDA, 2013).

Thinking more broadly about the meaning of urban and rural means transcending the definitions provided by government agencies. Though the thresholds change, all government definitions involve the basic idea of population size or density and physical space. As we noted, in the Census, there is growing inclusion of factors related to the built environment, as we see in the measurement of impervious surfaces and housing. While useful, these are only one part of the rich meaning we can attach to urban and rural.

## THREE DIMENSIONS OF URBAN–RURAL SYSTEMS

We identify three urban–rural dimensions. The first underlies government definitions, and is the *environmental demographic*. As noted, this is primarily concerned with the size of populations for a given geographic space. An example of this is the 1,000 persons per square mile rule used by the 2010 Census to identify central urban areas. As we saw before, the dividing line between urban and rural is where population size and density reach predefined thresholds. Where to draw this line has long been a subject of debate, and the arbitrary nature of finding it is perhaps unavoidable—a satisfactory answer may always be elusive.

What is missing is a logic on which to base a threshold. How can we decide that an area is too populated to be rural, and what does that mean? As we will discuss in the next chapter, this missing logic could be based on the ability of the natural environment to support the population—in other words, the potential for self-sufficiency. The ability to be a self-sufficient community is one of the defining features of rural communities in the urban–rural dynamics approach. Once populations overshoot their potential for self-sufficiency, they go into urban dependency mode, relying on imports of rural products for sustenance. Though difficult to pinpoint, the urban–rural systems approach provides a mathematical technique for determining the maximum population size for a given environment: the caloric well. Thus, the environmental demographic definition involving population size and density could be extended to consider the natural environmental resource base and a calculated carrying capacity (explained in the next chapter).

The second dimension is based on *political economy*. Central to the logic of political economy is the nature of work and occupations. For instance, in their classic discussion of rural-urban distinctions, Sorokin and Zimmerman (1929) define rural as working in agriculture, leaving all other occupations to fall into the urban category. This distinction is relatively narrow and limiting, as it leaves out forestry, mining, fisheries, and other traditional rural natural resource-based occupations. In the first published volume on political economy, Sir James Steuart (1767) provided a helpful distinction, referring to rural people as "cultivators" and urbanites as "freehands." Urbanites were free to put their hands to use on something other than cultivating the natural resources necessary for survival. As we will see, in urban–rural systems, rural production implies work that begins with natural resources, while urban production implies work that starts with rural products. Food is part of the natural resource base, but not its totality. Based on this political economic definition, urban–rural research could use data on occupational categories to classify urban and rural producers.

Urban domination of rural communities is central to the political economic perspective. It guarantees urban populations continued favorable terms of trade with rural communities on which they desperately depend. This domination was typically carried out with brute force in colonial days. While coercive power is still exercised, currently, it is more common for this urban domination to be secured through cultural means. The cultural production of various media is used to perpetuate the ideas of the inferiority of rural populations and legitimate urban authority. Measuring political domination of rural communities and people is more complex but not impossible if we consider using techniques regarding political freedoms used by political scientists, such as the Freedom House rankings applied to nations.

The above leads us to the third urban–rural dimension—the *sociocultural*. This dimension includes a focus on community social interaction, networks, and solidarity, and a concern for cultural norms, values, beliefs, and legacy. Rural communities are typically defined by patterns of social interaction with strong ties and mechanical solidarity, while showing *gemeinschaft* qualities; urban communities contain more weak ties and organic solidarity, while exhibiting *gesellschaft* qualities. However, these are variable, creating unique conditions for a given community. Importantly, each community is unique and significant. Trying to find cultural patterns that cut across communities will thus necessarily be challenging, but it is not impossible. One nearly universal cultural phenomenon is *urbanormativity* that attributes normalcy and superiority to urban life while viewing rural life as backward and deviant (Thomas et al. 2011; Fulkerson and Thomas 2019). Urbanormativity is the foundation of a place-based cultural hierarchy that sorts people into different rungs based on their urban–rural status.

The sociocultural dimension has a socially constructed foundation—a person or a place is urban or rural if and when we define it as such through social interaction. It adheres to the Thomas Dictum—that which we define as real will be real in its consequences—the closest thing we have to a law in sociology (apart from Michel's (1911) iron law of oligarchy). While socially constructed, it is anchored in objective reality. The environmental demographic and political economic dimensions position individuals and communities to have one kind of identity over another. It would be unusual for someone to grow up in a large city, work in an urban industry or service, such as finance, and then think of themselves as a country person. It is not impossible, but it is improbable.

As the most subjective dimension, the sociocultural is the most difficult to measure. We can examine available (objective) data on population density or urban/rural occupations, but a sociocultural perspective requires collecting subjective data from surveys or interviews, focusing on differences in social interaction and culture. For instance, the General Social Survey asks respondents where they grew up, with response categories that include large cities, suburbs, medium cities, small cities, in the country but not on a farm, and in the country on a farm. We can use data from this question to surmise the kind of place-socialization respondents received and study how this corresponds to other beliefs, values, and behaviors. The goal is to collect information on urban–rural identity, socialization, interaction, cultural beliefs, and values. Visual methods involving photographs may also be useful when examining the cultural character of a community.

Based on the three dimensions, it should be clear that categorizing a community or person as urban or rural is no simple task. It may be the case that a community is rural in the environmental demographic sense since it falls below the urban threshold in terms of population density. However, if none of its inhabitants work in rural occupations—those associated with cultivating natural resources—then the community is urban from a political economic perspective. Perhaps very few residents think of themselves as rural or rustic, which would not be surprising since most people derive their identity from their work (Gini 2013). In such a scenario, the place is rural on the environmental demographic dimension, but urban on the political-economic and sociocultural dimensions. This incongruous configuration is relatively common in the United States, where the proportion of rural residents working in rural occupations is relatively small. We could conclude that attempting to categorize communities as urban or rural is futile, or we could appreciate that these terms are more complex than usually recognized. The example also demonstrates some limitations of relying on a single dimension, such as environmental demography, as embraced by government agencies and the scholars who depend upon them. The danger is when we make assumptions about other dimensions for which we have no information. We cannot safely assume that a rural community is full of rural workers or people who identify as rural, simply because population density is low.

Hopefully, this discussion of urban and rural definitions has revealed the need for a more complete and nuanced understanding. The prevailing one-dimensional treatment motivated the development of what we now refer to as the urban–rural dynamics approach. As a trained rural sociologist, I have always found it disappointing how government agencies think about rural communities—essentially, as not urban. The embedded message here is that rural has no inherent meaning or value, so we are forced to define it by what it is not. Moreover, limiting the urban definition to places with high population density says little about the community. Areas described as rural and urban contain a great deal of variability. Rural communities specializing in farming are different from those specializing in mining or forestry. Urban communities can be characterized by dense apartment buildings or large lot residential neighborhoods in the suburbs. We can develop a much fuller picture of urban and rural by considering them through all three dimensions.

### Logic of Urban–Rural Systems

The logic of urban–rural systems reveals how the three dimensions are connected. The base of urban–rural system, as shown in figure 1.2, is the need for populations to access the resources required for survival—hence the foundation is environmental demographic. Initially, humans accomplished this through prior systems of nomadic foraging, agrarian settlement, nomadic pastoralism, and, finally, the urban–rural system, which began very localized and expanded with trade networks to encompass larger and larger regions. We review this evolution below.

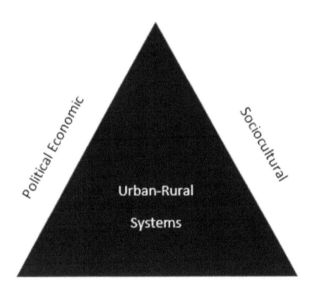

**Figure 1.2: Three-Dimensional Logic of Urban-Rural Systems.**
*Source*: Created by the author.

Though environmental demography is at the foundation of the logic, it requires two additional dimensions of support. The political economic dimension involves the crucial development of trade networks and political administration central to urban–rural exchange. Though originally forged through coercion, the recent expansion of trade in the modern world has been accomplished through peaceful negotiation. However, even in the contemporary world, many rural communities occupy a disadvantaged position. Only through the subjugation of rural communities by urban-centered nation-states can this continue. The primary instrument of control is not, however, coercion (though it remains an option) but ideology. Hence, the sociocultural dimension is necessary to achieve the ideological control of rural communities in ubiquitously urban-centric societies.

Another way of conceptualizing this three-dimensional logic of urban–rural systems is through the PECE model, an acronym for polity, economics, culture, and environment (Thomas and Fulkerson 2021). This handy acronym integrates all three dimensions. The environment refers to the supply of natural resources that service human populations. Since rural production exclusively incorporates natural resources, urban dependency is a built-in feature of urban–rural systems. Polity has to do with the administration of urban–rural dynamics, including decisions on facilitating the transfer of natural resources from rural communities to urban centers. This administration may include coordinating coercive measures, including military invasions or raids. Economy refers to trade circuits between rural and urban communities engaged in rural and urban production, consumption, and distribution. Rural production is defined as beginning with a natural resource in the environment. Urban production is defined as combining rural products to create emergent urban products that can be sold back to rural communities to acquire more rural products. Culturally, establishing urban superiority is the goal of the urbanormative ideology of urban–rural systems. It has the power to convince rural people of their inferiority to their urban counterparts, thereby justifying the devaluation of rural resources and the transfer of these resources for urban benefit. For the urban–rural system to work, urban domination must be protected since urban populations are dependent on rural people for the basic resources that drive their economy and sustain their population.

## SCALE AND COMPLEXITY

A limitation in current thinking about the definition of urban and rural communities is an exclusive internal focus. Turning the focus externally, we can observe that all communities are connected through wider urban–rural systems. Historically, urban–rural systems formed on a localized regional basis.

Over time, they expanded and created linkages to other urban–rural systems. Now, the world is a network of interconnected urban and rural communities linked together in a mega-sized global urban–rural system (Thomas and Fulkerson 2019, 2021). Within this system, highly populous urban communities depend upon trade with multiple rural communities for natural resources. Rural producers extract natural resources to sell as commodities, while urban producers purchase them to manufacture complex goods that are sold back to rural producers. Though potentially self-sufficient, rural communities have become entwined in urban trade to purchase an array of urban products, including automobiles, electronics, or other consumer goods. Urban communities, lacking the potential for self-sufficiency, have become dependent on these systems. Before going further, we should consider what is meant here by the term system.

Many sociologists have come to be repulsed by the system concept, which is an unfortunate accident of history unique to sociology. This revulsion is based on the history of sociology and the mid-century influence of Talcott Parsons. As observed by Lyon and Driskell (2012), for Parsons, a social system is defined as a:

> plurality of individual actors interacting with each other in a situation which has at least a physical or environmental aspect, actors who are motivated in terms of a tendency to the "optimization of gratification" and whose relation to the situations, including each other, is defined and mediated in terms of a system of culturally structured and shared symbols. (Parsons 1951, 5–6).

This encompassing definition is intended to capture all social possibilities, including but not limited to the community. However, Parsons rarely focused on the community level, instead moving between the individual and mass (national) society. Most problematic is his underlying assumption that human behavior is motivated by a hedonistic drive for gratification. Thus, the Parsonian definition has a rocky philosophical foundation. Understandably, contemporary scholars would reject this assumption, perhaps even with the risk of throwing the proverbial baby out with the bathwater. It is worth noting that there is little in Parsonian thought that requires acceptance of such hedonist or utilitarian foundations. Beyond the weaknesses of Parsonian assumptions about hedonism, is his broader proposition that social systems tend toward equilibrium—a state of normalcy. Parson believed that systems might go through temporary changes but will eventually revert. Conflict theorists challenge this assumption by maintaining that change is a constant (not provisional) state of affairs. Further, they suggest Parson's view had a conservative bias, subtly promoting stability and order over conflict and change. In the 1960s, when Parsonian sociology fell out of favor, it was because of conflict-oriented thinkers who offered such critiques, as noted in the introduction. With the waning of Parsonian dominance in sociology, many imagined the death of social systems thinking—but is it possible to reintroduce social systems in a non-Parsonian manner?

Thomas (2020) provides a solution by leading us toward a different foundation based on Complex Adaptive Systems (CAS). CAS grows out of complexity science—an umbrella that captures a range of multidisciplinary theories and approaches. These theories tend to share in common an emphasis on the properties of self-similarity, emergence, self-organization, and complexity (Lansing 2003). Thomas and Fulkerson (2019, 2021) use the CAS framework to describe urban–rural systems, the world system, and environmental demographic systems. While a CAS will adapt and change with time, there is always an element of uncertainty as when a change at one level can alter conditions on an emergent level—the butterfly effect. Path dependence means that once a change occurs, the system finds itself on a new trajectory that may or may not lead to equilibrium. We can only talk about systems because they contain emergent properties that do not exist at other scales. For our purposes, this means we cannot learn about communities by studying entire nations or individuals—these are different scales. We risk committing the ecological or reductionist fallacies when we generalize across scales. At the same time, different scales are connected in a continuous rather than discrete manner.

The logic of urban–rural systems is not reducible to separate urban or rural communities—only the system's political, economic, cultural, and the environmental (PECE) linkages or relations contain the logic. As we will discuss later, social interaction is a critical ingredient for community agency since interaction between individuals gives communities an emergent reality. Urban–rural systems exhibit autopoiesis, wherein they can create the components from which they are made—much like a machine that can regenerate by creating its replacement parts. If, for instance, a rural community stops producing a particular crop, the urban–rural system may identify another rural community to replace it, thereby allowing the system to continue. Further, urban–rural systems exhibit reflexivity, meaning that there are feedback mechanisms at work that would enable the process of adaptation. Adaptation is no guarantee of improvement since change can be for the worse. This brief overview of Complex Adaptive Systems is not meant to be exhaustive but should be sufficient for defending the value of thinking in terms of systems.

## EVOLUTION OF URBAN–RURAL SYSTEMS

Below is a very brief summary of the history that led to the creation of urban–rural systems—though a complete detailed account is provided by Thomas and Fulkerson (2021). Against this backdrop, we will see how urban–rural systems have evolved over time.

*Nomadic Foraging.* Long before humans lived in anything that might resemble a city or even a tiny village, they were roaming the environment as nomadic foragers, searching daily for the nutrients needed for survival. Small groups of twenty-five to thirty individuals would search for edible plants, roots, and fruits while hunting small game, fish, and insects. When the supply ran low, the group would pick up and move to a new location to make camp. This strategy reliably supported humans for thousands of years through the better part of the Paleolithic or old stone age. The late Paleolithic and dawn of the Neolithic included early attempts at creating permanent settlements supported by horticultural practices that evolved under foraging. It is a myth that foraging groups were incapable of cultivating food. While it was likely crude, late foragers had amassed a great deal of knowledge about the local flora and fauna that enabled a certain amount of control. While shepherding animals would take longer to perfect, planting crops occurred long before established farming communities emerged. Nomadic foragers would follow a predictable circuit and, knowing they would return at a future date, would plant seeds, leave, and return to reap the harvest.

Nomadic foraging is an environmental demographic system that enables mobile groups to remain highly self-sufficient. While some trade existed, it was not integral to survival, and usually focused on exotic goods to be given as gifts. Thus, the political economic system was rudimentary at best. Most experts believe that the life of a nomadic forager was far healthier than the first settled farmers because foragers ate a more diverse diet that more adequately addressed their nutritional needs—particularly after the broad-spectrum revolution. Moreover, foragers were thought to have led a life full of leisure time, as the work of hunting and gathering could be accomplished within a few hours. The social and cultural world of nomads is thought to be vibrant and informed mainly by religious beliefs. As these religions evolved, there would eventually be a desire to create permanent sites of worship, which was possibly one of the driving forces for creating the first settlements.

*Agrarian Settlements and Pastoral Nomads.* As humans increased their knowledge of horticulture, harvests grew more abundant, and settled life became possible. According to the archaeological record, the oldest known settlements in modern Turkey date to the late Paleolithic, though they were not successfully maintained. Though there are older sites of attempted settlement, such as in Çatalhöyük (roughly 7,000 BCE), the first successful agrarian settlements were in the Fertile Crescent of modern Syria and Iraq about 5,000 BCE. Large settlements have also been discovered in modern Greece, Pakistan, Bosnia and Herzegovina, and Ukraine—the latter part of the Cucuteni–Tripolye culture (Mantu 2000). Some of these large settlements may have been occupied seasonally by somewhat nomadic populations. Unlike their foraging ancestors, these nascent Neolithic farmers would need to work long, hard hours planting and harvesting crops while eating a narrower range of foods. This practice led to shorter, malnourished populations. Due to increasing population density, settled life accelerated the spread of disease, leading to the first epidemics and, later, pandemics. Though living in a permanent settlement based on agricultural production sounds like a safer option than nomadic foraging, life expectancy is thought to have declined initially. Despite the shorter lives of individuals, agrarian communities could host larger populations.

It is likely that the earliest farmers coexisted with bands of nomadic foragers and likely traded with them. Trade was one way to improve otherwise deficient diets, allowing for access to animal protein obtained from nomadic hunters since the first farmers could not risk raising animals that might consume their plant-based crops. It would be thousands of years before humans could master animal husbandry while maintaining fields of crops that were not devoured (early examples of domestication predate this, such as sheep and goat herding in Iran, roughly 8,000 BCE; the dog was domesticated over 30,000 years ago). As humans came to master both plant and animal agriculture—horticulture and pastoralism—they were able to create a bounty that exceeded their immediate needs.

Not everyone moved into a settled agrarian community. Some of the nomads formed mobile pastoral communities, such as the Proto-Indo Europeans, who would populate much of Europe (Anthony 2010). These mobile pastoralists often lived in large groups, numbering in the thousands, hence, not to be confused with much smaller bands of nomadic foragers. They acquired much of what they needed by trading with settled farm communities. They perfected the domestication of horses and used wagons to transport their wares. Some specialized in raiding and plundering settlements—a strategy mastered by the Scythians as early as the eighth century BCE, who could repel a powerful Persian invasion by the sixth century (Cernenko 2012). The profit of raiding was not very high when modest agrarian villages dotted the landscape. Later pastoral nomads became more potent due to the growth and development of cities attached to larger empires. The Mongols created the largest contiguous land empire in human history by the twelfth century C.E. using similar methods as the Scythians—but raiding larger and wealthier settlements.

Within settlements, the surplus that resulted from increased agricultural mastery enabled a small segment of the population to live outside the drudgery of cultivation. The first was likely religious figures in Ubaid temples, who could live off the labor of others. These were followed by political and military leaders. Eventually, more complex trade would ensue between settlements and a broader class of freehands. After a time, trade became so extensive that some settlements found they could exist without reliance on their own cultivation for survival. Thus emerged the first market towns and the birth of urbanization. Bear in mind that the first cities coexisted for an extended period in conjunction with agrarian villages, pastoral nomads, and nomadic foragers. Trade between cities was facilitated greatly by pastoral nomads. Thus, it is a mistake to think of these as distinct or mutually exclusive chronological stages.

*Urban–Rural Systems.* The first market towns we can describe as urban emerged roughly the fourth millennium BCE in the Fertile Crescent and included early Ubaid towns. These were sites on which traders from near and far could come together to barter and exchange goods. Such sites could exist in areas with less fertile soils since they were not dependent on farming for survival, thus making them the first experiments in urban settlement. Eventually, the size and complexity of market towns evolved into what we now call a city, the first of which is Uruk, in modern Iraq. We know about this ancient city as it was documented through the ancient tale, *The Epic of Gilgamesh*. At its peak, the city may have reached a population of 80,000–90,000 (Algaze 2013). The Uruk civilization reigned supreme for hundreds of years and included other cities of impressive size, such as Lagash, Umma, Ur, and Kish. Uruk would eventually be challenged by the Elamites of modern Iran and then by the Egyptian Empire, who would, in turn, be defeated by Macedonia and finally the Roman Empire. Through all of this conquest, the basic underlying structure of communities remained unchanged, with the bulk of people living in rural communities and a few in cities. As different empires moved in, the centrality of power often shifted, leaving once-dominant cities to rot and even collapse—a pattern that continues today.

With the birth of urbanization came the distinction between cultivators—including most of the population—and freehands—consisting of a small elite group (detailed in the next chapter). Over time, the freehands would develop trade and expand, while advances in agriculture would reduce the number of cultivators. Most communities remained agrarian and focused on self-sufficiency, but enough were producing a large enough surplus to sell excess agricultural products in exchange for urban products. When agrarian communities become so engaged in trade that they rely on agricultural exports as the basis of their economy, they become rural communities. It shifts from being independent and agrarian to being rural and trade-dependent—rural implies a political economic connection to urban communities.

## The Development of a Global Urban–Rural System

We have seen empires rise and fall through the centuries, always centered on one or more focal cities, be they Cairo, Athens, or Rome in the West, or Constantinople, Moscow, or Beijing in the East. The nobility occupying these central cities sat atop an elaborate network fed by countless rural communities, paying tribute and engaging in trade. Historically, rural communities have been exploited or enslaved, their subjugation being a prerequisite to the vitality of the more extensive urban–rural system of the empire. In many cases, the empire's collapse directly resulted from the deterioration of rural production, as occurred when Egypt's "breadbasket" was captured by invading Persians, thus damaging the Eastern Roman (Byzantine) empire irrevocably. A peace agreement was reached in 629 CE, returning Egypt to Roman (Byzantine) control, only to be lost again to invading Muslim armies ten years later. Losing its central food supply was a significant precipitating factor in the decline of the Eastern Roman Empire, with the eventual loss of Constantinople (Istanbul) to Ottoman Turks in 1453, thus marking the end of the medieval era.

The modern world system began to emerge after the fall of medieval Europe. The "discovery" of the New World, recentered global trade away from the Indian Ocean and toward Europe and the Atlantic (Abu-Lughod 1991). It was developed through colonial conquest that began with the independent European powers of Spain, Portugal, the Netherlands, Britain, and France. These empires had clear power centers in Lisbon, Madrid, the Hague in Amsterdam, London, and the Palace at Versailles near Paris. These empires fought with one another for centuries as they ambitiously set out to capture new territory they could exploit for resources and wealth. Rural and agrarian people, such as the Indigenous American, Asian, and African populations, were enslaved and forced to work to supply the empires. Coercion was long the strategy relied upon by urban-centered empires to ensure a steady and reliable flow of rural resources. Yet, coercion sows the seeds of its own demise, as colony after colony staged rebellions and revolutions that led, in many cases, to newly independent states throughout the seventeenth and twentieth centuries. For instance, the Portuguese Empire did not transfer Macau to China's control until 1999.

Two world wars solidified the end of the colonial era and laid the framework for greater international cooperation. The ensuing Cold War involved two competing systems, based on Western capitalism in Europe and North America and on Eastern communism based in China and the USSR. These competing empires established international relations by promising prospective nations favorable trade relations. Most scholars agree that the collapse of the Soviet Union was the birth of the singular global economy we know today. The ascendancy of China—once occupied by Japan—has shown the modern world system can offer all nations the ability to rise to the highest echelon, fall, and rebound economically. Unfortunately, many of the world's poorest countries, once subjugated by colonialism and plundered for decades or centuries, are in a poor position to achieve economic growth. The poorest nations are not coincidentally predominantly rural, highly dependent on the export of natural resources and agricultural commodities for their survival. Their place in the global urban–rural system remains vital as a source of rural resources, though their extreme poverty is unsustainable.

## EFFECTIVENESS OF URBAN–RURAL SYSTEMS

How well do urban–rural systems work? If all goes to plan, then terms of trade are fair, and urban and rural populations are adequately resourced and employed. However, urban–rural systems have a history of breaking down precisely because urban trade relationships tend to become lopsided in favor of urban advantage. The consequences are most pronounced in poor rural countries, where scarce arable land is dedicated to the production of high-priced commodities that will generate the highest expected exchange value (money) when sold to urban markets but offer little in terms of immediate use value (sustenance). For instance, while potentially providing a lucrative payoff when sold to a buyer, such as an urban textile company, cotton production cannot give the farmer a quick meal in an emergency. Urban–rural trade relationships have created devastating famines for rural communities when the anticipated prices for agricultural commodities fall below expectations—market prices set in urban centers of the highest order. If a rural farmer grows food for trade, they may calculate that the best way to survive the famine is to sell everything they produce, leaving nothing for immediate consumption. This decision may look counter-productive to an outsider, but it explains why nearly all famines occur in countries that are net exporters of agricultural commodities.

A devastating fungal infestation caused the famed Irish potato famine of the nineteenth century—*Phytophthora infestans*—that reduced between half to three-quarters of the potato crop to unusable mush. The few potatoes that could be salvaged were brought to market so farmers could attempt to pay off their debts and taxes. This meager harvest left nothing to feed the farmers, who experienced malnourishment and undernourishment. In the end, most could not pay off their debts and would lose their farms, prompting a mass exodus that we now know as the Irish diaspora. From an urban–rural systems approach, we can interpret this event as a collapse in the environmental demography involving Irish rural communities and the urban–rural systems in which they were participating. It was an environmental demographic failure since the population did not receive what it needed from the environment. Still, it was led by a failure of the political economic system that centers on urban–rural trade. The ensuing mass exodus transformed the sociocultural dimension of Irish communities and all the receiving nations that became home to Irish immigrants.

Urban communities rely on selling manufactured products that incorporate natural resources from multiple points of origin in exchange for vital rural resources used in making food, medicine, and textiles. Detroit, Michigan, for instance, is a city that came to rely on the manufacture of automobiles. As long as the political economic system functioned as intended, this urban population could maintain itself. However, as rival automobile manufacturers emerged in other urban centers worldwide, such as Tokyo, urban–rural trade networks shifted and reconfigured. Detroit started to lose out on urban–rural trade and soon found its population was not obtaining the energy required to maintain itself. As factories closed, workers were laid off. The city's vast infrastructure, paid for by taxes by evaporating wages, declined. Soon, those in the public sector were laid off. As public services fell, infrastructure collapsed, and much of the city became uninhabitable.

Unlike rural farmers, urban workers have a minimal capability to feed themselves. Yet, Detroiters made admirable strides in creating impressive urban gardens. While serving as an effective supplement, the math is not favorable for urban self-sufficiency due to large populations. The urban environment tends to have highly impervious surfaces and few natural resources. However, this too is changing in Detroit as peripheral city blocks are bulldozed and returned to a natural state. As these trends proceed, they look like a process of ruralization—the opposite of urbanization. Like Irish farmers, many Detroit autoworkers would have to respond to the collapsing urban–rural system around them by leaving their home communities. Such collapse creates devastation for local cultures and social relationships that developed over many years.

Given the risks associated with the impending possibility of collapsing urban–rural systems, it is reasonable to ask why we have organized our world in this manner. History can help us contextualize how we came to be a species that lives somewhere between urban and rural.

## SUMMARY

In this chapter, we began by thinking about the concepts of urban and rural as they are widely used and based on government definitions. We noted that these definitions were of an environmental demographic nature. We then explored other dimensions, including the political economic and sociocultural. Now informed of the three-dimensional meaning of urban and rural, we are prepared to understand the community as part of broader urban–rural systems.

We examined the historical evolution of environmental demographic systems, which ends with emergence of urban–rural systems. These grew alongside agrarian settlements and some remnants of nomadic foraging. We studied the composition of urban–rural systems today, operating within a larger and more encompassing world system. Finally, we questioned the system's effectiveness by considering examples of system failure. By now, it should be clear that all communities are connected. Each occupies a different node in a global network.

Returning to the discussion in the introduction, we may recall the community capitals framework. The capitals include the economic, political, natural, built, social, human, and cultural. Suppose we juxtapose these capitals with the three dimensions of urban–rural systems discussed in this chapter. In that case, we can find a close correspondence. The environmental demographic dimension includes natural and built capitals, the political economic dimension includes political and financial capitals, and the sociocultural dimension includes social, human, and cultural capital. What the capitals framework lacks is a logic connecting the various capitals. The logic of urban–rural systems provides the missing piece, explaining how the multiple capitals interact. In the concluding chapter, we will revisit how the capitals framework can integrate the logic of urban–rural systems through the Sustainable Capitals Pyramid.

*Chapter 2*

# Environmental Demography

In the fourteenth century, Ibn Khaldun underscored the logic of environmental demography by observing that human populations can only be supported through organized cooperation (in Abdullahi and Salawu 2012):

> The power of the individual human being is not sufficient for him to obtain (the food) he needs and does not provide him with as much as he requires to live. Even if we assume an absolute minimum of food . . . that amount of food could be obtained only after much preparation. . . . Thus, he cannot do without a combination of many powers from among his fellow beings if he is to obtain food for himself and them. Through cooperation, the needs of several persons, many times greater than their own number, can be satisfied.

Ancient humans never lived like tigers, who are primarily solitary in adulthood. The earliest humans lived in small groups, who combined their powers to hunt and gather food for collective survival. Khaldun anticipated that more elaborate strategies would be needed to support larger populations, such as those we find in cities. When we approach community from an environmental demographic perspective, we consider organized cooperation that enables the population to find what it needs from the environment. The central principle of *carrying capacity* is that the environment, at a local level, can only support a limited population based on the availability of finite resources.

The notion of carrying capacity has been around since 1933 when Aldo Leopold wrote a textbook called *Game Management*. Leopold's interest was in monitoring wildlife populations by studying the interdependent predator-prey relationship, such as between wolves and moose. Environmental limits to population growth are as applicable for humans as for wildlife, so the concept's relevance for humans was not hard to infer. Odum (1953) made the connection explicit and added a mathematical formula that showed how carrying capacity followed a logistic S-curve function—the curve levels out at the point where the population approaches the limit set by natural constraints.

If the population overshoots local resources, growing past natural limits, stabilizing mechanisms will be activated. The population size must be reduced, or more resources must be produced. One option is for some individuals to relocate to a different area with available resources. Another option is involuntary—population will decline due to undernourishment or malnourishment. Other factors, such as diseases, can also reduce populations, though they are unplanned. War has long been a source of death globally, and it often results from competing populations vying for the same resources. Thus, ideas surrounding population and the environment have been circulating for centuries, focusing mainly on overpopulation when population exceeds natural limits. We will consider the social and environmental consequences of overpopulation before considering ways to plan resilient communities.

## SOCIAL CONSEQUENCES OF OVERPOPULATION

Most scholarly discussions of environmental demography begin with Thomas Malthus, one of the pioneering thinkers on the subject. He was influenced by his contemporaries, including Condorcet and Godwin. He should not be regarded as the first to fear the negative social consequences of large populations growing seemingly without limits. In the United States, Benjamin Franklin considered the issue decades before Malthus. He took a more optimistic view that placed faith in human ingenuity and the benefits of living in large cities. These ideas were offered in his *Observations Concerning the Increase of Mankind* in 1751. In a short essay of 3,000 words, the goal of Franklin's argument was to direct British colonial policy toward expansion into the Americas since Europe had become too crowded. Franklin was a pragmatist and innovator, and the solution to overcrowding was to create a release valve—to send people to areas with low populations. Unfortunately, this translated into the horrors of colonial expansion, leading to conflict with Native Americans and other colonial powers, such as the French. Eventually, the colonists would revolt, ironically, led by Franklin. The logic of a release valve, when considered in the contemporary world, encourages the emigration of citizens from one nation to another when population grows too large. This remains viable and prudent, though there is often resistance to such policies raised by the receiving nations, who may view immigrants as threatening. For instance, even the most socially progressive nations, such as Denmark and Sweden, have had their share of xenophobia toward North African immigrants.

While not the first to write about population, Malthus offered one of the most complete treatments in his 1798 treatise, *An Essay on the Principle of Population*. To understand his views, it is necessary to understand the world in which Malthus lived. Residing in the United Kingdom at the close of the eighteenth and beginning of the nineteenth century, he witnessed firsthand the exploding populations that resulted from the emerging industrial revolution. Unlike Franklin, he feared that population growth could result in complete disaster not easily alleviated by simply relocating portions of the population. Eventually, the planet would be too full. His central thesis was that population grew geometrically while agricultural production grew arithmetically. As a result of the differential growth rates, he estimated population would eventually overshoot the food supply, leading to what he referred to as population checks.

Population checks were, for Malthus, nature's way of reducing population and included the trio of famine, disease, and war. Famine would be the immediate result of an insufficient food supply. In the late eighteenth century, farmers were exhausting their soils from overfarming and lacked the knowledge and means for applying fertilizers or rotating fields. The pressure was high to keep planting, in large part, to feed troops fighting in a perpetual war machine. Malthus reasoned that war itself resulted from dwindling food supplies, which created competition and fighting by different factions seeking to capture what scarce resources were available. Most of Europe was engulfed in warfare during Malthus's lifetime, living through colonialism, the American and French Revolutions, the rise of Napoleon, and the invasion of France by a coalition of nations that included Russia, the Ottoman Turks, and Prussia. Malthus, like his contemporaries, tried to connect the dots by linking population to agricultural crises and perpetual warfare. The third population check, disease, is more complex since it is more closely related to population density than size. Disease is particularly troublesome in cities, where transmission rates are highest. Malthus probably understood that the pandemics of his time, including yellow fever, malaria, and smallpox, were connected to population density. Though there was little scientific knowledge about disease—bloodletting was still in use as a treatment, for instance—there was some basic understanding of spread, the need for quarantine, and efforts to promote inoculation, which meant exposure to a live sample. War provided incentives to have soldiers inoculated against smallpox since it was one of the leading causes of death on and off the battlefield.

Malthus's view was that immorality was the source of the population problem—and hence, all of its negative social consequences. More to the point, he believed foremost that humans needed to exercise sexual restraint to limit reproduction. His solution would promote moral reform and abstinence, informed by a Christian religious doctrine. He placed most of the blame for overpopulation on the poor, whom he thought the most morally bankrupt, irresponsibly reproducing with no way to feed the new mouths brought into the world. He vehemently opposed England's Poor Laws, which provided a meager social safety net to help feed and house the poor. He believed such laws only perpetuated the problem of population and argued it was preferable to allow the poor to perish and thereby reduce the population. While these views may seem extreme or even absurd, one can still find similar arguments being made today in the political sphere, either explicitly or implicitly, as a justification for slashing social spending on programs that aid the poor.

After scrutiny, many of Malthus's theories and mathematical calculations have been debunked and falsified. He was wrong about both the growth rate in agricultural productivity and population growth. Humans have proven more innovative than he expected, creating technologies and knowledge that would expand agricultural productivity to continue to surpass the overall global demand for food. The population grew faster than Malthus anticipated—it grew exponentially. We can credit Benjamin Franklin, who correctly anticipated this growth function. Though highly variable by nation, fortunately, the overall population growth rate globally peaked in the 1960s and has been falling ever since. It was not because of a moral crusade, although birth control campaigns have successfully reduced fertility in nations such as Thailand. The most urbanized nations would wind up with the largest populations and the lowest fertility rates. Urbanization itself, it turns out, provides a disincentive for having large families since children become economic liabilities rather than the assets that they are as workers on farms. Poverty also tends to increase infant and child mortality, creating an incentive to have more children in the hopes of some surviving into adulthood. Improvements in access to health care can reduce infant and child mortality and remove this incentive, leading to lower fertility in rural areas.

Today, nearly all global population growth occurs in a handful of primarily poor rural nations in Sub-Saharan Africa and parts of Asia, such as Afghanistan. Nevertheless, the ability of these remaining nations to achieve population stability has been stymied by continual poverty endemic to a farming economy, even though rates of urbanization are very high in most of these rural nations. For example, Uganda is one of the most rural nations. Only one in seven people live in an urban area yet has an urbanization rate greater than 5 percent—five times that of the United States. The future of the global population rests on the futures of these poorest rural nations. However, despite Lester Brown's (2008) call for "wartime mobilization" of resources to mitigate global poverty and stave further population growth, we have not seen the collective global response necessary to curb population growth.

The most crucial contribution we received from Malthus was his insight on the limits of population growth relative to what the environment could supply—the logic of carrying capacity and the basis of the energy economy (explained later). Humanity needs to move toward a more sustainable balance between population and the environment. However, there is no way to get around the fact that a world with nearly eight billion humans and growing is hard to sustain. We may see Malthusian population checks emerge as a result of overpopulation. At best, Benjamin Franklin's escape valve logic would mean that overpopulated communities can survive by sending part of the population away to inhabit a new community at a local level. Migration can be an effective local policy, though it is not without its own challenges. Conflicts emerge when populations invade territories, resulting in armed conflicts or other forms of cultural and social conflict. Unless space exploration becomes a reality, at the global level, the escape valve remains an elusive option.

The worst and least valuable part of Malthus's legacy—though it endures—lies in his blaming of the poor. While it is true that poor agricultural families tend to be larger—more kids mean more hands in the field, is a logical adaptation more than a failure of morality. The poverty of farm families is a direct result of urban exploitation. Corporations seek profits by selling products at a low price and leaving almost nothing to pay farmers. Urban populations enjoy the products of cheap rural resources produced afar, even as their consumption perpetuates rural poverty, population growth, and the social consequences of famine, war, and disease. Perhaps no one was more critical of Malthus's blaming the poor than Karl Marx and his associate, Friedrich Engels.

## Marx and Engels's Critique of Malthus

Writing a short time after Malthus, in the early nineteenth century, Marx and Engels were critical of Malthus's blame of the poor for overpopulation and ensuing misery. They found his moral argument to be deficient. For Marx (and Engels), human misery was a function of capitalist exploitation. Marx and Engels witnessed the same dire conditions in industrial Europe as Malthus. Engels lived through a time when workers in Europe were forced to labor under some of the worst industrial conditions imaginable, prompting him to write, *The Conditions of the Working Class in England*. This volume provided a snapshot of Manchester, England, between 1842 and 1844 and would become the basis of a lifelong collaboration with Karl Marx. Engels's analysis may be regarded as one of the first community studies emphasizing a political economic perspective.

During the industrial era in England, many children were spending their waking hours in dangerous and hot coal mines since they were small enough to fit through the vent holes created to release heat and gas from the mines (Rhodes 2018). Other children and adults labored in dark factories, enduring injuries and fatigue. For Marx and Engels, these atrocities were not the result of overpopulation but calculated profit margins and capitalist control over the means of production. Marx and Engels were aware of how capitalism transformed humans into alienated beings. It turned agriculture into an industrial process that exploited soils to depletion. Marx became an avid follower of the soil scientist Justus von Liebig, who provided the science necessary to understand soil nutrients and how to create and apply synthetic fertilizers. Marx had additional concerns about how urbanization led to environmental catastrophes such as the pollution of waterways, as raw sewage was funneled directly into the Thames and other rivers of Europe. These two problems— deficient soils and sewage-filled waterways—were interconnected for Marx, leading him to theorize a "metabolic rift" in the natural cycling of nutrients between humans and soils (Foster 1999). We return to the ideas of Marx and Engels in the next chapter.

## ENVIRONMENTAL CONSEQUENCES OF OVERPOPULATION

In the 1960s, biologist Paul Ehrlich became a national figure for his grim projections of human misery after what he called a population bomb. Along with Rachel Carson, he was instrumental in motivating the modern environmental movement—one of the most successful social movements in recent history. Recall that the 1960s witnessed peak population growth rates globally, which would have created a great deal of alarm in the absence of knowledge about future trends downward. Many suggested Ehrlich was channeling the ghost of Malthus. Unlike Malthus, however, Ehrlich was aware of the limits to the Malthusian argument and was more concerned with the environment than the social consequences of overpopulation. Malthusian predictions were not borne out worldwide in terms of social consequences, though there were isolated disasters that seemed to provide at least partial evidence. For example, one could interpret the devastating famine that struck China between 1959 and 1961 as proof. It led to an immense loss of life, with estimates ranging from ten to fifty-five million deaths. Though nature was partially at work, such catastrophes could have been avoided through better and more careful planning. China's Great Leap Forward included poorly advised agricultural and food distribution policies that created famine more than nature—it was a failure of the political economy.

Neither Malthus nor Ehrlich could have predicted agricultural innovations in the 1960s Green Revolution under the direction of such individuals as Norman Borlaug. Borlaug developed different varieties of crops that were more resilient to drought and pests, had higher yields, and allowed productivity to increase dramatically. The result was a more robust food supply than previously imagined. While that was the overall outcome, the results were less successful at the local level in some cases—discussed further in chapter 8.

Though many view Ehrlich's (and Malthus's) legacy as one of miscalculation, his enduring influence may be found in the brilliant insight he developed in his IPAT model. In this model, environmental Impact is proposed as a function of three factors: population, affluence, and technology. Ehrlich suggested that it is not sheer population size that determines our future. Technology has proven to be a formidable ally in holding off Malthus's population corrections. At the same time, energy-producing technologies, such as those associated with nuclear fission, have led to catastrophes in Chernobyl and Three-Mile Island. Fossil fuels are implicated in climate change and global warming, and practices like strip mining and mountain top removal (MTR). Ultimately, affluence has more to do with consumption patterns than population since a large poor population will consume less than a small affluent population. We get a much fuller picture of environmental impact by adding affluence and technology to our consideration. These impacts come in two primary forms: adding pollutants and withdrawing resources. In the long run, the damage done to the environment can become relevant to the social consequences predicted by Malthus since a depleted and degraded environment cannot produce enough to support a large, affluent, and technologically irresponsible population. Though technological innovation has done much for the food supply, solving at least temporarily the problem of overpopulation. We should note that Borlaug himself cautioned that we may have only bought a few more years since the supply of freshwater used in irrigation is dwindling. Concerns of population outstripping natural resources have not gone away.

Environmental sociologist William Catton, Jr.'s (1982) book, *Overshoot,* added a cultural dimension to our understanding of the environmental consequences of overpopulation. Catton expressed that many risks of overpopulation could be averted if Western culture became more ecologically enlightened. His collaborator, Riley Dunlap, contributed to this idea by developing a survey instrument measuring the NEP, or New Ecological Paradigm (Catton and Dunlap 1980). The NEP involves a package of beliefs and values that acknowledge the limits to growth. At the base of the argument for Catton and Dunlap is that culture is to blame. Catton explained that the Western worldview was informed by a vision of manifest destiny and the belief that resources were infinite—perhaps following Franklin's advice to move if the resources get low.

Moreover, there was a general belief that humans were exceptional beings that could overcome natural limits. This view would later be referred to as the Human Exceptionalist (or Exemptionalist) Paradigm (HEP), which was the polar opposite of the NEP. When these ideas were developed, a massive global social movement was underway focused on the environment, which must have looked like evidence that the New Ecological Paradigm was taking root. They could not foretell the ups and downs that characterized the environmental movement through the 1980s and beyond.

## THEORY OF THE ENERGY ECONOMY

To help grasp the relationship between population and the environment, Fulkerson and Thomas (2021) developed a theory of the energy economy that was further elaborated in Thomas and Fulkerson (2021). This theory focuses on the concept of energy balance between population demand and environmental supply. The term *energy* here refers to the entirety of goods consumed by a population—some of which will meet needs, and some that are luxuries. All consumed goods have a foundation in natural resources that must be harvested, gathered, collected, or mined—activities we describe as rural work. The natural environment is where stores of energy can be discovered and utilized. Goods production begins with rural workers obtaining energy sources from the environment and selling them into more complex urban products. We define urban production as beginning with rural products. Human labor is one of the only sources of energy originating in urban areas, though rural products are needed to support this labor energy. Urban-rural systems include complex trade networks that facilitate circuits of urban–rural production, as we elaborate on in the next chapter.

As we noted in the previous chapter, long before humans lived in sedentary communities, they learned how to survive collectively in small groups of nomadic foragers. These small groups would continually move through the environment, going to natural energy sources and consuming them immediately. Since then, humans have met the energy challenge by settling into agrarian villages, developing systems of pastoral nomadism, and eventually creating the urban–rural systems that allow massive populations to live in cities with almost no local energy production. Everything is obtained through a complex circuitry of trade. These environmental demographic systems offer alternative ways to accomplish the same goal: achieving energy balance. Some require the community to remain mobile, which expands the resource horizon. Others require a more intensive approach to accessing sufficient calories from within the same locale, negating the need for mobility. The sedentary community is a recent invention in the long history of *Homo sapiens*, but innovations have enabled populations to grow to sizes unimaginable in earlier times.

For a population to sustain itself, the ratio of energy demand to supply should be at parity (one-to-one). If the ratio falls short, the population experiences a deficit. It must adapt by consuming less energy or importing more of what it needs to increase supply. If the ratio exceeds parity, there is a surplus, and the population may consume more. It may alternatively save the excess resources (if nonperishable) and export the surplus through trade. Surplus means that a population is successfully sustaining itself. Rural communities differ from agrarian communities in their reliance on trade. While agrarian communities engaged in some level of trade—it was never the basis of the energy economy, just a supplemental way to obtain goods otherwise impossible to produce locally.

Any form of work or labor requires an expenditure of energy. Hiring someone means trading the fruits of labor for the cost of labor's energy expenditure. The dollar amount assigned to labor is a matter of political economy and is based on the economic value of the work. If someone is hired to paint a portrait, then the cost of the portrait will include the labor cost and possibly more to create a profit. Marx defined profit as the exploitation of labor since it meant the worker was not receiving the total value of what they produced—surplus value went to the owner of the means of production (in this case, the paint supplies and studio facilities).

## Estimating Energy Balance: The Caloric Well

One of the most significant contemporary innovations emerging in analyzing the environmental consequences of the population is the ecological footprint, created by Wackernagel (1994). The ecological footprint is a useful measure as it quantifies the resources required of populations as land area. This estimate is essential for monitoring the overall demand for resources. Demand can then be compared to estimated supplies in the environment. Rees (1996) and Wackernagel and Rees (1998) provide an example of how to apply the ecological footprint. However, they are reluctant to describe the footprint in terms of energy—something directly dismissed by Wackernagel (1994). Using the ecological footprint, they claim that at the current consumption rate in the United States, if the rest of the world were to follow suit, would necessitate six Earths. While useful, the ecological footprint is not as mathematically precise as we would prefer.

Thomas (2020) and Fulkerson and Thomas (2021) offer an alternative way of estimating energy balance. The basic idea behind the caloric well is that every person in a population has a minimal energy requirement for survival, starting with a diet of 2,000 calories per person per day. Of course, this is a conservative estimate of how much energy individuals need to survive at a bare minimum. In addition to food, individuals require building materials to support their homes. They require a minimal amount of clothing to keep warm and protected from the elements. They require a certain amount of energy used for heating and cooking purposes. All these energy demands can arguably be quantified in terms of calories, a unit of energy. Fulkerson and Thomas (2021) provide a detailed discussion of how the caloric well can be itemized. Based on this minimum caloric need per individual, if we multiply it by population size, we arrive at the Total Energy Demand. If 100 people are living in a village, this will amount to 2,000 * 100 = 200,000 calories of energy per day. Fulkerson and Thomas (2021) also consider the amount of energy available based on different land uses. For instance, they estimate the amount of energy generated by an acre of corn, which is one of the most productive crops. If we multiply the caloric output per acre by the total area in which the population lives, we can estimate the Total Energy Supply. For instance, one acre of corn can sustain approximately three people for a year (roughly 2.19 million calories). Finally, when we compare the Total Energy Demand to the Total Energy Supply, we arrive at the Energy Balance Ratio. For our village of 100 people, we would need thirty-three acres of land worth of calories for one year of support. If the available land were lower than thirty-three acres, the population would be in overshoot. The caloric deficit can be overcome by importing energy supplies (food, clothing, building supplies, etc.) from external regions—typically rural regions with excess Total Energy Supply. The boundary of the environment needed to support the population is referred to as the resource horizon. As populations grow, the resource horizon expands.

## THE ENVIRONMENTAL DEMOGRAPHY
## OF URBAN–RURAL SYSTEMS

When considering the environmental demography of urban-rural systems, it is important to recall all three dimensions, including the political economic and sociocultural features, which will be discussed in the following chapters. As noted in the last chapter, it is possible to be a rural community on one dimension but not on the others. When we say "rural community," do we mean a place with low population density, a place where most people are cultivators or do we mean a place where most people identify as rural, participate in rural culture, and participate in predictable patterns of social interaction? In the United States, rural communities usually refer to places with a low population density that host only a small proportion of people working in rural occupations. It can be deceiving to drive through a rural community where one can find evidence of rural work. For instance, farms may occupy much of the landscape. However, it is a mistake to assume this means most people are farmers in this particular community. The nature of agriculture in the United States is highly mechanized and so does not employ a large number of individuals. While about sixty million people live in rural areas (defined by population density), only 2.6 million people work in agriculture, less than one percent of the national population, and only 5 percent of the rural population. Further, a lot of farmlands is absentee owned and corporate, meaning that nobody in the community is benefitting. In addition, we lack data on the sociocultural aspects of communities, though it can be collected.

The central question of environmental demography is whether a given population can sustain itself. A community with a relatively small population with access to large tracts of land and natural resources has a high potential. Nevertheless, as we noted, only a small percentage of rural communities are engaged with the energy economy—most rural residents are best described as freehands. Therefore, they can be described as urban, even though they may live in an area with a sparse population. Many rural communities function as suburbs, where residents generally commute to a nearby city for employment. Of those working in rural occupations, what are they doing with the resources they harvest? Most are selling to large-scale buyers tied into urban production. Farmers often have contracts with corporations that require a quota sold at a predetermined price. Contract farmers are not typically providing their local community with access to the bounty of their harvest. Conventional farming revolves around a narrow range of crops, which would probably be inadequate for local needs, but ideal for urban industrial corporations that manufacture goods such as soda. The beverage industry requires large amounts of corn to create fructose syrup as a sweetener. Rural farmers may use the money they earn selling corn to soda corporations to buy their sweetened beverages, thereby closing the loop on urban–rural trade. According to the USDA, farmers receive about eight cents for each dollar consumers spend on food and beverages. Another way of viewing this is to note that urban producers capture 92 percent of the food and beverage industry value. However, without rural resources like corn—products like soda would not exist.

Today, few communities practice agrarianism, which means steering agriculture and other rural work toward meeting local demand. Many Amish communities strive for self-sufficiency—though there is a great deal of diversity among the Amish, with some groups more willing to engage in urban–rural trade. In the developing world, there is more potential to find rural communities engaged in self-sufficient or peasant farming, who have not yet converted to commodity agriculture.

## Urban Dependency

Few people in urban communities need to worry about working in the energy economy. Urban life exists because of the development of complex trade networks that siphon resources from rural areas, send them to other urban communities for processing, and get shipped to the local area for retail trade, consumed as finished products. Thomas (2012) defined this expansion of trade as urbanization, suggesting that it preceded the arrival of cities. Almost everything that precedes retail is hidden from view, so the assumption that an infinite supply of goods may flourish provided one has the means to buy what is needed and wanted.

As discussed earlier, urban areas are unique for their large hungry populations situated on a small unproductive territory. Unlike rural communities, they can flourish only if a steady supply continues to flow in from external rural areas. At least, in theory, rural communities can achieve some level of energy balance internally since they host small populations living on relatively large swathes of productive land. The potential energy of the environment exceeds the small demands of the population. Rural communities are usually established historically to harvest energy from the environment—though many have ceased such work.

Unfortunately, many urban areas are food deserts, lacking access to either grocery or restaurant options. Some may even lack access to convenient stores or fast-food restaurants. Such areas emerge from political economic processes that leave entire neighborhoods without viable employment opportunities. In such cases, we see the worst of urban existence on display—the entire arrangement of depending on trade for rural items such as food has collapsed since the means to trade (money) cannot be acquired. In the modern capitalist world economy, the ability to find success in urban–rural systems hinges on the ability to pay and, thus, employment. Urban–rural trade occurs through financial transactions rather than direct barter. Food prices, meanwhile, are a function of global markets that can fluctuate greatly, at times rising as a result of inflation.

## Limits of Urban–Rural Systems

The environmental demographic perspective applied to urban–rural systems is helpful for understanding community change but can also be essential in the area of planning. The ubiquity of urban–rural systems has created an implicit faith that energy balance can be achieved for populations entirely through trade. While true in theory, urban–rural trade often fails the populations it was designed to serve. In the United States, the wealthiest nation on earth, a large segment of the population is considered food insecure. According to the US Department of Agriculture's Economic Research Service, as many as one in seven Americans have lived with food insecurity over the last decade—at best, one in ten. Between 3 and 6 percent are experiencing very low food security. Since the United States has a population of roughly 330 million, over the last decade, between thirty-three to fifty million people have lacked

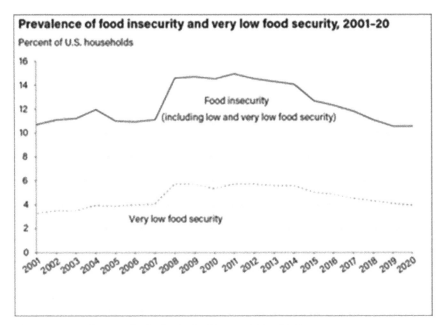

**Prevalence of food insecurity and very low food security, 2001-20**

Percent of U.S. households

Food insecurity
(including low and very low food security)

Very low food security

**Figure 2.1: Food Insecurity in the United States, 2001–2020.**
Source: (USDA, 2022).

sufficient food, while ten to twenty million live in a dire condition of inadequate food security.

When we observe large segments of urban and rural populations living with a caloric deficit, it is difficult to declare that urban–rural systems are working sustainably. Much of its explanation is political economic—the subject of the next chapter—but we can make a few observations here. The freehands in urban communities need something of value to sell for participating in trade. Usually, labor is sold, which is then used to create other goods and services that support urban–rural trade. This only works if someone is willing to pay for the labor—in other words, there must be employment. If there is little to no employment (or employers), urban workers have little recourse. Public policies that provide a safety net can help protect urbanites in this precarious situation in the short run, but a more systemic solution is desirable for the long run. Safety nets are meant to fill in gaps for temporary setbacks and not serve as permanent correctives to systemic failure.

One of the significant disadvantages of living in an urban food desert is the inability to access energy in the environment directly. Most urban areas have extensive impermeable, paved surfaces and very little soil to grow food. In some cases, the scarce land resources that exist, perhaps found in parks, can be used to create urban gardens that can serve as a helpful food supplement.

Some forms of farming are possible in urban environments, including insect farming, mariculture, and greenhouses. All of these measures should be considered, as should the initial investment required which can be substantial. The math, however, is difficult to reconcile in the absence of a population reduction and implies that immense urban centers should evaluate the Franklin solution—using release valves to lessen pressure.

On the other side of the coin are rural communities that paradoxically may host rural production activities in farming, forestry, and mining. However, the population, as a whole, sees little or no benefit and winds up dealing with poverty and caloric deficits. Rural communities have a much greater ability to meet local energy demands using local environmental resources. However, current commodity farming practices are generally not suited for this purpose. The possibility of turning to fishing or hunting or growing a garden in the rural environment can yield sources of food outside of the market. This is more difficult in urban environments, where such opportunities are scarce.

## PLANNING CONSIDERATIONS

Environmental demographic planning is primarily an accounting exercise. We can approach this through the footprint or the caloric well method. The population can be estimated by using census data, which are generally available for all nations worldwide. Finding accurate population data at the local level may prove more challenging since censuses are conducted infrequently. Knowing the size of the population, we can estimate caloric need, beginning with the bare minimum of food—2,500 calories per day per person. From this, a Total Energy Demand (TED) can be estimated. Next, data on the community's land area can estimate energy productivity (see Fulkerson and Thomas 2021). Once we know the average potential productivity per unit of land, such as the acre, we can estimate the Total Energy Supply (TES). By examining TED/TES, we can arrive at the Energy Balance ratio, which will inform planning and insight on the potential to be self-sufficient—helpful, even if the goal is not self-sufficiency.

On the supply side, planning what to produce is critical. Rural communities should consider more careful use of agrobioculturally diverse farming methods that meet local demand. For those rural residents who are farming, it may be necessary to receive technical assistance that can help convert current farming operations from traditional commodity production, suited for urban industry, to sustainable agrarian farming methods. Beyond farming, communities should inventory all available energy supplies, including water, textiles, wood, fish, and metal ores. Many rural communities in upstate New York were able to achieve a modest level of industrialization 200 years ago by harnessing running water, which could power mills. Local hydropower is no longer utilized to the same degree, save for educational purposes, as when children visit an old mill site on a historical field trip. Perhaps the potential energy of water should be revisited at the local level, alongside wind, solar, and geothermal options. Harnessing local energy sources is vital for local environmental demographic sustainability. If the basis of economic value is energy, then generating more energy should lead to a more vibrant economy.

Land tenure and ownership policies must also be considered. If most productive land is privately owned by a few individuals, then the remainder of the rural community is prevented from using the local environment. Worse yet, absentee corporate ownership of land leads to a faceless entity that converts farmland into a commodity to be bought and sold on international markets (Ashwood et al. 2020). These markets fuel global land grabs whereby a community may find the bulk of its land owned by a nation thousands of miles away. In less-developed countries, land tenure laws may allow farmers to use public lands for peasant farming (self-sufficiency as the goal) or commodity farming (trade as the goal). However, the international community and national governments have pressured farmers toward commodity production, despite the horrific trade terms resulting from grossly undervalued rural products that leave these farmers destitute and starving. The public structure of land ownership enables farmers, but global commodity markets can cause grave damage. The global Via Campesina (Peasant Way) movement is one of the most extensive collective efforts to promote peasant farming in less developed countries, reducing reliance on global urban–rural trade. Even if peasant communities are not entirely self-sufficient, having at least some survival method without complete reliance on unpredictable markets that coordinate urban-rural trade is a sound policy. Maintaining public lands is critical to allowing this shift to peasant farming, as privatized land would render peasant farmers squatters or trespassers, likely leading to their forced expulsion.

On the demand side, achieving energy balance for an urban community may require a reduction in population if it is simply too high. Infrastructure can play an essential role in facilitating population deconcentration. For instance, high-speed trains can transport workers between an urban office and a rural home within a reasonable commuting timeframe. The increasing adoption of videoconferencing, such as Zoom or Teams, and other web-based technologies, means that people residing in distant rural communities or isolated urban neighborhoods can find work that is not local. Similarly, rural residents living in a community with few employment opportunities would be able to access external job markets rapidly if viable commuting options were to open up. The historical overreliance on the automobile to achieve these goals has added a financial burden to rural households and contributed to environmental problems such as climate change. Moreover, traffic congestion and inefficient transportation routes make automobiles impractical in many urban settings, greatly elongating commute times and reducing social interaction with family and friends, leading to a lower quality of life for the individual and the community. The spatial organization of many urban areas has been disrupted by automobile accommodation.

In summary, planning for energy balance at the community level is a multifaceted and complex task, but also one that is vital. What is remarkable is that environmental demography is not typically considered in mainstream community planning and development frameworks. That in itself is evidence of a generally high level of confidence in the reliability of global urban–rural systems. However, we have ample evidence for questioning this confidence, including the problems of food deserts and overspecialization commodity farming. Very little is required to examine energy balance, since population data and geographic data are readily available. We can apply a caloric output value to generate a supply estimate to the estimated caloric demand of the population. If there are other natural resources available, we can attempt to quantify the energy value of those resources. The more local resources harvested for local consumption, the more secure rural communities will be, and the less dependent they will be on urban–rural trade to support them. Participation in urban–rural systems can be risky, but there are measures that protect communities from severe consequences without reliance on costly safety nets.

*Chapter 3*

# Political Economy

While environmental demography focuses on balancing population with environmental resources, political economy refers to the systems of power (politics, law, government, and military) through which humans administer and organize the production, distribution, and consumption of resources (economy). The federal and state government control the parameters of the economy by setting fiscal and monetary policy that sets interest rates on loans, controlling currency and inflation, and financing debt through bonds. Laws regulate and govern economic activity by enforcing contracts and patents, governing treatment of the environment, and ensuring the health, education, and safety of the population. Further, the government employs workers directly and indirectly (through contracts) in the military and civilian sectors. All of these activities rely on sufficient revenue. While some government functions generate revenue, such as national park tourism, train service, and postal service, it is also necessary to raise corporate, property, sales, and income taxes. At the local level, many individuals and communities depend on government employment, whether through public education, law enforcement, military service, conservation and environmental protection, the post office, transportation, or other services.

Political economic organization takes place on multiple levels. Currently, much energy is directed toward thinking about national and global political economy. At the global level, there is no governing body beyond limited power of the United Nations and partial alliances or treaties such as NATO (North Atlantic Treaty Organization). Thus, global economics, organized by multinational corporations, operate in response to the laws governing individual nations. While national governance is responsible for most of the functions described above, local communities vary substantially in the extent to which they can raise revenue and provide services. The overarching austerity trend has been to reduce or eliminate local government taxes and services in favor of private solutions. Community needs and wellbeing are often subjugated in favor of national or global interests—either because of a lack of power or an absence of planning. In this chapter, we will emphasize ways in which communities can strengthen their political economy, part of which hinges on the ability to gain control over local environmental demography. Indeed, it is possible to have sufficient local resources to support a population and fail to effectively produce and distribute them, leading to deficits in consumption.

This chapter considers how different political and economic systems have historically coincided with environmental demographic systems, providing a trajectory toward the present. We will consider classical political economic theories that explain the relationship between urbanization and capitalism. Marx and Engels's critique of these theories reveals the endemic problems of alienation and exploitation. Contemporary theories add to this critique by highlighting the social and environmental costs of capitalist growth and urbanization. We will consider how macro-level issues manifest and dominate the local political economy through growth machine theory. A review of local political dynamics will provide a fuller understanding of how community power structures become either vulnerable or resistant to the formation of growth machines. The chapter will conclude with planning considerations for a more sustainable community political economy, considering civic capitalism, the potential role of cooperatives and other locally oriented business models, and promoting pluralist or diversified political structures.

## POWER, AUTHORITY, AND POLITICAL ECONOMY

Max Weber (1978, 53) famously defined power as the ability to act, even against the resistance of others: "the probability that an actor in a social relationship will be in a position to carry out his own will despite the resistance of others, regardless of the basis on which that probability rests." The central mechanism for enforcing power from a Weberian perspective is violence, and Weber (1946) defined the state as having a monopoly on the legitimate right to use violence. The agents of power are thus the combined activities of uniformed military and the civilian police force. The important question is not how, but who has the power to marshal these forces? This requires us to consider the structure of authority and political systems. Since power is at the root of political systems, and since this power can be wielded over economic actors, the economic system is subservient to the political system. However, at times, it looks as though the reverse is true.

Weber offered insights on different types of authority: traditional, rational–legal, and charismatic. Traditional authority is when political power is achieved through custom, which usually involves a right to power bestowed by kinship. An heir can thus assume the reins of power because of their lineage. Rational–legal authority is political power granted to someone based on their position within a hierarchy—usually as part of a bureaucratic organization. This is how democracies function, as a combination of appointed and elected officials rising to different positions of power. Finally, charismatic authority is power achieved by persuasion—as when groups identify someone they wish to follow because they are deemed to possess desirable qualities. Traditional and rational–legal authorities may possess charisma, enhancing their effectiveness, but charismatic leaders often emerge outside of the conventional power structure, as part of emerging social movements. For instancy Martin Luther King, Jr. was a charismatic leader who rose to power through the civil rights movement.

Different types of authority correspond to different political systems that include tribalism, monarchies, oligarchies (rule by a group), dictatorships/autocracies, and democracies. In the contemporary world, most nations can be located on a spectrum from dictatorship to democracy, while the space between these extremes can been described as anocracies, which are theorized to be unstable and prone to civil wars (Walter 2022). Democracies tend to use a rational–legal basis for authority. Monarchies and oligarchies often rely on systems of traditional authority. Dictators often rely on charismatic authority, which creates challenges in the transfer of power, and thus may also incorporate traditional or rational–legal bases of authority. The type of political system is relevant to the kind of economic system that is implemented.

When we consider economic systems, Marx and Engels offered a staged evolutionary typology. It begins with the early stage of primitive communism, which involves the equitable combining and sharing of resources. This is replaced by imperial slavery, as the first empires emerged, and inequality began to grow based on the exercise of raw power and military domination. This stage is replaced by feudalism, which involves a landed aristocracy allowing a peasant class to use their land for subsistence in exchange for tribute. Marx and Engels theorized that private entrepreneurs would lead a revolt against feudalism that installs capitalism—pointing to the French Revolution as evidence. They projected a future transition into socialism, led by workers against the capitalist class, which transfers ownership of all private land and capital to the state. The Bolshevik Revolution had this as its goal, leading to the formation of the USSR. However, there is some debate about whether this was a truly socialist economy, and not just pure imperialism. Russia was a feudal economy, and many doubted socialism could emerge without capitalism. The final economic stage of communism implements a system of collective ownership, but it is poorly understood. While a useful typology, Marx and Engel's assumption of staged progress is problematic. We must avoid the temptation to characterize human history by thinking of discrete categorical stages. What we have are ideal types, hybridized forms, and messy combinations. Each of these are Complex Adaptive Systems and should be conceptualized accordingly. Moreover, the timeline of their evolutionary history ignores important facets of the archaeological record, which suggests that ancient history was more complex.

## POLITICAL ECONOMY AND ENVIRONMENTAL DEMOGRAPHY

Environmental demography, the focus of the previous chapter, should be understood as the substructure for political economic systems. Political economic systems are designed to accomplish the primary goal of the energy economy—to match environmental resources with the needs of a population. The mechanisms for achieving this outcome can vary substantially, and each environmental demographic system has its own unique blend. Politically, traditional authority dominated most of human history, with the occasional charismatic leader emerging. Weber's rational–legal authority has become more widespread along with bureaucratic organization in the contemporary world. The economic foundation has evolved from almost universal primitive communism to one that is predominantly capitalist. When we examine environmental demographic history, we can observe that economic stages do not occur linearly, nor do they coincide naturally with forms of political rule. Table 3.1 illustrates the various possibilities of political, economic, and environmental demographic systems and how they may be configured or combined with authority types.

The table should not be read strictly across rows as distinct combinations, as the types do not necessarily align. Instead, several combinations are possible. Some are unlikely, such as if we try to imagine a nomadic foraging community implementing a capitalist economy ruled by a rational–legal dictator. Other combinations are more likely, such as a nomadic foraging groups

**Table 3.1. Possible Combinations of Systems and Authority**

| Environmental Demographic Systems | Economic Systems | Political Systems | Authority Types |
|---|---|---|---|
| Nomadic Foraging | Primitive Communism | Tribalism | Traditional |
| Pastoral Nomadism | Imperialism and Slavery | Monarchy or Oligarchy | Charismatic |
| Agrarianism (Peasants) | Feudalism | | |
| Urban–Rural Systems | Capitalism | Democracy | Rational–Legal |
| | Socialism | Dictatorships | |
| | Communism | Anocracies | |

with a system of primitive communism and a tribal political system guided by traditional authority. However, things become murky when we consider agrarianism, pastoral nomadism, and urban–rural systems, which have each experienced considerable variety. Each environmental demographic system requires examination.

## Nomadic Foraging

Under nomadic foraging, the energy economy is most closely aligned with the informal political economy. Nomadic foragers generally organize in a tribal manner, led by a traditional authority figure, who is usually chosen based on kinship ties. Individuals cooperate to collectively ensure that everyone in the group has adequate nourishment and other supplies needed for survival. The economic system was simple: nature was the production system, and everyone capable worked to harvest natural resources. Distribution was fairly equitable as resources were combined and shared without much difference in portion. Consumption was immediate and mainly for survival, leaving little room to amass wealth or luxury. Power was distributed equitably, based on tribal organization with clearly defined leaders. In addition, there were typically religious figures who enjoyed some privileges. The limited ability to generate surplus ensured that resources and power would remain at a basic equitable and minimalist level. At times groups would cooperate with outsiders to engage in trade for unique items that were part of a gift economy that could span a surprising distance, often exceeding hundreds of miles. As participants in a gift economy, trade was not essential, meaning it was not relied upon for provisioning the needs of the population. The political economy of nomadic foragers has been described as primitive communism, though the term primitive has negative connotations. It resembles the hallmark of communist organization, characterized by Marx: from each according to their ability, to each according to their need.

## Agrarianism and Pastoral Nomadism

Agrarian or peasant communities, the first sedentary environmental demographic system, was focused heavily on the energy economy, with most people involved in planting and harvesting crops—horticulture—for consumption. The first agrarians coexisted with nomadic foragers, who had access to a broader range of foods, including wild animal meat, which was hard to come by, and thus created valuable trade opportunities. Eventually, the nomadic hunters domesticated animals and became pastoral nomads. Pastoral nomads formed a complementary nonsedentary environmental demographic system that carried forth some of the same traditions of nomadic foragers and were valuable trading partners for agrarian settlements. Trade expanded from rare and unique gifts to essential food and other items of the energy economy. The increased surplus of agricultural products, such as grain, led to a greater capacity for trade and increased inequality. The political economy of early agrarian settlements was likely very similar to that of nomadic foragers, though the rise in trade implies a form of capitalism.

Eventually, agrarian communities would master settled pastoralism in addition to horticulture, reducing their reliance on pastoral nomads. Meanwhile, pastoral nomads began to specialize in raiding settled communities, taking what they wanted by force, rather than trading—implementing an imperialist economy. A decline in trade likely fueled the motivation to raid or demand tributes. Some became so proficient that they built large empires. The Mongols, for instance—late pastoral nomads who specialized in horses, hunting, and warfare—created the largest land empire in human history. They would eventually merge into various settlements, ruling as the Yuan Dynasty in China.

Late agrarian power structures grew more elaborate as settlements became organized for protection, leading to a military class, who, in addition to religious figures, would enjoy privileges. The wealth of ruling individuals and families would grow with a mounting surplus. Citizens were offered protection for tribute, contributing to a feudal economy ruled by monarchies. Most community members lived at the level of subsistence, farming what was needed for survival. Cooperation with other communities was increasingly crucial as warfare became more elaborate and coordinated, paving the way for modern nation-states. Peaceful trade served as a mechanism for cooperation but was challenged by power grabs internally and externally. Politically, traditional and charismatic authority characterized agrarianism and pastoral nomadism. Eventually, this shifted from small tribal authority to large complex systems of monarchy.

## Urban–Rural Systems

As humans came to live in the bifurcated realities of urban and rural life, cooperation remained critical, though many challenges emerged. All goods on which humans depend for the range of their consumption begin with some element of nature, and thus rural work, whether it be for food, fiber, energy, fuel for heat, or minerals. Farming food, often the first image one has when thinking of rural workers, requires depositing seeds into the soil, applying water, fertilizer, and various pesticides. Farming has become increasingly industrial, yet the work of nature is crucial—we depend on seeds to germinate and grow into a desirable plant that yields some food or feed product, or perhaps a fiber or energy product, such as oil from cottonseed. Humans can feed and water a seed but cannot make it grow. Another icon of rural work, coal miners are also dependent on natural processes that turn ancient plant matter into coal. What separates the rural from the agrarian farmer is trade—rural producers have the goal of selling or trading what they produce. In contrast, agrarian producers have the goal of consuming what they produce. The different orientations influence what and how rural work is done, including selecting crops to grow, animals to rear, and energy sources to harvest.

Urban economic activity is defined as beginning with the import of rural products—generally from diverse points of origin. The first urban settlements were minor market towns where trade was the focus. We might describe this as an early form of mercantile capitalism, though this is a term usually associated with medieval Europe, rather than the ancient Fertile Crescent around 4,000 BCE. Urban industrial capitalism occurs when rural products become arranged to create more elaborate and complex goods. Industrial capitalism is often considered a product of the industrial revolution, but the basic model was in place for at least a millennium earlier, when the Chinese manufactured pottery that was exported as far as the East African coast (Hansen 2020). Since urban production cannot occur without rural products, it is uniquely separated from the energy economy and completely trade-dependent. Services facilitating trade and transport—the hallmarks of capitalism—are therefore crucial to the overarching urban–rural system. If a large urban center suddenly lost all of its trading connections, it would quickly implode, sending its population away or leaving it to face Malthusian population checks. If rural communities lose trading relationships, they can revert to agrarianism (Schwartz and Falconer 1994).

While the first ancient cities were market towns, in many respects, the emergence of larger cities was a response to a desire to mount sufficient resistance to invading armies, often comprised of pastoral nomads (Thomas 2010). The need for more elaborate urban–rural trade grew over time, from more localized areas to encompassing nearly every part of the modern world system. Between the most basic urban–rural systems of the Fertile Crescent and the modern day, we find a lengthy process wherein the development of widening trade networks led to city-states and empires (Thomas and Fulkerson 2021). In this context, the first currencies were created to facilitate the movement of goods—coins with images represented, for instance, heads of livestock. Trading livestock physically is a much more challenging logistical feat than exchanging coins.

What distinguished the colonial imperial or feudal powers from land-based warrior nomads was mastery of the sea. The Portuguese and Spanish empires—remnants of the Western Holy Roman Empire—sent armadas to settle and plunder the Americas. They were followed by the Dutch, French, and British navies—all feudal monarchies—who turned their sites to Asia,

Africa, and the Americas. These European powers competed with and fought one another in perpetual wars to claim as much territory and resources as possible and become the most powerful empire. As capitalism replaced older forms of feudalism, rational–legal authority came to supplant traditional authority. Amid colonialism, on the cusp between old monarchies and emergent democracies, were attempts to understand the inner workings of capitalism. Early scholars recognized that examining urban-rural trade was crucial. It may thus make perfect sense that the first works of political economy grew out of one of the most powerful colonial empires—the British.

## THEORIZING POLITICAL ECONOMY: CAPITALISM AND URBANIZATION

The first book to use the term *political economy* in its title was written by Sir James Steuart—a contemporary competitor with the better known Adam Smith. Writing in the eighteenth century, Steuart observed a colonial world dominated by European powers, with a nearly universal agricultural, rural economy—driven by trade with urban populations. He witnessed the rise of urban centers employing new forms of industrial production using the many rural resources that were being funneled to cities through trade and brute force, as was standard under colonialism. The British Empire reigned supreme in his lifetime. However, revolutions in the United States and France showed that older forms of traditional authority rooted in feudal monarchies would face challenges both from within and outside the empire. The British had already established a constitutional monarchy following its civil war in the seventeenth century, limiting traditional authority and creating a parliament that would rule through rational–legal authority. Similarly, the Dutch had established limits to the crown's power by transferring governance to the Hague.

Steuart (1767) observed that the rise of industrial goods production needed to happen in areas with strategic trade advantages. Writing before the rise of railways or highways, this meant having access to seaports. Because they began their historical evolution in colonial times, most of today's major cities are coastal. Since urban existence was still novel and unusual in this predominantly rural world, urban workers were described as "freehands" who were fed by the mass of "cultivators." Steuart could not imagine a society or world where the vast majority of its citizens would be urban freehands. While today's economy has succeeded in employing more people in urban than rural production, the fundamental insight of the dependency of freehands on cultivators remains in play (Thomas 2005; Fulkerson and Thomas 2021). Two significant components emerge from Steuart's political economy. These were the economic advantages in trade that accrued based on location and the advantages of a developed division of labor, both within and between the cultivators and the freehands.

Adam Smith's, *Wealth of Nations* (1937[1776]) did not contradict Steuart on the importance of urban location for trade advantages. Smith went further to explain historical patterns of economic evolution and urbanization, noting some of the central features of early cities. Smith also expanded on the idea of the division of labor, which is how economies come to accommodate more and more urban workers, with each occupying different locations and roles. He anticipated the industrial model that breaks down complex tasks into smaller subtasks to enhance productivity. He introduced the concept of absolute advantage, based on the idea that the most competitive producers are those who make the most productive and efficient use of labor. For Smith, a prosperous economy combines rational self-interest with competition, which will maximize productivity and profits over time. In this way, he is often considered the father of both modern capitalism and the field of economics.

One of the misunderstood components of Smith's contribution is the notion of the invisible hand. Smith rarely used this term himself, though many interpret his ideas with the perspective that Smith believed the economy functioned best of its own volition without any intervention—laissez-faire capitalism. In a closer reading, Smith reveals that he saw a need for political oversight and intervention to prevent markets from collapsing. While Smith appreciated the principle of absolute advantage, he also noticed that it might become a problem for workers. He anticipated that overspecialized workers engaging in mundane and repetitive activities—now associated with much industrial work—could become alienating.

## SOCIAL CRITIQUE OF CAPITALISM: EXPLOITATION AND ALIENATION

In the previous chapter, we introduced Marx and Engels, who were critics of Malthus. Generally, Marx and Engels were highly critical of capitalism and its proponents. However, in many ways, they did not challenge the basic ideas outlined by Steuart or Smith, as they sought to explain the logic of capitalism. They understood that capitalism was the logical replacement for feudalism in their theory of economic evolution. However, they challenged the morality and wisdom of the capitalist system, which they thought would eventually fail. For Marx and Engels, capitalism continued to promote class conflict while exacerbating the exploitation and alienation of workers. Under feudalism, class conflict was based on land ownership, with the landed nobility pitted against peasant farmers forced to pay tribute for their use of the land. This conflict led to rebellion and revolutions. Under capitalism, the class conflict is based on the private ownership of capital—the machinations of industry. Class was based on ownership of capital instead of land, creating the elite bourgeoisie and unfortunate proletariats forced to sell their labor to survive. Marx thus viewed private property as a recipe for exploitative class relations since the owning class would have an incentive to pay workers a wage that was less than the value they produced, creating surplus value or profit. The owners would continually look for ways to build profit at the expense of the working class, forcing them to work harder and faster for less money—to be more productive. Thus, Smith's idea of absolute advantage, of maximizing worker productivity through competition, would be viewed by Marx and Engels as highly exploitative. In the *Economic and Philosophic Manuscripts of 1844,* Marx and Engels (2009) went much further than Smith in critiquing the alienating qualities of labor in the capitalist system, outlining several forms, including alienation from 1) the end product (what was made by the worker), 2) the process of work (how it is made), 3) decisions about what is produced (forced to produce specific goods), and 4) other workers (in competition). Ultimately, Marx and Engels called for the abolition of private property since this was the crux of the problem in capitalism (ownership of capital) and feudalism (ownership of land). Only when the workers control the means of production can labor be freed from exploitation and alienation. Under socialism, private property is transferred to the state.

Thus, for Marx and Engels, capitalism reorganized class conflict between the owners of the means of production and the working class. Since this is a built-in feature of the system, nothing short of a complete and total restructuring would solve the problems of exploitation and alienation. These concerns motivated their (Marx and Engels 1967) 1848 publication of *The Communist Manifesto*, a short book designed for the working class that had the goal of rallying workers to join ranks and take control of the means of production to move their country toward socialism and later, communism.

## ENVIRONMENTAL CRITIQUE OF CAPITALISM: DEPLETION AND POLLUTION

Much of the discussion so far has been with urban communities and the social welfare of workers in mind. It is fair to say that Marx and Engels were predominantly concerned with the conditions of workers in urban communities, with comparatively less thought given to rural workers. However, Marx and Engels were aware of rural cultivators' risks in specializing in capitalist agriculture by growing commodities designed for trade rather than consumption (self-sufficient agrarian farming). These views were most fully expressed late in their careers, in the third volume of *capital*, which Engels published after the passing of Marx. Marx was influenced by the chemist and soil scientist von Liebig, who described modern agriculture as the "robbery economy" because of the way the soil is depleted of all nutrients until it is completely exhausted and incapable of production. The capitalist mode of agriculture encourages the farmer to take from the soil without giving anything back or protecting it for future generations. He was, indeed, approaching the notion of sustainability through these critiques of environmental degradation. Marx states:

> From the standpoint of a higher socio-economic formation, the private property of particular individuals in the earth will appear just as absurd as the private property of one man in other men. Even an entire society, a nation, or all simultaneously existing societies taken together, are not the owners of the earth. They are simply its possessors, its beneficiaries, and have to bequeath it in an improved state to succeeding generations as *boni patres familias* [good heads of the household]. (Marx, 2000, p. 1038–1039)

Foster (1999) noted that Marx and Engels were concerned with urban areas' environmental conditions during the nineteenth century when toxic industrial emissions poisoned the air. For instance, reliance on coal instead of wood led to a thick smog forming over most significant industrial cities in Europe. Marx drew an interesting connection between the problems in cities and the problems in the countryside, which he summarized through his notion of metabolic rift. The basic argument here is that humans once existed in a natural metabolic relationship with nature. Humans would consume materials found in nature, absorbing nutrients they needed while returning unused nutrients to the soil through waste. Marx observed that when people moved into urban industrial cities, this nutrient cycling experienced a rift. For cities, vast quantities of raw sewage emptied into local rivers, creating an awful stench, concentrating spreading water-borne diseases like cholera, and making the water unfit for consumption. For rural communities, the loss of waste disrupted nutrient cycling, thereby creating deficient soils that made farming increasingly challenging. Marx thus thought of urbanization as an unnatural byproduct of capitalism.

Building on the Marxian perspective, O'Connor (1988) emphasized two contradictions of capitalism related to the crises of underproduction and overproduction. The crisis of overproduction implies a social risk. A system that chronically underpays its workforce will be incapable of buying the products the system needs to sell to function, resulting in an oversupply. The second contradiction, the crisis of underproduction, implies an environmental risk that results from the vociferous appetite of capital for natural resources, which exist in a finite supply. As production increases, natural supplies diminish, sometimes to the point of total exhaustion, as was nearly the result of the whaling industry during the 1970s and '80s. The mythical Lorax created by Dr. Seuss embodied the conscience of nature as the last Truffula tree was cut down to make more thneeds—a lesson in the second contradiction.

One might look upon these contradictions as temporary problems with obvious correctives that would salvage the capitalist system. The innovation of Henry Ford, to pay workers enough money to buy a car, was one way to address the crisis of overproduction. Ultimately, this policy has struggled to survive in the competitive automotive industry that exerts heavy downward pressure on auto workers' wages. Lumber companies, reliant on trees for their livelihoods, often realize the need to practice restraint in the desire to clearcut forests, thereby averting the crisis of underproduction. But they compete with more scrupulous organizations willing to ignore the inevitable exhaustion of forests. It would seem that correctives, while possible, often lead to lower levels of competitiveness that may spell doom for individual organizations or firms.

The organizational logic of capitalism is explained well by Schnaiberg (1980) through his theory of the Treadmill of Production. Schnaiberg argues that organizations in a capitalist economy are engaged in fierce competition to achieve the highest possible profits—not simply out of greed but out of a legal obligation for organizations publicly traded on the stock exchange. Efforts to pay workers more wages or reduce environmental impacts will necessarily reduce profits, making the organizations less competitive and more likely to go out of business. Diminishing profits will likely trigger a sell-off, and eventual bankruptcy, leaving the less socially and environmentally responsible organizations to carry out the contradictions noted by O'Connor. All of this points to the futility of capitalist organization, implying the need for a restructuring.

## TRENDS AND THEORIES OF GLOBAL CORPORATE CAPITALISM

Marxian-inspired scholars such as O'Connor and Schnaiberg observed that capitalist ownership has evolved into a corporate model that includes shareholders and a sizeable managerial class that has more in common with wealthy owners than the proletariat. More importantly, corporate ownership has evolved from national to multinational or global. Thus, to understand current political economic trends, we need to look at the global corporate capitalist economy, which is markedly different from the privately owned national or regional firms of the nineteenth century. Multinational corporations engage in high volume trade flows between nations, though often within the same organization, referred to as foreign direct investment (FDI). The extent of global trade cannot be exaggerated. For instance, in the spring of 2021, a large cargo ship traveling through the Suez Canal in Egypt ran aground. Unable to budge, it blocked all passage and trade through the canal for several days. Experts estimated the blockage resulted in nearly $11 billion in losses each day, with a total cost exceeding $100 billion. Incidents such as these remind us how global our economy has become and how fragile and vulnerable it remains.

When it comes to theorizing the political economy of the world system, we may look to Lenin's (1948) prescient observations in 1916 about capitalism and imperialism—when colonialism and feudalism led to the first world war. Lenin was influenced by and extended Marx and Engel's class analysis to an international level. In the 1960s and '70s, development scholars created two theories for understanding how the global economy was organized called dependency and world systems theory. These theories grew out of observations about the poor terms of trade confronting Latin American nations that seemed to affirm Lenin's predictions in the postwar era (Prebisch 1950). In short, Dependency scholars suggested that poor peripheral nations' rural resources were being devalued and plundered. They were unable to secure acceptable terms of trade with wealthy core nations of the world, making urban products unattainable. The paradox is that many rural countries are endowed with incredible natural resources for which there is massive urban demand. However, the rural population is rarely compensated fairly for exporting these resources—part of something referred to as the resource curse (Sachs and Warner 1995; Ross 1999). Some of the most vulnerable workers are migrant farmers who lack basic protections or adequate compensation. For instance, Cambodian migrant farmers in Thailand were dispossessed and deported following a 2014 coup (Nuricka and Hak 2019).

Frank (1966, 1967) suggested that peripheral nations typically host a satellite metropolis—usually a capital, which may be a third-order city—that exploits the countryside so it can collect and export resources to generate revenue. The cities benefiting from these cheap rural exports were located in wealthy nations, where value was added through manufacturing. This was also noted by scholars working from a world city system framework (see Friedman 1986; Alderson and Beckfield 2004), who maintain that the power of core nations is carried out through a network of highly connected global cities.

According to world systems theory, the world's nations are divided into different strata. At the top are the wealthiest nations with the most robust and diverse economies, called the *core* countries. At the bottom are *peripheral* countries, the world's poorest nations with an economic dependency on a narrow range of natural resource (rural) exports. In between these extremes are *semi-peripheral* nations forming a middle layer with hybrid characteristics—partial reliance on rural exports and fledgling urban industries that are more diverse than those in the periphery yet not nearly as robust as what may be found in the core. The size of the economies of nations in these three strata is exponentially larger, going from bottom to top. If measured by per capita gross domestic product (GDP), typical peripheral countries might hover near $400, semi-peripheral nations near $4,000, and core nations near $40,000 per capita.

As noted, peripheral nations rely on exporting natural resources, such as minerals, ores, and timber. They also depend on exporting agricultural commodities, such as produce (e.g., grapes, bananas, etc.), sugar, palm oil, and coffee. Natural resource extraction and agriculture both bring widespread social and environmental damage. The laborers often live at or below subsistence level, depending on fluctuating commodity prices. These natural and agricultural products are imported to semi-peripheral nations, where they are transformed through value-added processing into other products—for instance, coffee beans are roasted, and palm fruit is processed to make palm oil. Semi-peripheral industries are often unwanted in the core because of the harmful social and environmental byproducts they create. Core countries import either the value-added products of semi-peripheral nations or the raw materials directly from the periphery, providing their industrial processing. The core, however, is mainly engaged in the service economy rather than the good economy on the production side. The superior purchasing power of core nations allows them to be the world's consumers without being the world's producers. In this way, many of the social and environmental consequences of production are externalized, while the benefits are enjoyed.

Urban-bias theory (Lipton 1973, 1977, 1984) took a different approach than focusing on the development strategies of national governments in mostly rural peripheral nations. It suggests that poorer countries strive to urbanize and industrialize by exploiting their rural populations. In such places, the strategy is often explicit: generate and capture revenue from the export of rural products, then use the proceeds to invest in urban industry. This strategy sounds good in theory, yet it is a recipe for national development that depends on the harsh exploitation of the world's poorest people: peripheral rural farmers and farmworkers. The only way for the strategy to work is if these poor rural workers are severely underpaid, and the resulting surplus-value is transferred into urban industrial development projects.

## LOCAL POLITICAL ECONOMY:
## GROWTH MACHINE THEORY

Now that we have examined the dynamics of the global corporate capitalist economy, we must now consider how this plays out at the local community level. One of the best theories for providing this view is growth machine theory—one of the most productive and widely used contemporary frameworks for understanding urban development and social change (Molotch 1976; Logan and Molotch 1987). This theory focuses on the coordinated efforts of private companies, local governments, and various supporting actors, such as media outlets, who create a growth consensus in the local community. This consensus views any form of economic growth as positive and beneficial. The process begins when a private interest approaches a municipal government with a development project in mind. Usually, these are grand-scale projects, such as sports stadiums, shopping malls, factories, hospitals, or large housing developments. These large-scale projects are attractive to the private interest because of their potential to generate profits. In other words, private interests operate based on exchange values. Municipal governments, eager to add private business and additional population to the tax rolls, work diligently to make the community attractive for investment. This may include offering a set of policies that provide tax incentives or guarantees of low regulation in the areas of the environment and labor. The media, including local newspapers or radio stations, eager to grow the population and expand its base of consumers, promotes the proposed development projects as desirable for the community. It is a growth consensus because there are no objections to economic growth—even as the welfare of the public is not usually considered.

Residents of a community considering a development project must also sign on to the project, or the government and private investors may face resistance. The media play a vital role here in promoting the benefits of economic growth. Residents, however, do not operate based on exchange values since it is not them who will profit from the development project. Instead, they work based on use values corresponding to the quality of life. People want to live in safe and clean communities that offer a range of amenities. The growth consensus tries to obscure the line by equating the exchange values of private investors with the use values of public residents. The reality is that these often come into conflict.

One area of such conflict is environmental. If a development project was geared toward industrial development—the construction of a factory, for instance—the by-products might include air, water, and land pollution. These problems undermine the quality of life in communities and undercut public use values. When a sports arena is constructed, the amount of urban landscape required for demolition can be immense. As the wrecking balls go to work, they begin clearing away infrastructure, along with its history, legacy, and cultural capital. This may not concern residents if the area is universally viewed as undesirable. But even under these conditions, there are usually at least some properties of historical significance. Losing history and culture undermines the quality of life and use values. Sports arenas also sporadically magnify traffic congestion, leading to calls for the expansion of roads. The inconvenience and noise of the traffic are one thing, but the costs of improving infrastructure are usually passed on to taxpayers.

One of the most impressive facets of growth machine theory is its staying power—it continues to find empirical support. For instance, Gasteyer and Carrera (2013) discovered an interesting phenomenon when growth machines collide. Their examination of south-central Illinois found competing interests vying for access to underground coal deposits versus interests that were promoting agriculture for corn ethanol biofuels. Members of the local farming community considered the health and environmental risks, organized opposition to coal development, and promoted the continued farming of corn.

Pick up a local newspaper in nearly any community, and you will often find that ambitious development projects are touted as the best hope for improving life in a community. Economic progress is continually equated with social progress. Unfortunately, the benefits of these grand projects often flow to a minimal number of beneficiaries. At the same time, the costs accrue to the majority of residents who must now live in a degraded environment, have inferior working conditions, or experience a declining quality of life.

## LOCAL POLITICS: ELITISM VS. PLURALISM

When Alexis de Tocqueville (1982) visited America and published the first volume of *Democracy in America* in 1835, he made several insightful and optimistic observations about the democratic system that was taking shape in this young and mostly agricultural nation. He argued that the organization of the country into countless villages and small communities, each with its local government and foundation of independent farmers and businesses, was an unbreakable mixture. In short, the success of the democratic system was derived from its rootedness in local political participation. Yet, in his publication of volume two in 1840, Tocqueville warned about the threats of rampant individualism, racial inequality, and the industrial aristocracy. Individualism threatened the community orientation that made local politics strong in America—the rise of urbanism was not something he could foresee. Racial discrimination prevented full equality from forming, which undermines a central premise of democracy. Such pervasive inequality continues to plague democracies in America and other parts of the world. Finally, Tocqueville worried that the economic sphere would infiltrate and jeopardize American democracy by corrupting its institutions. Perhaps he anticipated growth machines.

Picking up on these concerns, C. Wright Mills (1981) coined the term *power elite* to describe what he thought characterized the highly centralized power structure of the United States, which comprised top economic, political, and military leaders of the country. In his view, these individuals made most of the important decisions for the country. They would need to at least perpetuate the illusion that the public has input for this to work. A power elite that wishes to advance its agenda may deceive the public by promoting propaganda that serves their narrow private interests—the dynamic noted by growth machine theory. Mills's theory of the power elite undermines the idea that there is a functioning democracy, providing a counternarrative to what can be described as pluralism. The notion of pluralism suggests power is widely distributed across actors, with each part of the system providing checks and balances against the others. At a local level, as noted by Lyson (2006), Mills and Ulmer (1946) conducted a significant research project for the US Senate that showed the relation between big business and community welfare. They concluded with a call for investment in a diverse array of locally owned and operated businesses since these were associated with greater community welfare compared to communities dominated by large manufacturing employers. Their research confirmed the fears expressed by Tocqueville of economic infiltration.

There has been a long debate about how political power is organized and used in the United States and whether it is truly a democratic nation. When we turn to the local community level, we will find a great deal of variation. Some communities are highly active in politics, engage in critical discussions and debates, and arrive at solutions in a collective and representative manner. In contrast, others may be inactive in local politics altogether. In between these extremes are communities that are active politically but lack adequate input from representative segments. These communities may be dominated politically by a localized power elite. Generally, communities experiencing the growth machine are dominated by an elite that wishes to control the agenda and force their economic interests on the community, even against their objections.

In the 1950s, a group of researchers led by Floyd Hunter (2017 [1953]) developed a method for mapping out the power structures of communities called the reputational approach. It involved interviewing members of the public and asking them who you had to go through if you wanted to get something done in the community. The researchers took the feedback from separate individuals and triangulated between them to find agreement on specific names. In the end, they would be able to characterize communities' power structures as concentrated in a few hands (elite) or as being widely dispersed (pluralist). These were alternatively described as the monolithic versus diversified power structures. Beyond the reputations of particular leaders, Hunter observed that diversified structures were more likely to emerge in communities with several small locally owned firms than a small number of large employers.

More recently, Robert Putnam (2000) emphasized the importance of various organizations supporting civic engagement and local political participation. Among them were voluntary associations and fraternal groups such as the Rotary, Elks, Masons, and Moose. Membership in these groups was declining across the country, leading to a lower level of civic engagement. However, the reality for individual communities is likely to vary quite substantially, with some having a higher level of civic engagement and supportive institutions and organizations.

In addition to having supportive organizations and institutions, there's also been some research by Oldenburg (1991) that suggests the need for third spaces, defined as nonwork and nonfamily spaces, such as a local bar, café, drugstore, barbershop, or grocery store. Communities vary in the extent to which third spaces exist, and some communities lack any public space whatsoever. This can present challenges to supporting and promoting public dialogue and debating issues affecting the community. The loss of a local school can spell the end of public space. A community center can fill this gap, which may be formed in an abandoned school building.

To solve the problem of growth machines, treadmills of production, and power elites, we must identify the best way to level the playing field and promote a democratic process. One of the foremost pragmatist philosophers, John Dewey, wrote a thought-provoking argument in *The Public and Its Problems* that questioned the prospect of democracy amid an increasingly complex world. He observed that the average citizen in a democracy lacks the expertise necessary to grasp and provide meaningful input on complex and technical issues. While prizing democracy, he questioned the value of public information if it was grossly uninformed or misinformed. He then considered the role of experts who possess the ability to grasp and provide helpful input on complex issues, which makes an appealing case for a move toward technocratic rule—the rule of experts. A technocracy, however, suffers from the fact that the public will bear out the consequences of expert decisions. He concludes that the best way through this was to have open lines of dialogue between experts and members of the public. The experts could help tutor the public on the complexities, but the public would be responsible for decisions. The media, for Dewey, was the primary channel for this communication, but he warned against the potential for propaganda to jeopardize this tenuous arrangement. Of course, these warnings now seem almost naïve, living in a world in which propaganda is daily perpetuated through social media and conventional media, seeking to warp popular understandings to advance the private political economic agenda of an elite. Yet, the grave needs to limit misinformation and disinformation to create a clear line of communication between the public and experts remains. Perhaps the best place for this to occur is at the community level.

## PLANNING CONSIDERATIONS

One of the most significant problems with the critique of political economy offered by Marx and Engels is the absence of a clear path forward. *The Communist Manifesto* provides general ideas more than specific steps toward creating a communist economy or the preliminary socialist economy. Earlier in their careers, these were considered stages of evolving economies, which would have to progress independently. It was unclear how a primarily agricultural feudal economy in Russia, for instance, could leapfrog the stage of capitalism and move directly into socialism. Therefore, the Bolshevik revolution, which brought about the USSR, was not something that Marx and Engels could have foretold. The result was not something consistent with a Marxian vision. In the contemporary world, as growth machine theory reveals, there remain several challenges for communities that participate in the global corporate capitalist economy, constantly facing pressures to chase economic development at all costs.

Fortunately, such global participation is not mandatory at the local level—though it is often assumed or taken for granted. One alternative vision for community political economy was formulated in the late 1990s and early 2000s, around the notion of civic capitalism, with a series of studies spearheaded by Charles Tolbert III (Tolbert, Lyson, and Irwin 1998; Tolbert, Irwin, Lyson, and Nucci 2002) and the late Thomas Lyson (2004, 2006). The core idea of civic capitalism is valuable when thinking about a more sustainable community political economy. The central focus of the approach is restoring economic activity to "Main Street" by leading communities through a process that simultaneously disinvests in corporations and businesses that are global in scope while promoting ways to enhance local investment. Relevant to this approach are studies that consider practical ways to make local investment a reality. Among these approaches are various cooperative models—worker coops, owner coops, and so on. Other approaches consider generating startup capital by enhancing the local financial sector or creating community grants or loans. The success of businesses often depends on generating sufficient startup capital, which allows a company to develop and grow to its capacity.

One of the clear benefits of the civic capitalism approach is its logic. While global corporations may serve a community as a large employer for a time, they have no local commitment that guarantees long-term viability. Large corporations have repeatedly demonstrated their willingness to relocate if cost savings are anticipated by moving operations elsewhere, leaving an extreme economic shock rippling through the community. Once vibrant economies in cities such as Detroit, St. Louis, Utica, Rochester, and Cleveland have been severely damaged by corporations closing down operations. In most cases, these corporations made profits when decisions to leave were finalized. Still, the prospect of greater profits lures corporations away if, for instance, the new location offers a lower price for equally productive labor—Smith's absolute advantage. When confronted, most managers and decision-makers in corporations point out their logic, which is the responsibility they have to their shareholders to ensure they are maximizing profits. The shareholders and managerial class making these decisions reside far outside of the affected communities facing closures. The damage to workers and their communities, which begin to face a fiscal crisis (explained later), are secondary concerns to the interests of the owners of stocks. If there is backlash from these communities—perhaps residents refuse to buy products from these corporations—the effect is minimal on the corporations' bottom line since they operate at such a large scale.

The logic of a locally owned and operated business departs significantly in several ways. First, the owners are usually not absentee but are firmly embedded in the community they serve, maintaining social ties to both workers and customers, simultaneously economic and non-economic. In smaller rural communities, business owners and operators know their workers and customers through local schools, youth sports, religious organizations, civic groups, and other community groups. As a result, local businesses are not as eager to pick up stakes and move to another community, even if the economic prospects are more promising. Leaving would mean laying off workers who are personal friends and family members. It would mean leaving customers, friends, or family without the goods or services once provided. Creating damage to these relationships would harm the business's reputation and its owners and operators. The line between the owning and working class is not as neatly drawn as in larger enterprises.

Under cooperative business models, the Marxian line of owners and workers may be erased when workers are simultaneously the owners. Worker-owned cooperatives offer individuals with limited startup capital an opportunity to pool their resources to launch a business. For example, instead of a sole proprietor coming up with $250,000 to start a business with four employees, a cooperative business may have these five employees come up with $50,000 to own a one-fifth stake in the business. While the personal profits will be lower if the business succeeds, the potential risks would be significantly lessened if the business fails. In most cooperatives, each worker-owner is an equal shareholder, and decisions about the business are made democratically. It would be highly unusual for the worker-owners of a local business to propose abandoning the community in which they operate.

Alternatively, if customers own a cooperative business, they usually pay a subscription fee and receive some allotment from what the business produces. The subscription will allow the customer to receive a certain number of groceries each month if it is a grocery store, for example. In this model, the customers get to vote on conducting the business. Once again, it would be implausible for customer-owners to decide to relocate such a business since doing so would end their access to what the business provides.

Not everyone wants to participate in cooperatives as workers or customers, but other options exist to jumpstart local businesses. Community grant programs offer a way to finance a new business that is a sole proprietorship without the owner shouldering the risks that could be devastating if the business fails. Again, if individuals were required to come up with $250,000 to start a business, they may take all the wealth they own and put it on the line. For most people, this wealth comes in the form of their homes as collateral. If the business succeeds, the loans are paid, and the owner eventually owns both their home and the business. But if it fails, the owner could lose their home. A community grant is ideal since it would not require repayment, provided specific criteria are met. It is prudent to require a business to receive such a grant to remain open to the community for a predetermined period—perhaps one year. This way, recipients cannot open and close, pocketing unspent funds. Carefully managed grant programs can pump new life into Main Street businesses without exposing the owners to potentially devastating risks. Rather than a grant, the financing may be provided as a loan that is forgiven after making payments.

In general, if a business opens in a traditional way of a sole proprietor obtaining a personal loan from a financial institution, another critical consideration is whether this financial institution is itself a local operation. Global, national, or even regional financial institutions may be less willing to grant loans or forgive missed payments should the business have a lull. Local financial institutions operate by the logic of local businesses—there maintain social ties to the community. It is more challenging to turn down a borrower who is your child's grade school teacher than a perfect stranger. Moreover, suppose a local financial institution were to create a reputation for being scrupulous and unforgiving. In that case, local customers may react by terminating their accounts, which would probably be the end of the local financial institution. Unfortunately, there has been a great deal of consolidation in the financial sector, and local financial institutions are increasingly scarce. Local credit unions offer one model to maintain a local financial institution if there is interest, and these often operate within a cooperative business model.

The often-overlooked benefit of the localizing strategies above is that they overcome many of the problems raised by Marx and Engels in the critique of capitalism. Their critique made assumptions about the kind of business model that defines capitalism. While this assumption remains valid when we consider the current trends toward the global political economy, the logic of civic capitalism calls this assumption into question. The conflict between workers and owners, if not erased, can be significantly reduced through alternative business models suited to the local community.

Beyond planning for a better local economic future, should be equal concern for promoting a more pluralistic power structure and identifying and encouraging a supportive system. Scholarship suggests that local politics benefit from civic capitalism (Blanchard and Matthews 2006), or having many diverse locally owned and operated small businesses, a network of organizations that encourage sociability, and a selection of third spaces for members of the community to have dialogue. In chapter 5, we will return to this point when we discuss attractor points. One of the best ways to ensure a representative local government is by forming a community council comprised of representatives of all groups or segments of the community. Local decision-making will be viewed as illegitimate if not the product of a representative body. Nor will it be considered legitimate if an elite controls the political process. Ensuring that there are spaces for public dialogue is something that the community should consider supporting. There should be an inventory or assessment of available spaces that are currently open to the public or that could be. This space should provide community members with a forum to voice concerns, provide input, and generally participate in local politics.

*Chapter 4*

# Culture

Culture refers to the beliefs, values, norms, lifestyles, customs, heritage, history, language, and material artifacts shared by a group of people. Local culture is highly layered, as every community exists within larger regional, national, and global cultural systems, even while maintaining a unique local history and identity. Some communities host subcultures or even countercultures; some may be described as diverse, while others are more homogeneous. Sometimes local cultural differences are minor, while in other cases, they can be striking, as is evident when comparing an Amish community with a nearby suburban or exurban rural community. The way people dress, their language, their customs, and lifestyles can vary drastically within a relatively small geographic space. This contrast is evident in urban settings in which different neighborhoods may be organized along ethnic lines, as we find when we go from Little Italy to China Town in Manhattan, New York. Our interest in this chapter lies in unpacking the notion of community culture while generating ideas that can inform sound planning designed to protect and promote local community cultural capital and diversity.

Learning to live in an ever-changing and complex world is not easy, and thus another vital element of culture is the process of socialization. Socialization refers to the formal and informal training and education individuals receive. It is how we provide someone with an instruction manual for how to live within a culture, which is partly offered through formal training and partly offered through lived experience, including the lessons that are taught in a household by parents or guardians. It includes children's formal schooling into the basics of what is deemed relevant and essential. The extent to which local cultures are emphasized in either the informal or formal education of children varies substantially across schools and districts.

In many cases, children growing up in smaller rural communities are not presented with much locally relevant knowledge or information about their community, leaving them with a sense of place insignificance. There is a growing awareness within rural education of the need for greater place literacy. When asked to say where they are from, students from rural areas often produce a reluctant pause, followed by disclaimers like "it's in the middle of nowhere" or "it's not important." How people come to feel pride or shame in their communities are matters of place literacy and socialization.

Nevertheless, every community has its own culture, identity, historical legacy, and significance. Making sweeping generalizations about the cultures of urban or rural communities is haphazard. However, some crucial patterns emerge in communities based on the population's size, density, and diversity. In rural communities, with smaller populations and lower density, one is more likely to see someone familiar out in public. In large dense cities, one is more likely to encounter total strangers. Familiarity may bring a sense of belonging and personal significance to individuals in the rural community. Alternatively, it is not unusual to feel small, alienated, invisible, or insignificant in a large city.

Urbanites value the privacy they gain from being a stranger and the sense of freedom to be an individual. Rustics may feel pressure to conform to community standards that inhibit personal expressions. Thus, the way individuals process urban-rural differences varies, as some people are more private and enjoy the relative anonymity of urban communities. Others have a greater need for visibility and the sense of belonging they experience in a rural community.

## THEORIZING URBAN–RURAL CULTURAL PATTERNS

Georg Simmel's (1950) classic essay, "The Metropolis and Mental Life," explored some of the social-psychological experiences of the city versus small-town life. He noted that one of the effects of living in the city is the constant bombardment of stimuli, such as the sounds of cars honking, sirens, people talking, vendors selling merchandise, dogs barking, pigeons cooing, and so on. Simmel was writing about nineteenth-century Europe and thus had no idea how much additional stimulation would be created in the ensuing century with the advent of digital technologies. For instance, picture bright billboards beaming advertisements across Times Square while taxis and buses drive and honk their way through hordes of pedestrians walking, talking on phones, blaring music, and taking pictures.

Simmel claimed that the only way to navigate the overload of information and data in cities was by blocking it out by creating a blasé attitude. Such an attitude is an adaptation designed to protect the psyche of urbanites. Thus equipped, urbanites may coldly step over the homeless in sleeping bags lying on the sidewalk. Crimes committed in broad daylight in front of hundreds of witnesses might go unreported—the diffusion of responsibility effect is exacerbated in urban settings. People in New York City and Paris sometimes have a reputation for being rude. This reputation was probably developed by people who had experienced a culture shock due to interacting with urbane populations with blasé attitudes. While Simmel offered thought-provoking essays, his contemporary, Ferdinand Tönnies, would create the most comprehensive framework for understanding urban-rural patterns in community cultures.

Tönnies's (1957) classic framework of *gemeinschaft* (urban society) and *gesellschaft* (rural community) argued that two guiding wills competing for dominance in a community. Urbanites are guided primarily by the rational will (*kürwille*), while rustics are guided mainly by the natural will (*wesenwille*). The natural will, for humans, is an inclination toward what Simmel would call sociability. It is fundamental to personal relationships with family and friends and focused on quality and content. The rational will is the inclination to make carefully considered choices, weigh pros and cons, and optimize decisions. It is associated with impersonal or transactional relationships, such as a customer–cashier relationship in a store. The emphasis is on quantity instead of quality and efficiency over content. Small rural communities rarely host impersonal transactions since there is a higher level of familiarity with people in the community. This absence of impersonality can change when rural communities experience spikes in visitors, temporarily raising the population to urbane levels.

The rational and natural wills should be considered the yin and yang of close and distant relationships—as related to Simmel's notion of social distance. Tönnies suggested that everyone is guided to some degree by both of these wills. Rustics, while oriented toward familiarity and sociability, are still capable of making careful and rational calculations with strangers, as much as the urbane are capable of making small talk and being personable despite the constant pull toward a colder form of transactional rationalism. Displays of trust between strangers may be interpreted differently due to the competing wills.

For instance, my wife and I saw a couple in New York City awkwardly trying to take a selfie with the city skyline. We offered to take the picture for them but were surprised when the couple declined our offer. They smiled and conveyed a sense of regret that they could not (rationally) trust a stranger who might steal their camera. There are, in fact, several con artists in New York City who prey upon trust to swindle people out of money or other goods, so distrust is understandable as a rational response. However, it would be a mistake to walk away thinking these were rude people—they were rational people and perhaps a little blasé. We made the offer because we come from a smaller community where stranger trust is less risky. Offering to take someone's picture falls within normative and even rational behavior. Due to the small size of our community, it is difficult for con artists to operate since their status as outsiders is usually apparent—a fact not lost on the local police department. A couple refusing to allow a picture from a stranger in our small community would probably be viewed as rude since the rational basis for distrust is absent. This may be why urbanites are sometimes disliked in rural communities, as they have been socialized into a different set of rules or norms that are context-specific to the city.

The brilliant insights of both Simmel and Tönnies were also influenced by Max Weber's work, who focused much of his attention on rationality, emphasizing its cold, harsh reality, as captured in his image of the "iron cage." Weber applied much of his examination of rationality not to communities but to his study of organizations as bureaucracies, which he contrasted with traditional or personalistic organizations. For Weber, the strict rules and regulations, clearly defined levels of hierarchy, formal communique, and formal titles that announce position in the hierarchy—all characteristic of bureaucracies—were a rational response to the need to coordinate the actions of a large number of people in an organization. Small privately owned businesses would look very strange if they exhibited these features. Hence, they tend to be guided by personalized, warm relationships that Tönnies would describe as consistent with the natural will. Thus, Weber's views on organizational differences parallel Tönnies's views on communities.

A scholar influenced by these classical thinkers is Louis Wirth, who wrote "Urbanism as a Way of Life" (1938), building on urban-rural comparisons discussed above. Wirth encourages us to move beyond the census and stop equating urban with a physical entity delineated by arbitrary political boundaries in his pioneering article. For Wirth, cities are more than large population centers with a high-density level, though these features significantly affect social interaction and the mode of group association. Also significant is the heterogeneity and diversity that cities support, particularly when hosting various immigrant groups. As with Weber, Simmel, and Tönnies, Wirth observed that urbanization leads to a greater need for structure and order to help coordinate intricate social activity and a complex economy. Like Simmel, Wirth was a Jewish minority living in a noninclusive society, leading both scholars to experience some level of alienation, discrimination, and exclusion. Its lack of intimate personal relationships defines Wirth's description of urbanism and the "segmentalization of human relations which are largely anonymous, superficial, and transitory . . . " (Wirth 1938, 1)—features consistent with the notion of gesellschaft and rational will. The implied typological comparison is that rural areas do not segmentalize human relations. They treat individuals as whole beings and offer more opportunities for deeper, more meaningful, and more long-lasting intimate personal relationships with a greater sense of belonging and personal significance. Wirth (1938) points out that the speed of urbanization does not lead instantly to cultural changes or the fast replacement of traditional rural modes of association with pure urbanism. He suggests that this takes place gradually over time. Moreover, once developed, urbanism no longer needs to stay confined to the city and may spill well beyond the urban borders into the countryside. He correctly anticipated that rural communities could be dominated by urbane norms, values, and beliefs—magnified through advances in contemporary digital telecommunications and media.

In sum, the urban–rural cultural patterns and ways of life we have considered are helpful if we think of them as Weberian ideal types. As ideal types, we would not expect them to exist in reality in a pure form but only to show a tendency toward exhibiting such characteristics. Only then can we observe general cultural patterns in communities.

## CULTURE, POLITICAL ECONOMY, AND ENVIRONMENTAL DEMOGRAPHY

Community culture is tied to communities' environmental demography and political economy, and it can transform both. Developing new technologies, such as the plow or the domesticated goat, is a cultural act that can transform environmental demography. It is hard to imagine vast urban–rural trade networks functioning without the innovative use of transportation and communication technologies that are now more sophisticated than ever and central to the world capitalist political economy. Computers handle complex logistics in an automated manner, such as when a customer purchases an item in Walmart, and the inventory is automatically updated when the sale is completed at the register. When the inventory is updated, orders for replacements are automatically issued, leading to requests from manufacturers and other producers to create more of the item. The producers, in turn, import more natural resources by trading with rural producers, who then collect and harvest more natural resources. We rarely think of the incredible series of rippling innovations or circuits of production and trade when we purchase an item at a store.

The cultures of prior environmental demographic systems have varied intriguingly, which becomes evident when studying religious beliefs. The classic thinkers did not consider the almost universal cultural hierarchy that falls along the urban–rural line. Generally, urban areas enjoy the benefits of existing on top of the cultural hierarchy, as urbane lifestyles (urbanism) are viewed positively as forward-looking. Cities and the people who live in them are generally regarded as intelligent and cutting-edge progress and innovation. Florida's (2019) thesis about the creative class underscores this perception. Rural or rustic communities are at the bottom of the cultural hierarchy, often viewed as quaint, home to simple people who are generally backward or stuck in time. Few fashion magazines suggest looking at the trends sweeping rural communities—they almost universally point to urban hotspots for fashion trendsetting. The implication is that rural areas are not a source of cultural creativity or progress; hence, the creative class would not find such places appealing.

Fulkerson and Thomas (2019) discuss the many stereotypes that have been applied to rural people and places, identifying three themes of rural as wild, escape, and simple. By wild, rural people are likened to animals, closer to nature than urbane humans; so too are they unpredictable and potentially dangerous. As an escape, rural communities are understood as places of refuge for urbanites to visit. This view limits the value of rural communities to their utility for urban visitors—not their inherent value. As simple, rural communities may be viewed as offering a slower and less complicated pace—a positive characteristic, especially when combined with the notion of rural as an escape. Unfortunately, rural as simple also implies a general lack of intellect, innovation, or other features associated with urban enlightenment. Hayden (2021) adds that rural can also be thought of as a source of horror, noting the enduring myth of rural inbreeding and presumed genetic deficiencies that give rise to hideous rural monsters routinely evoked in the rural horror film genre. The cultural representations of rural people and places can be found across a range of media sources, from mainstream television shows (Fulkerson and Lowe 2016), reality shows (Jicha 2016), books (e.g., Smith 2014; Ching 2016), and movies (Hayden 2021; Thomas, Lowe, Fulkerson, and Smith 2012).

The ideology of the urban–rural cultural hierarchy is urbanormative. As noted previously, Thomas et al. (2012) first defined urbanormativity as the view that urban life is normal while rural is deviant or abnormal. When we read a newspaper that uses the "we" voice to tell a story about a rural community, the implied referent in "we" is the urbane population, while the rustic is the other. For a rural person to encounter such an implied urban bias can be alienating and demeaning, even in the absence of the more pronounced rural stereotypes that remain alive and well. Rural populations experience an open season, in some respect, for caricatures, stereotypes, and tropes. As a class, rural people are not protected from the same sensibility that stands to prevent stereotypes along other dimensions of identity, including race, gender, sexuality, and ability. There is a general assumption in the United States that rural people are always white, very conservative socially and politically, and less educated. As with many stereotypes, there may be a vague grain of truth since rural people are more likely to fall into these categories. However, the problem with stereotypes is that they are overly general and overbroad. Such generalizations deny the existence of rural racial and ethnic minorities, diverse rural sexualities, the variation across rural communities in educational outcomes, and other sources of rural diversity. A genuinely intersectional approach will incorporate the urban–rural dimension.

Stereotypes of rural Americans ignore rural areas in the United States with a pronounced black population in counties stretching from Texas to Virginia, forming a region described as the Blackbelt South (Wimberly and Morris 2002). Increasingly, agricultural regions of the south and west have experienced a growth in the Latinx population, leading to a more significant cultural influence from parts of Central and South America. The United States is one of the largest Spanish-speaking countries globally, and that is not due entirely to urban populations. Therefore, rural communities in the United States are more diverse than popular stereotypes would have us believe. The perpetuation of the white rural stereotype eliminates rural racial and ethnic minority groups from the public imagination while reinforcing the parallel assumption that urban can be equated with black or Latinx populations. The black population in northern cities of the United States is largely the product of the Great Migration that occurred in the early to mid-twentieth century. During this time, millions of rural black southerners sought to escape Jim Crow laws and repressive southern culture following the Civil War and Emancipation (Tolnay 2003). However, as the continued existence of the Black Belt region reminds us, the Great Migration was not total—a substantial number of southern rural black residents decided not to move north, unwilling to leave their homes and communities behind. The history of the Great Migration in the United States is thus vital to present-day understandings of black cultural legacy and heritage.

The ideology of urbanormativity has several cultural consequences, but it is also essential to consider its effect on political economy. The belief that rural people are less important reinforces and justifies their exploitation within capitalist urban–rural systems. One consequence is the obscenely low wages given to farmers both nationally and internationally, many of whom are women and children and often racial and ethnic minorities. We must appreciate the power of urbanormativity to understand how the interests of urban populations continue to take priority over rural populations, which are vital to the perpetuation of urban–rural systems.

## IDENTITY, REPUTATION, AND REPRESENTATION

Culture and historical change become intertwined to create community identity. Just as the individual's biography portrays their identity, a community's history informs its identity. Communities vary in how they construct a narrative with a historical sense of significance by denoting notable people, events, and other artifacts of the past. In New York State, one can find tiny blue signs along most major and minor county or state highways that cut through the countryside. Each sign tells of a historically significant fact. Even remote rural communities may have blue signs paying some form of tribute.

Some community historical narratives focus on military histories, denoting important battles and military figures. For instance, in upstate New York, many places were significant in the Revolutionary War. Historical narratives may claim to be the first in something important, like housing the first pub in the county, state, or nation. Sometimes inventions or works of literature or art are celebrated. Many of the local historical markers in New York pay homage to the Indigenous population, providing important reminders to those now living in their absence and serving as a form of cultural preservation. In Central New York, we learn about the Mohawk and Oneida, while the Delaware were the dominant group just south of us. There are periodic signs denoting significant indigenous burial grounds or gathering spots.

While every community may have a history, not every community plays an active role in constructing a narrative, marking historical sites, or appreciating the uniqueness they possess. The result of such inattention contributes to the sense of insignificance felt by many rural residents. Urban communities may also face the threat of historical amnesia as pressures to gentrify mount, potentially disrupting their historical legacy to build something entirely new. For instance, in rebuilding downtown Detroit, many blocks of buildings have been bulldozed. In the rubble lies significant places where people used to live, work, and meet socially, such as local jazz clubs that thrived in the 1930s and '40s. Preservation of these sites holds the potential for a wealth of cultural capital, though this is not always considered. Rural boomtown communities may experience a similar effect when urbanites move in and overwhelm the cultural identity of the existing small population. Rural gentrification likewise erases the community's legacy. As discussed in chapter 6, the built environment often embodies the local culture, and altering or demolishing it is a form of cultural destruction.

It is vital to appreciate the layered nature of culture and note how macro-regional and national cultures incorporate local variations. In some cases, communities can develop a reputation or "brand" that makes them attractive and distinctive to the broader region—thereby bolstering significance. Tourism and hospitality often depend on favorable branding that will reliably attract visitors, creating a steady revenue stream. As a result of its reputation and branding as the birth of baseball, Cooperstown is home to several baseball-related specialty stores and restaurants. Nearby Hartwick Seminary also benefits from proximity and hosts several chain hotels that would otherwise not have a reason to exist. They also host the Cooperstown

Dreams Park, a baseball camp that draws well over 100 teams per week, creating a more sustained, though seasonal, positive economic impact.

On the other side of the coin are communities stigmatized as places to avoid. Communities or neighborhoods in urban areas may develop reputations for being undesirable, mainly if they take on the brand of being "inner city" (Wacquant 2007, 2008). Once again, community cultural reputations matter since they have real political and economic impacts. It is nearly impossible to attract visitors to places with a reputation for being dangerous, polluted, backward, or otherwise unpleasant. How communities come to develop bad reputations is itself a point of interest. Hayden's (2014) analysis of Seabrook, New Hampshire, sheds light on community stigma in a rural context. Anyone from Seabrook was referred to pejoratively as a "Brooker." This label became a synonym for redneck or hillbilly—unflattering rural stereotypes that implied such ideas as incest and genetic deficiency.

As noted by Anderson (1983), communities are cultural artifacts. Communities may actively work to shape the narrative of the community, actively managing its reputation. Alternatively, outsiders can impose a representation on a community that effectively erases its legacy and wipes the slate clean—the basis for gentrification. For some, these actions may appear beneficial since gentrification can produce shiny new communities that meet the expectations of the new residents. Neglected are the voices of those who inhabited the old community that is being erased. Actively maintaining a local narrative and legacy can serve as a preventative to gentrification efforts, which are as cultural as physical.

Generic cultural notions about attractive bucolic rural settings motivate urbanites to visit the countryside on vacation and sometimes entice them to buy second homes. Communities may emphasize rustic charm by actively generating images and experiences that match urban expectations. Thomas et al. (2012) coined the term *rural simulacra* to describe these efforts to present a generic rustic image. Rural simulacra are unique because they do not emphasize locally significant histories. They exist like a Disney theme park, creating a pleasant illusion to draw in and please visitors without including anything about a unique local history or identity. However, maintaining a generic image creates the impression that nothing of real, local significance or importance exists. This impression can also pave the way for rural gentrification. In chapter 6, we will return to this concept when we discuss how rural simulacra fit into the built environment.

## Quality-of-Life, Satisfaction, and Attachment

A community's image, reputation, or brand is significant for what they tell the outside world. For community members, the insiders, quality of life matters, including the kinds of values, norms, and lifestyles the community wants to support. What people find desirable in a community is mainly subjective and will not appeal to everyone. Someone might live in Cooperstown who hates baseball—and such a person would probably have a lower rating in their level of community satisfaction. Importantly, this same person might be highly attached to the community because they have extensive social ties.

Not everything is entirely subjective, as there are more objective quality-of-life elements that can make a place undesirable, such as the presence of environmental hazards. It is hard to imagine someone wanting to visit or live in a community with high levels of toxic waste—though there is probably some range in how much tolerance there is for toxic waste across communities. Research in environmental justice has shown that some communities become so desperate for economic activity that they accept unwanted land uses such as toxic waste dumps or prisons (Bullard 2018). Old steelworkers in Gary, Indiana, would often appreciate the smog in their city since it was a sign of economic activity and were much more tolerant of air pollution. This kind of tolerance is rare. Poor, predominantly African American rural communities in North Carolina exist close to enormous hog farms, which create an unmistakable rancorous odor. The waste lagoons on these farms will fill, leading the farm operator to spray the water and fecal matter into the air to dissipate it downwind. The result is a raining down of water and hog waste on community members in nearby areas. It is hard to imagine a more disgusting experience than walking out the front door to be showered in pig dung. Residents in these communities are understandably unhappy and may score very low on a community satisfaction score.

While community satisfaction or dissatisfaction can factor into the decision of residents to remain or to flee a particular locale, there are other important factors to consider. When one leaves a community, they are not just leaving behind the undesirable elements. They leave behind relationships, organizations, workplaces, schools, churches, and other elements that make life desirable. The decision to move is therefore complex.

The previous chapter discussed growth machine theory, which has a distinct cultural theme. As the theory suggests, one of the universal beliefs that cut across communities is that economic growth is desirable, regardless of the social or environmental costs. Unfortunately, if a community decides to host a dangerous or dirty economic activity, it may injure its cultural reputation, perhaps becoming stigmatized as dangerous or undesirable. It is challenging to attract visitors as tourists or second homeowners if such a reputation develops. When this happens, other related sources of economic growth are endangered, thus contradicting the original reason for allowing the activity in the first place—economic growth. Decisions about how to develop a community's economy emerge from the local culture.

## COMMUNITY CULTURAL CAPITAL

In many ways, history and identity can be considered the cultural capital of a community. Not just because they provide a sense of legacy and purpose for its residents, but because historical significance can lead to investments that have returns—often in the form of tourism. For instance, thousands of people descend on Cooperstown, New York, to attend the induction ceremony at the Baseball Hall of Fame every summer. Every fall, thousands of visitors will stop by Sleepy Hollow, New York, to celebrate the lore of the Headless Horseman on Halloween. These are highly seasonal events but significantly boost the local economy. These examples illustrate that culture can create significance, even when history does not—the Headless Horseman is a myth created by Washington Irving. However, tourism revenue based on the myth is significant. These events and the stories that surround them provide meaning and color to the identity of communities, which in turn provides residents with a greater sense of place significance.

The notion of cultural capital has remained one of the most elusive community capitals mentioned in the introduction. Pierre Bourdieu (1986) may be credited with coining the term, and he used it to explain how social class and financial capital came to be reproduced by elites through cultural means. In his book, *Distinction* (2019), Bourdieu pointed out how elites demonstrate their status by how they carry themselves—their habitus, which includes how they walk and talk. Their cultural capital involves specialized knowledge that only an elite possesses, such as an appreciation for and the ability to discuss abstract art. Through their habitus and cultural capital, elites can signal to one another their shared status. This concept is not unlike Veblen's notion of conspicuous consumption, which provided elites a way to demonstrate their status through their consumption patterns. Bourdieu would emphasize that only the elite would spend large sums of money on eclectic art forms, which the general public would find difficult to understand. These insights help grasp cultural capital at the individual level but are less instructive at the community level.

In their discussion of community cultural capital Flora and Flora (2015) emphasize the role of legacy. They note that every community has a unique history, traditions, and, in many cases, language. This distinctiveness is particularly pronounced among indigenous communities, who often find it challenging to maintain a legacy of language and tradition. Policies have been designed to strip native populations of their language and traditions, including the Dawes Act, which compelled attendance in school, western dress, and religious conversion to Christianity. These horrible events underscore the need to protect cultural legacies.

An edited volume by Seale and Mallinson (2018), *Rural Voices*, shines a light on rural linguistic variation and its intersection with cultural capital. As in the example of the Dawes Act above, the dominant group in a society or community often imposes its language, customs, and norms on everyone else. Sociologists refer to this as cultural leveling or assimilation. Rural linguistic variations or dialects are often defined as negative cultural capital in urbanormative society. Urban dialects, alternatively, often signal elite status, thereby serving as a form of cultural capital for individuals in an urbanormative context.

At the community level, the ability to demonstrate cultural capital occurs through projecting a particular image or identity that embraces local themes. As noted, rural communities often appeal to urbanormativity in the desire to boost tourism and enhance the local economy. They do this by projecting rural simulacra that convey generic rustic charm while saying little about the local distinctiveness. Providing a Disneyfied rural image may boost economic growth, but it may also undermine local efforts to carve out a distinct identity and harm the local sense of place. Rural communities may be put on the map due to their distinctive histories. For instance, Kitty Hawk, North Carolina, claims to be the birth of aviation since it is where the Wright brother flew their first successful flight. The Wright Brothers National Memorial and Museum informs visitors about the significance of early aviation while pointing to the actual site where the flight occurred. Such unique characteristics can serve as a draw to encourage tourism, which is helpful if that is the goal of the community. Creating community events or permanent fixtures, such as museums, can provide information and history that can be effective strategies for enhancing both cultural and financial capital.

Sometimes it is more important to consider *how* tourism will be accommodated rather than *whether* it should be allowed. The question for the community to consider is about reputation and image—are museums and other facilities devoted to visitors the kinds of things residents want to see in their community? If visitors come away with an appreciation of the local history and legacy of the community, this is an indication of respect, which can reflect well on the local population. However, popular tourist sites can transform a community and often overwhelms the infrastructure, as we see in the case of growth machines. Some of these issues can be addressed through careful planning.

## PLANNING CONSIDERATIONS

As the previous sections should clarify, each community has historical significance and image upheld by those inside and outside the community. Thus, historic preservation is an important planning consideration. Since it is crucial to a community's identity, planning efforts should develop a process for constructing and projecting local history. What significant events have taken place, which influential individuals have lived here, what was the indigenous history, what are some of the "firsts" to take place, what is the community best known for, and why would someone want to visit? These questions offer a beginning toward efforts at constructing a narrative. History should be written, shared through storytelling, and displayed so that individuals from within or without can learn. A simple way to accomplish this is through signage—much like a museum tells a story by offering signs placed adjacent to significant artifacts. Not every community will have the resources to commit to creating a museum of local history, but there are ways to simulate the museum experience in public spaces.

Another vital planning consideration we have discussed is based on the careful maintenance of reputation and image. Whether based on fact or fiction is of little matter; the consequences of the local reputation will be significant. Members of the community should have conversations about what image they have of their community and what they wish to project to the outside world. Avoiding the temptation to appeal to generic rustic sentiments is advised. The appeal should draw attention to the community's uniqueness since nowhere else is like it. As rural scholar Gene Theodori once quipped, "When you've seen one rural community, you've seen one rural community" (p.1).

A related consideration for planning is having a conversation about the role of outsiders. We have discussed tourism and the political economic benefits accompanying a positive community image or brand. However, it is a mistake to assume that all communities want to host throngs of visitors. While this may present economic opportunities, it may also drastically undermine the local quality of life, by magnifying traffic, putting strain on the local infrastructure, and interfering with the normal flow of life in the community. Community members should discuss the extent to which they want to open their doors to the outside world and how best to accomplish this.

Balanced against pleasing outsiders should be the more critical conversation pointed at pleasing community members by maximizing their sense of place, attachment, satisfaction, and quality of life. Community members deserve to live a life they find rewarding and should have conversations about what they want to happen locally to make their lives fuller and more complete. What activities are currently offered and appreciated? What is not appreciated? How do the lifestyles of the community align with the local history and image?

Once communities decide on strategies for promoting local community satisfaction and figuring out how outsiders might be incorporated, more conversations will be needed about creating a supportive infrastructure. Roberts and Townsend (2016) suggest that one of the most critical factors for a community to consider if it wants to attract a creative class is giving them access to urban markets. Rural communities are generally small and thus have a limited demand for the products of creative workers, such as abstract and fine art. Roberts and Townsend suggest that the simple act of providing internet connectivity is vital to making distant urban markets accessible. Their message is clear: do not let a deficit in digital capital create a deficit in cultural capital. If communities embrace tourism, the ability to host large crowds requires significant infrastructure in terms of roads, sidewalks, bridges, the electrical grid, water and sewage, and so on. Many rural tourist destinations rely on well water and septic systems. As a result, development is necessarily dispersed. Creating a water district and providing sewage treatment services are necessary to have the kind of dense development that successful tourist spots can offer.

Our discussion of community cultural capital has highlighted urban–rural dynamics. We showed its relation to environmental demography and political economy and considered reputation and identity relative to local history. We examined local ideas of community satisfaction and quality of life and how these need to be weighed against pressures to be open to outside interests. We reviewed planning considerations that take these factors into account. In the next chapter, we will focus more closely on social interaction and solidarity, which are closely related to culture and the capacity of communities to exhibit agency and put planning activities into motion.

*Chapter 5*

# Social Interaction, Networks, and Solidarity

Social interaction refers to social contact and communication geared toward influencing mutual thought and action (Sorokin 1928; Gillin and Gillin 1948). Social interaction occurs through social networks, composed of actors and their relations (Giuffre 2013). Such actors may be individuals, groups, or other social entities—in the context of communities, we are mainly interested in individuals and the social groups to which they belong. The configuration of social networks within and between social groups has implications for the kinds of solidarity that may form. Solidarity refers to the ways individuals and social groups are bound together. Conditions of anomie (normlessness) and social disorganization may result from a breakdown in community social interaction, networks, and solidarity, leading to factionalism, clientelism, or hyperindividualism. Interactional breakdowns may result, at least partly, from physical, social, and epistemic distance.

When defining community, scholars generally agree that social interaction is of central importance. Bruhn (2011) proposes that interaction alone comprises the entirety of community. While it is hard to imagine a community without social interaction, scholars diverge in fully equating interaction with community. Wilkinson's (1999) theory of community as an interaction field comes close to this view, though the geography of community (as imagined by individual actors) factors into his definition. Kemper (2002) identifies social interaction as the process of community, distinct from a community's organizational structure. Kemper's definition incorporates the structure-process dichotomy that is common in social theory. We will take a broad view of the community that considers social interaction within political economic, sociocultural, and environmental demographic dimensions.

In our model of urban–rural systems, the sociocultural dimension conceptually links culture and social interaction. Cultural norms, values, and beliefs are a product of social interaction and shape future social interaction in a dialectical feedback loop. The cultural work of defining a local legacy and identity is accomplished through interaction, as community members strive to construct a narrative that will be reinforced and reproduced. As a product of interaction, the local narrative is fluid and evolving to accommodate new conditions and write new chapters in the local history. Culture and interaction vary within and between social groups in communities based on levels of diversity and integration.

In terms of prior environmental demographic systems, small nomadic foraging groups were generally characterized by strong ties within singular groups. However, these may be connected through more extensive tribal networks, usually related to kinship lines. Larger agrarian or pastoral nomadic groups usually maintained internal strong and external weak ties. Within urban–rural systems, urban areas are defined by a preponderance of weak relative to strong ties, and rural areas by a preponderance of strong relative to weak ties (Wilkinson 1999). The reality of interaction amid weak ties ensures frequent encounters with individuals we have little knowledge or acquaintance with, while strong ties ensure more familiarity. Divergent cultural outcomes result from these interactional differences, as discussed in the previous chapter—the cold, transactional, and rational qualities of gesellschaft versus the warm, familiar, and friendly qualities of gemeinschaft (Tönnies 1957). These characteristics are thus based in part on the strength of social ties that prevail.

The political economic dimension also shapes sociocultural outcomes. The primitive communism of tribal chiefdoms promotes egalitarian norms of sharing and mutual reliance. This departs from imperialist and feudal monarchies' unequal, predatory, and coercive relations. Now the world is dominated by the global corporate capitalist economy's alienating and exploitative social relations. Changing political economic relations will influence the formation and integration of social groups, thus the levels and types of solidarity.

## COMMUNITY AS INTERACTIONAL FIELD

In *Community in Rural America*, Kenneth Wilkinson (1999) proposed a theory of interactional fields that offered a sharp break from evolutionary and systems thinking prevalent in prior community theories. According to Wilkinson, when people interact based on their community, they construct a community field. This field is necessarily broad and general and should not be confused with narrower fields that emerge around different subgroups with special interests in communities. For example, if two neighbors interact on the sidewalk about attending a community festival, they engage the community field. If they are both parents of kids who play soccer and wind up discussing the next practice, they are now participating in the social field of the soccer parent subgroup rather than the community in general. This subtle difference is significant.

Using this definition of community as an emergent interactional field, they participate in the community field whenever people discuss their community. The referent of this interaction is usually a politically defined territory, such as a hamlet, village, town, county, or city. Suppose two neighbors bump into one another while on vacation in South America and wind up discussing the next mayoral election back home. In that case, they are participating in the community field, far removed from the territory of their conversation.

Community field theory also explains how it is possible for people who reside within close territorial proximity to lack community—in the absence of social interaction, no community field can emerge. This plays out frequently in so-called bedroom communities, where people might live and sleep but not work, shop, or identify as home. Living in a large city suburb, a resident may think and talk about the large city as their community, never considering the suburb a separate entity with its own identity, legacy, or history. The idea that one can live outside of their community would be strange if we accepted a strict territorial definition, but the interactional field definition allows this to happen. Such suburban communities are often designed to promote individual privacy and suppress public interaction due to cultural preference (Oldenburg 1991).

Going a step further, Bradshaw (2008) suggests the emergence of the postplace community. As social interaction grows increasingly virtual, individuals may find that they experience a greater sense of belonging with a group of people with whom they share no physical co-presence. However, the notion of a virtual community runs contrary to the theory offered by Wilkinson. Suppose one spends all day writing posts for a Star Trek fan club Facebook Group. In that case, they are fully engaged in a special interest group by Wilkinson's definition, though participating in a postplace community, according to Bradshaw. Implicit in Wilkinson's understanding of the community field is a physical place on which the interactional field is oriented. Wilkinson's theory does not reject physical territory as a community component.

The problem with ignoring physical space and place altogether is that crucial environmental demographic and political economic issues become neglected or ignored. Even in neighborhoods with minimal social interaction or public engagement, people expect running water, paved roads, clean air to breathe, and social order. A homeowners' association may provide these services as a private entity, but that is still a form of community governance that members pay for and support. If the expected services are not provided, homeowners may complain to the association and voice their concerns, thereby initiating social interaction based on the community in which they live—the community field.

We should acknowledge that there are people who take very little interest in participating in the interactional field of their local community precisely because there are so many avenues available to interact virtually with anyone, anywhere online. In this respect, we could view advances in social media and other online technologies as barriers rather than facilitators of community interaction. However, a new type of social media platform, Nextdoor, attempts to facilitate virtual interaction among people living in physical proximity. It is unclear whether this approach will be successful in the long run. However, it appears to be helpful as a platform for neighbors to share information about locally available services, like finding a local person to watch their pets, fix their plumbing, or shovel their snow. I have observed people using the Nextdoor app to introduce themselves to their neighbors by offering a little history and narrative about their arrival and time in the community. These introductions appear sporadically and usually elicit some back and forth, including mostly welcoming comments. Is this the future of virtual community interaction? Can virtual interaction coexist with or even support local community interactional fields?

Perhaps most importantly, when people fully participate in the community interactional field, the community experiences a growing capacity for action or agency. For example, if someone has a problem finding groceries, other community members may identify with them. They may interact with the local political figures to develop a strategy for attracting food retailers or generating a local business to meet the community's needs. If nobody is interacting with their community, it is nearly impossible to imagine how a community could practice agency to overcome the problem of food deserts. Suppose community members stay in their homes, ignoring the local place. In that case, the community loses its capacity to act and be responsive to the needs and wants of the local population. Luloff and Bridger (2003) noted, "Local capacity to address important issues and improve local well-being depends upon the strength of the community field." From this perspective, community development is the process of building the community field, as will be elaborated in chapter 8. Objective measures, such as improving local employment outcomes, while important, are secondary to creating the community field since it is this field that makes the possibility of agency and future improvement possible.

## NETWORK TYPE AND STRENGTH: BONDING
## STRONG AND BRIDGING WEAK TIES

Social interaction is how people create and maintain networks or ties to one another with different levels of intensity or intimacy. We can use the terms offered by Granovetter's (1973) groundbreaking article on the "Strength of Weak Ties" to refer to our connections as either strong or weak ties. Strong ties refer to those connections we have to individuals in our primary group, while weak ties refer to those between groups. Strength refers to higher emotional intensity, intimacy, and time invested in the relationship. Granovetter also suggests that the strength of ties has a basis in similarity—the principle of homophily. While the value of strong ties is nearly self-evident—close relationships meet many basic social and emotional support needs—the value of weak ties is often less appreciated. While weak ties do not meet the same needs as strong ties, they offer something else, a gateway to new information and opportunities embedded in extended networks. An individual may serve as a bridge between groups, providing a vital link in the diffusion of information and ideas. Burt's (1992) theory of structural holes builds on this notion by focusing on the critical value of bridging individuals, arguing that more competitive social networks contain individuals who can fill the hole between parties who would benefit from sharing information and ideas. Burt is primarily concerned with economic competitiveness. The implications of his theory could be interpreted at the community level to mean that the presence of bridging weak ties increases the community's economic competitiveness.

The advent of social media has shown people that weak rather than strong ties link most individuals in their networks. The General Social Survey has repeatedly shown that most American adults admit to having only one or zero close personal friends they can call on in times of need. Nevertheless, they may have hundreds of friends in their social media network. While some sites are designed for general social interaction—Facebook was meant to facilitate social interaction between friends initially—others have adopted the goal of improving professional networks, such as LinkedIn. Sites like LinkedIn are successful because people know the value of weak ties for their professional aspirations. The more people one knows, the greater the probability of gaining insight or opportunity that helps with professional growth. A vast research literature has now subsumed research on social ties and networks as a potential source of value around the notion of social capital.

Fulkerson and Thompson (2008) found in their meta-analysis of social capital definitions that there are at least two different ways of defining this concept—one that focuses on resources obtained by individuals through their personal ties and the other that involves the normative assets required for collectivities—groups, organizations, communities—to overcome their collective action problems. The two definitions are somewhat compatible since a community that provides its members with valuable social ties—strong and weak—may also be a community that can exercise agency to solve collective action problems. Earlier, we discussed community fields as representing the capacity of a community to exercise agency. We can think of them as being relevant to community social capital in this respect. According to Brehm and Rahn (1997), individual-level social capital creates community-level social capital. Putnam et al. (1993), who popularized the notion of social capital, claimed that shared norms of trust and generalized reciprocity were centrally important.

Flora and Flora (2015) describe community social capital as a precursor to an important goal of building entrepreneurial social infrastructure (ESI). In order to achieve ESI, Flora and Flora claim that there must be a balance in the community between bonding social capital, made of strong ties, and bridging social capital, made of weak ties. They argue that too much bonding or bridging can lead to factionalism (too much bonding) or clientelism (too much bridging). Not having enough of either type can lead to individualism, undermining the whole notion of community. Once again, there can be no social ties without social interaction, and without social ties, there can be no community. When individuals are embedded in bonding strong ties, they have the support they need to help them succeed emotionally and psychologically. When they are embedded in bridging weak ties, they have access to information and opportunities they need to succeed in growing professionally and personally. A community that encourages individuals to become embedded in strong and weak ties is a community that is optimal for action that will benefit both individuals and the broader community.

Perhaps most important to understanding community social capital is not its causes but its consequences for the community. Recker (2013), for instance, has found that having a high level of social capital—especially bridging social capital—is vital for improving the quality of life in communities, based on both objective and subjective measures. Moore and Recker (2017) found that having higher levels of community social capital could help reduce the crime rate. Besser et al. (2008) found that social capital could increase a community's level of resilience, following in the wake of a "shock" that caused some level of damage, such as when a major employer closes down operations in a community that leads to unemployment. Laycock and Caldwell (2018) found that community capacity was necessary for rebuilding in the wake of extreme weather events, such as tornadoes. There is value in social interaction and social ties, particularly when they create solidarity.

## SOLIDARITY AND THE DIVISION OF LABOR

In sociology, most discussions of solidarity begin with Emile Durkheim (2019) and the ideas he outlined in his magnum opus, *The Division of Labor in Society*. For Durkheim, interest in studying the division of labor was not political economic. Instead, he focused on what the division of labor meant for social solidarity, which he considered one of the most fundamental sociological concepts. Although he did not invent the term *solidarity*, he developed an explanation for two types he called organic and mechanical solidarity.

According to Durkheim, as observed by Adam Smith and James Steuart long before, growth in population density, and thus urbanization, encourages the development of the division of labor in society. The more freed people from cultivation and rural work in the energy economy, the more freehands there are to pursue other ends. Some become shoemakers, while others make candles, learn to bake bread, master blacksmithing, and so on. While Smith and Steuart studied this phenomenon to understand political economic implications and the optimal functioning of a capitalist system, Durkheim examined how the division of labor altered the way humans interact with and relate to one another socially. He observed that if the division of labor is minimal, as is the case when community members are all working in the energy economy—nomadic foragers or agrarian farmers—each individual can relate very closely to the others because their lives are so similar. What emerges is a form of solidarity that Durkheim referred to as mechanical. In contrast, when everyone works in a different occupation, the ability to relate diminishes, and the mechanical bond weakens. In its place is a different kind of organic bond that results from mutual interdependency.

As people left the energy economy and division of labor progressed, there was a bourgeoning of trade in increasingly complex goods. People soon found they could identify with only a few individuals, while the number of strangers working in different occupations grew drastically. The level of division encouraged specialization. It was one thing to learn blacksmithing, but even the kinds of blacksmithing would evolve. Differences emerge between metals and products, from weapons to more pragmatic goods like nails and horseshoes. Even within the occupation of blacksmithing would emerge a division of labor and a lost sense of sameness. Blacksmiths would one day be replaced by industrial processes that reinvented metalworking based on a factory model, breaking the craft into separate subtasks carried out by different individuals and machines.

Durkheim noted that amid all of this division and specialization was growing mutual reliance between community members. If someone is not a farmer, they still need food. In turn, the farmer may find their job easier if they can acquire metal pitchforks and field plows from metal workers. They, in turn, sell their food to acquire these items. Of course, this exchange is rarely carried out through direct barter but mediated through the exchange of currency, which may obscure the mutual interdependency. Again, the political economic aspects of the division of labor were not Durkheim's concern. While mechanical solidarity depends upon strong ties between people with a shared worldview and experience, organic solidarity depends upon weak ties between people performing different specialized functions, each contributing to the overall interdependent functioning of the community, region, or broader national society.

So, where do organic solidarity and the highly specialized division of labor take us over time? Durkheim's thought was greatly influenced by the social evolutionary framework developed by Herbert Spencer, whom Charles Darwin influenced. After reading Darwin's work, Spencer coined the phrase "survival of the fittest," although the phrase is sometimes misattributed to Darwin. Darwin's theory of natural selection specified a primary mechanism of speciation—of different species evolving from other species. Speciation is based on the division of labor in nature. We call the different stations occupied by species niches. In the human world, not by mistake, we often refer to someone's line of work metaphorically as a niche. Spencerian evolution extends Darwin's model to human society, suggesting that humans evolved from simple to complex work, culture, and social organization forms. Durkheim extended speciation to explain the division of labor.

Durkheim's theory is based heavily on the Spencerian evolutionary framework. As the division of labor advances, urbanites continue to rely on rural cultivators for essential natural resources that produce food, clothing, and other materials. Rural cultivators rely on urban producers to create goods and services not locally available. However, in the contemporary world, we find that rural areas have also experienced a significant deepening of the division of labor. Few people living in rural communities in the United States (or other economically advanced nations) work in the energy economy. That means organic solidarity is taking hold within and between urban and rural communities. Most rural people work in healthcare, education, industry, or other governmental jobs. Even among traditional rural farmers, specialization has left them highly vulnerable and dependent on monocrop agriculture. Some farmers specialize in corn and soy, others in wheat, and others in cotton. Farmers have less in common, and they may also come into conflict when developing agricultural policy (Winders 2009). Conventional farming can be described as industrial farming, suggesting that rural areas may not be spared the same experiences as urban areas. However, the smaller rural communities may offer a greater sense of familiarity and *gemeinschaft*, even with an advanced division of labor.

An emerging trend in farming is adopting agrobiocultural techniques, which emphasize the sustainable cultivation of a wide variety of crops of plants and animals for both consumption and trade (Carolan 2016). This is happening, arguably, because highly specialized industrial farmers are finding that they cannot count on others to provide what they need to function—a failure of organic solidarity. The high costs of farm equipment and inputs, including seed, fertilizer, and pesticides, coupled with the low prices for agricultural products, make farming difficult. The low price signifies a devaluation of rural work. The global peasant movement encourages farmers to practice some level of self-sufficiency. It pushes back against low prices and pressures to specialize in commodity agriculture by encouraging a return to agrarian environmental demography focused on growing a variety of foods, thus restoring mechanical solidarity. These developments underscore one of the central flaws of evolutionary thinking—the assumption that social change is a unilinear form of progress. Humans have the capacity for agency and planning and are not condemned to play out a trajectory that does not serve them well. At the same time, a lack of understanding, planning, and organization can result in negative consequences if current patterns are not challenged or reversed. The question then becomes a matter of community action or agency. How can communities leverage solidarity in a way that creates improvements in the lives of its members?

## BARRIERS TO INTERACTION: PHYSICAL, SOCIAL, AND EPISTEMIC DISTANCE

Given the importance of social interaction, networks, and solidarity, we must consider potential barriers within and between urban and rural communities. Fulkerson and Thomas (2019) explored this question, arriving at a discussion of distance—physical, social, and epistemic—as a barrier. As we live in a world spatially divided into urban and rural communities, the reality of physical separation is significant. Rural communities are usually founded in locations that can take advantage of the energy economy, harvesting some environmental elements. Maybe there is dense forest land, fertile soil, or a mine containing metals or energy sources like coal and oil. Deposits of natural resources may be located in remote, hard-to-reach places. Thus, a central challenge to the urban–rural system involves logistics. How do we move the desired rural product from the countryside to the city? This has meant transporting by water, loading goods onto boats or ships, and moving them to a collection point, usually within a city of significant size. If not by water, goods have also been moved by rail and road.

In some cases, as with island nations, there is a fair amount of air trans-portation. These elongated trade networks achieve a system that ensures rural people remain physically removed from urban populations. Physical distance helps lay the foundation for social distance and epistemological distance.

Social distance does not necessarily require physical separation. Social hierarchy and stratification dimensions, based on class, ethnic, racial, gen-der, sex, age, religion, or other social differences, have become stigmatized. Urbane and rustic identity can operate in this way, creating social distance. Social distance is present when two people can sit in the same room in physical proximity and yet feel miles apart. Sociologists have long known that one of the surest ways to overcome social distance is by promoting and facilitating social interaction. Once social interaction occurs, the many layers of stereotypes and prejudice may begin to melt away. What happens when physical distance is combined with social distance? The odds of contact and communication are diminished, which means that stereotypes and prejudice can flourish, unchallenged by the information that would result from engag-ing in social interaction. Since urban and rural people physically reside in dis-tant communities, the physical distance is a challenge that must be overcome if there is to be more social interaction and less social distance.

What are the consequences of physical and social distance? The cultural consequences are perpetual stereotypes and misrepresentations, along with the formation of epistemic distance. Epistemology is a term used by philoso-phers to describe how individuals come to understand the world. To the extent that our past experiences shape these understanding processes, do we develop place-specific epistemologies. Someone raised in a rural setting will have a set of experiences that may be vastly different from someone raised in a dense urban setting. The basis and content of social interaction may be starkly dif-ferent. Hence, when coming into contact with someone with a very different lived experience, the feeling of unfamiliarity may cause an uneasiness that reinforces social distance. One of the worst consequences of epistemological distance is the moral dimension. We are more likely to feel sympathy for and common cause with those who have lived lives, not unlike our own—those with whom we have mechanical solidarity. Those who have lived a very different kind of life may find others foreign and unworthy of compassion, which could result in moral indifference, social disorganization, and anomie.

## SOCIAL DISORGANIZATION AND ANOMIE

As a theory, social disorganization approaches social development and social problems from the perspective of a system of norms communicated and reinforced by interaction in a community. The theory has roots in the

Chicago School of Human Ecology (reviewed in the next chapter) and grew out of observations about how different norms align with different zones of an urban environment. More specifically, in parts of the city, disorder and crime seemed to flourish, which were understood as a breakdown in localized norms. Social disorganization theory is commensurate with Durkheim's concept of anomie, or the condition in which norms and interactions breakdown leading to social disorder. Anomie is often the state of affairs when communities experience rapid urbanization and industrialization, hindering social interaction, networks, and solidarity.

According to Kubrin (2009), the basic tenets of social disorganization theory are that highly organized communities will display advanced levels of solidarity, strong bonds, social integration, and healthy social interaction among residents. Such communities will be well-positioned to solve collective action problems, preserve social order, and prevent crime (Shaw and McKay 1931, 1942). Alternatively, social *dis*organization is marked by the absence of these qualities, leaving communities without the capacity to overcome social problems and vulnerable to a descent into chaos.

Social organization is vital for supporting a sound educational system, robust employment opportunities, and reliable health care services. Recent research has suggested that educational success depends heavily on supportive community norms and expectations (Kay, Shane, and Heckhausen 2016), particularly amid a shifting rural economy (Sharp et al. 2020). When students attend school amid high expectations, they are more likely to succeed—perhaps a self-fulfilling prophecy. Social disorganization undermines educational success by introducing new problems, such as crime, that may socialize children into alternative deviant norms that devalue education while promoting illegal activity (Trinidad 2019). Kelling and Wilson (1982) suggested that foot patrol officers helped residents feel a greater sense of order and safety, allowing them to go about their routines with less hassle. They advanced a "broken windows" hypothesis that the street's orderliness depended on keeping up appearances or order. Once one window is left broken, soon the rest will follow. They suggest that broken windows indicate a loss of community social control. This argument's base is the premise that fear inhibits social interaction, and declining social interaction undermines normative control.

A critique of social disorganization theory is that it subtly promotes social conformity while denouncing all forms of deviance as inherently harmful. Social deviance can serve positive functions, as when there is a need to change the existing social order because it encompasses inherent flaws. We witnessed this in the 1960s in the United States, when protesters began challenging racist and sexist laws and norms by purposely and visibly defying them. Rosa Park's refusal to move to the back of the bus became an iconic symbol of civil disobedience that inspired others to follow suit in a widespread movement toward civil rights. Critics of the civil rights movement feared the disruption to norms would be damaging while downplaying that existing norms were already causing damage. The civil rights movement's goal was not to upend social order but to break it down to remake it more inclusively, underpinned by social interaction that cuts across racial and ethnic lines.

Thus, social disorganization theory can be critiqued because it views social disruptions as threatening to the prevailing social order, even when the social order perpetuates injustice. Klein et al. (2017) tested the hypothesis that introducing new immigrants to a community—a potential social disruption—would lead to the predicted adverse outcomes of a descent into social chaos and upheaval. Klein and colleagues found the opposite. In urban communities, based on the Uniform Crime Report, they discovered that crime was lower in new immigrant communities. The story for rural communities was more varied, leading the researchers to conclude no relationship between rural immigration and crime. They added that the addition of immigrants to rural communities usually contributed economic benefits to those communities by reinforcing the labor pool. Rural areas are typically saddled with an aging population and a dearth of young workers, and new immigrant groups tend to offer young and reliable workers. We might speculate that the community experience varies considerably based on how prepared communities are to receive, welcome, and incorporate immigrant groups into existing interactional networks. It is most likely the case that the prejudice and discrimination targeting new immigrants can become a source of social disruption. Residents display suspicion and distrust against their new neighbors, which inhibits social interaction. A culture of openness may be the best remedy for such communities as it creates pathways for interaction, which allows the community field to emerge.

Social disorganization can be avoided by promoting the community interactional field. The field enables the agency to empower communities to overcome problems, threats, or shocks while improving the quality of life. However, inequalities must also be overcome, even when embedded in the social order. If they persist, the need for disorganization will emerge, which is why social justice is a guiding principle of sound planning.

## PLANNING CONSIDERATIONS

The importance of social interaction, building the right balance of strong and weak networks, investing in community social capital, and promoting different forms of solidarity should now be evident. Collectively, we can describe efforts to improve these as investments in social infrastructure. The term *infrastructure* usually implies physical components we find in the built environment, such as roads and bridges, which will be the subject of our next chapter. Social infrastructure implies the less tangible but equally important social organizational structures that support the operation or functioning of the community. Though one cannot see a social network, they are as real as a network of sidewalks. Though community solidarity is not directly observable, it is as real as the concrete foundation of a skyscraper. So, what can communities do to promote and encourage social infrastructure?

Part of the answer should be to tear down barriers to interaction rooted in social, physical, or epistemological distance. Closing distance may require planning efforts to create a physical space for social interaction. Such spaces can be temporary, as they emerge during a farmer's market or community event. Alternatively, the space may be more permanent, as when a facility is constructed to promote social interaction. These facilities can be municipal, including schools, community centers, or civic centers. They can be hosted by nongovernmental organizations, such as the YMCA; the Elks, Moose, and Rotary clubs often erect buildings with space dedicated to social interaction. Religious organizations, such as churches, temples, and mosques, can be virtual spaces to develop ties. There can also be privately owned meeting places devoted to social interaction, as noted by Oldenburg (1991) in his observations about the role of third places—cafés, beauty parlors, general stores, and bars—so named since they come after one's home and workplace as sites for social interaction. Oldenburg was concerned with the decline of public interaction spaces in American communities since postwar suburban development has tended to avert the creation of public interaction spaces by privileging and protecting the privacy of individuals and their households. Thus, one of the most pressing planning considerations is making space for public interaction and dialogue. Ideally, this will include an evaluation of attractor points, as explained in the next chapter.

Communities should take stock of what kinds of interaction emerge in different spaces—do they promote weak or strong ties, or possibly both? Recall the notion of entrepreneurial social infrastructure, suggested by Flora and Flora, as a balancing of bonding and bridging social capital or social ties. This should be the general goal when it comes to assessing interactional space. Some changes will require alterations to the built environment. However, not everything is a problem with space—there is also a cultural pattern that could prevent the development of social interaction. As Putnam (1995, 1996) notes, Americans are no longer "joiners." We go through a periodic fluctuation, alternating between extreme individualism, amoral familism, and more public community engagement and cohesion forms. He suggests that we are currently experiencing intense individualism after decades of community decline in the 1960s. However, Putnam (2021) also claims that we have some reason to hope that the tide is turning, and we might be headed for an "upswing." He reminds us that Americans were equally individualistic in the late nineteenth century when industry and urbanization took hold. It took years of momentum to build a sense of community, and even then, it was not a fully inclusive form since social inequalities remained pervasive. Putnam cautions that it will take considerable planning and effort to develop what we are referring to as social infrastructure. Importantly, from a planning perspective, we must ask what good is it to have a space for interaction if nobody wishes to use it? The cultural idea that places value on coming together must become a priority.

Technology is another important consideration for planning for more social interaction. As we have noted, many scholars believe that current technologies have made it possible to develop social ties utterly independent of local geography. However, what are the benefits and costs of this digital networking? A growing body of research suggests that our digital lives alienate and promote loneliness (Turkle 2017). Turkle (2017) claims that humans need face-to-face contact for their social-emotional development and that young people, in particular, are being deprived. Other studies suggest that social media sites can be a source of factionalism, leading to conditions that are dangerously ripe for a level of conflict that could spiral into a civil war (Walter 2022). It is prudent to approach digital postplace virtual communities warily with these findings in mind. While technology can act as an enhancement, as Nextdoor offers, it also holds the potential to be corrosive or a replacement for in-person communications.

Finally, steps should be taken to promote the value of community solidarity and social interaction. Public meetings and dialogue about the value of interaction and organization could help address concerns and provide an alternative to individuals who may have never considered what they could gain from investing in their community. Putnam's (2021) advice is to encourage a proliferation of voluntary activities on behalf of the community, contributing to the quality of life. Even small acts, such as working in a soup kitchen or participating in a cleanup effort, can reinforce the power of working together.

*Chapter 6*

# Built Environment and Spatial Organization

The built environment refers to physical components, including housing, commercial and industrial properties, public facilities, and infrastructure that supports life in the community. Infrastructure includes water and sewage, roads and bridges, the electrical grid, telecommunications (internet, mobile phone towers, phone lines), parks, public transportation, emergency services, education, health, and other services. Communities vary in their ability and desire to deliver a full range of services. Fiscal considerations are a constant worry for communities, and fluctuations in political economy or environmental demography can impact public finances. Within every community's built environment is a system of spatial organization, which is, in some ways, the physical manifestation of its underlying social organization. The amount of planning that goes into designing and creating the built environment varies considerably. Some communities are responsive to shifts in social organization, while others struggle to adapt. It is easier to change cultural ideas than tear down physical buildings and facilities to build something new.

Attempts to understand and plan the built environment go back thousands of years. Ancient Greek philosophers—Plato and Aristotle—contemplated the design of ideal communities, balancing population size with political functions and social familiarity while specifying the physical layout, including a central agora or acropolis surrounded by residential space and other functions. These ideas would inform the design and function of the Greek Polis (Keller 2003). Many of these ideas carried over into the Roman empire, which contributed to significant advances in physical infrastructure, such as erecting complex aqueduct and road systems. Over the past two centuries, scholars have proposed theoretical models designed to optimize the layout of communities and regions in ways that could not have been imagined by the ancients, owing to changes in culture and technology, political economic shifts, and environmental demographic change. We will examine essential theories of spatial organization, the built environment, physical infrastructure, and their underlying logic to inform more purposeful planning.

## URBAN–RURAL REGIONS: THE VON THÜNEN RINGS MODEL

One of the earliest models of spatial organization was proposed by von Thünen in 1826 in his book *The Isolated State.* The regional model (figure 6.1) involved concentric rings with an urban market at their center. The market is surrounded by a ring with dairy farming and the gardening of produce and flowers. These items perish quickly and must therefore have proximity to the market, where they may sell quickly. The next ring includes forest land, which acts as a buffer zone and provides wood resources for energy and heating purposes. In the early nineteenth century, wood was the primary energy source for most communities, though coal and oil would later be adopted. Beyond the forest are grain and field crops, which can be transported slowly to the market since they do not spoil quickly. This ring is surrounded by the outermost with ranching and livestock grazing. It is prudent to keep large herds of animals away from gardening activities, as they may consume the high-priced produce. Though not shown in the figure, the entire series of rings is surrounded by wilderness. Presumably, we eventually encounter another similarly situated isolated state beyond the wilderness.

The ring model was proposed for several pragmatic logistical reasons, with much of it dependent on the need for managing short-range transportation on foot or by horse. These were the realities of village life in the early nineteenth century. Most of Europe remained under the rule of feudal monarchies, and neither trains nor automobiles had been invented. The model remains one of the only to reveal the interconnectedness of localized urban and rural

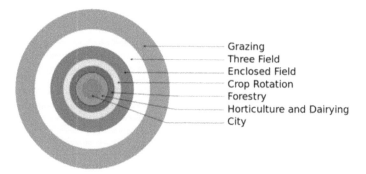

**Figure 6.1: Von Thünen Model.**
*Source:* (Wikimedia Commons, 2014).

functions. Rural areas provide critical natural resources from afar, and the urban center provides the market for trade and industry to process these resources into other goods and services. The ring model was offered primarily for planning purposes, and von Thünen's work was greatly overlooked or even ignored by the scholarly community in his lifetime.

While the von Thünen model remains insightful, context always matters. Advances in railroad and automobile technologies have altered the spatial logic upon which this model rests. The distance between the urban market and the rural landscape has now be greatly elongated—even globalized. Further, advances in refrigeration, storage, and containment allow such products as dairy milk to be produced much further afield and transported by refrigerated rail cars and shipping containers. These advances are the main reasons we rarely find a localized urban–rural system.

Though changes in technology have altered the context, it would be a mistake to dismiss the von Thünen model as obsolete. As with any such model, it can remain a useful analytic device as long as we understand its scope conditions. It maintains practical value if viewed as an idealized self-sufficient regional urban–rural system model. The environmental demography of such a region must be balanced if caloric demand is kept low by limiting population and consumption and the local environmental supply remains suitable. The model is helpful for anyone seeking to plan an autonomous, self-sufficient region. Current trends toward localization and sustainability are giving rise to such planned communities, many of which seek to create a lifestyle without automobiles or fossil fuels, thereby eliminating carbon emissions to address the climate crisis.

Unfortunately, von Thünen does not make explicit the location of houses, public buildings, roads, bridges, or related infrastructure. We can probably imagine that the urban market center has many public buildings and functions that would be missing or uncommon in surrounding rural areas. Housing is likely dense in the urban center, while it would be dispersed in the rural countryside. There would likely be roads and paths radiating from the central market to various spots in the hinterland, but this will depend on other factors. If we were to zoom in on the central market, we would be focusing on the urban space exclusively—the object which the Chicago School has explored. Most subsequent theories and scholarship on spatial organization and the built environment have examined urban or rural spaces internally without considering their connections.

## URBAN–RURAL SETTLEMENT PATTERNS

From the field of geography, we find models that describe the physical shape of settlements. These shapes are influenced by natural features, such as lakes or mountains, and organized around human-made features, including highway systems or ambitious development projects like sports arenas. The four settlement patterns include dispersed, nucleated, linear, and isolated, as shown in figure 6.2.

As a matter of degree, most rural areas display an isolated pattern, where one may not see more than a single household at a time. This pattern develops where this is a great deal of farmland or other protected natural areas, such as forests. Protecting these productive areas for rural production was the initial logic creating this pattern. If we add a few more households, we begin to approach the dispersed pattern, which can also accommodate widespread rural production activities, though sprawl may begin to threaten natural resources. Depending on population size and density, small towns, classified as rural or small urban communities, often demonstrate a linear pattern with a single road cutting through a somewhat dense collection of buildings, including businesses, government buildings, and households. Linear patterns are

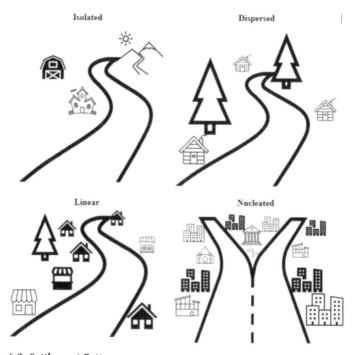

**Figure 6.2. Settlement Patterns.**
*Source*: Created by the author.

often found along state or county roads that wind through the countryside and are often identifiable by a decreased speed limit. Some linear settlements are more prominent and may result from constraints on urban nucleated development due to the natural terrain. Communities that host a large body of water or perhaps steep hillsides cannot readily develop a nucleated pattern, even when the pressure to add more depth is present.

As towns grow, they typically develop the density and depth of a nucleated settlement. Large rural communities may have nucleated organization, but it is a pattern more typical of urban areas. Nucleated settlements can vary internally, depending on the street pattern followed. Cooley's transportation theory (1894) offered an early comparison of such systems. Some cities use a grid system, making it easy to move about on foot. Other cities might have a radial street pattern, where main roads begin in a central district and are dispersed in a pattern approximated by a hub and spokes. This design is more favorable to cars than to people because it is more land extensive.

Beltway highway systems have become more common. Their characteristic doughnut shape allows cars to travel around a nucleated settlement while stopping off at the radial lines that grow farther apart moving away from the city's center. For instance, this pattern may be found in Raleigh, North Carolina, where the 440 beltway surrounds the central city, offering exits to the major roadways like spokes. Inside the beltway is a nucleated pattern, while linear development forms along the major roads outside of the beltway. Continuing further out is a second beltway, 540, which traverses a vast area,

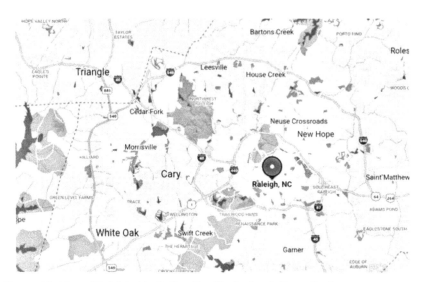

**Figure 6.3. Map of Raleigh, North Carolina Illustrating Beltway Design.**
*Source*: Microsoft Bing.

still offering exits to the major roads, which are now spaced very far apart. The additional space leads into suburban communities situated outside the inner beltway. Outside of 540 is dispersed housing and, eventually, isolated housing patterns surrounding the Raleigh area entering an agricultural area. Beyond that, an isolated settlement may transition into a dispersed settlement until arriving at a nearby community.

Other cities, such as Boston, have variations on the nucleated settlement with roads that curve, wind, or cut diagonally, making it more challenging to navigate than the grid system. New parts of the city tend to adopt the grid system. The kind of street system in place often hinges on historical evolution and the period in which the system was planned. As with many older cities originally designed for pedestrian foot traffic but now must accommodate automobile traffic, the result is a system in transition. Historical factors played a role in New York's famous Broadway layout, which has become iconic for its live theater. This road began as a Native American trail that allowed passage through Manhattan Island long before European arrival. It was widened and incorporated into the original Dutch fort erected in the seventeenth century, called Gentleman's Way, in what was then New Amsterdam. The British gave it the name Broadway after assuming control of the Dutch colony. The road was maintained through the destruction of the original fort. Thus, Broadway long predates and continues to defy Manhattan's otherwise neatly organized grid pattern, maintaining its historic course.

Identifying a settlement with one of the above shapes is simpler when there is a buffer separating one community from another. In some urban areas, settlements have grown into one another, making it difficult, if not impossible, to identify a boundary. What were once nucleated areas with miles of sparse development between them have become more or less contiguous, with linear development emerging along the connecting roads. The four settlement types help us understand the primary forms of urban–rural settlement in the contemporary world, which depart significantly from the world of von Thünen. At this stage, we will benefit from examining the internal spatial patterns and built environments of urban and rural areas.

## URBAN SPATIAL ORGANIZATION

The Chicago School is the source of the original formulation of human ecology theory in sociology. The scholars at the university treated the city of Chicago like their own private laboratory, investigating it to understand the inner workings of the urban environment. The original research team consisted of Park, Burgess, and McKenzie (1925), who approached the city of Chicago like a plant ecologist approaches a field in the countryside.

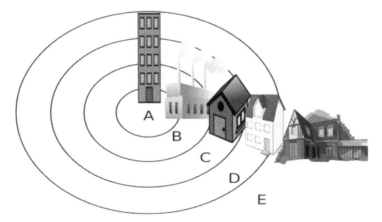

**Figure 6.4. Concentric Zone Theory.**
*Source*: (Wikimedia Commons, 2006).

Concentric zone theory (figure 6.4) is an obvious adaptation of Clements's (1916) model of plant succession, designed to explain how plant species spread in a given ecosystem. Rather than explaining land-use patterns of plant species, Park and colleagues sought to explain how different social functions would come to inhabit various parts of the city. The result was a five-zone model. At the center is the central business district (CBD), where land values are high, as are returns on investment. It is where most major employers are located. Zone 2 (B) is the transition zone that contains some residential and commercial spaces. There are typically vacant buildings here because the area's purpose is in flux. In zone 3 (C), we find the inner-city/working-class neighborhoods consisting of single-family tenements. Beyond that, in zone 4 (D), the single-family homes become more prominent and often appear more suburban, with green lawns and greater affluence. Finally, zone 5 (E), because it is so far from the CBD, consists of commuters.

Concentric zone theory resembles von Thünen's ring model, with its different circular functional zones. What is different is that the entirety of CZT is made entirely of urban space, containing none of the rural functions identified by von Thünen. We might imagine the entirety of CZT's five zones to be found within the area described by von Thünen as the urban market. However, the context of Chicago in the 1920s and '30s is notably different. Many of the rural functions that von Thünen thought would surround the urban market are now far removed from the city, and the city has grown more than von Thünen could have imagined. Indeed, one of the significant reasons Chicago grew to be a major city is that it became the terminal point where much of the nation's agriculture—grown in the West and Midwest—is processed, packaged, and shipped eastward through the Great Lakes corridor or southbound down the Mississippi.

Upton Sinclair's, *The Jungle*, provided a harrowing and often gruesome window into the working-class conditions of meat processing and packaging in Chicago in roughly the same era that the Chicago School was studying the built environment, which was the decade including and following World War I. The characters in Sinclair's novel would likely have resided in zone 3, where working-class housing may be found. The agricultural products arrive in Chicago through extensive railways and steamships. Since fresh meat cannot travel far—a point not lost on von Thünen—live animals had to be transported to Chicago's slaughterhouses. When Sinclair was writing, Chicago was slaughtering prodigious quantities of livestock using a factory-based approach that provided the necessary speed to keep up with demand. It also created some of the most horrific working conditions in the history of the United States, as exemplified by Sinclair's characters and their struggles.

Although concentric zone theory is the best-known to emerge from the Chicago School's Human Ecology approach, it was not the only or even the best theory. Later contributions, such as urban sector theory (Hoyt 1939) and multiple nuclei theory (Harris and Ullman 1945), provided better approximations of the actual contours of cities. One of the critiques of CZT is that it superimposes an idealized geometric shape that rarely resembles the actual layout of any city. It does not account for natural features, such as Lake Michigan, which encroaches on some of the zones of Chicago. Multiple nuclei theory contributed the insight that there is usually more than one central place within a city, though some of these centers may not be as primary as the CBD. There is typically a historical reason for this—as noted, many large cities are formed by smaller communities growing into one another through coalescence.

Urban sector theory added that different functions in the city usually follow a radial pattern that aligns with transportation routes moving out of the center toward the periphery in a hub-and-spoke pattern. Between the various spokes are the sectors of the city. Different sectors correspond to different functions, including industrial, entertainment, residential, retail, and commercial sectors. Several cities have such sectors or districts and provide evidence for the theory. Though these later theories offer better approximations, they too are limited in scope to certain cities at particular points in time. For instance, cities that have developed with or after the widespread adoption of automobiles usually never form the kind of dense settlement pattern and street grid system that we find in places like Manhattan that cater to foot traffic.

Leaving the accuracy of these models aside, the general effort to attempt an understanding of the spatial organization in cities is the lasting legacy of the Chicago School. Their imperfect ideas are still taught in most academic programs that address community development and urban or regional planning. New models could likely be developed that better reflect the realities of the twenty-first century, but these too would one day become less applicable. The quest for a generalizable theory of spatial organization remains elusive—it may be the case that we will always be limited to the logic of specific times and places.

## RURAL SPATIAL ORGANIZATION

Attempts to model and theorize rural communities' spatial organization and built environments are rare. Perhaps it is because it is difficult to grasp a periphery as an independent settlement space, as we might do if we ignore the central market in the von Thünen model. Nevertheless, as we observed, contemporary rural communities are not typically adjacent to the urban markets they serve. Several are moving away from traditional rural production practices, thereby altering the logic that created isolated to sparse settlement patterns. Such rural communities are more likely to experience linear development patterns or full-blown nucleated development. An example of linear development may be found in Mount Vision, New York.

In Mount Vision, much of the linear development is residential, though there is a place of worship and a theater created from an old church. There are no shopping or food options, making it a food desert. The nearest grocery is a Dollar General located about three and a half miles away—requiring access by car. The surrounding landscape is primarily made of agricultural and forestland. The crossroads consist of a state route and a county route.

A growing concern for environmental protection and conservation has led to a persistent concern for limiting development in the countryside. Parks or preserves are often used to halt or stifle settlements from encroaching on natural spaces, as we see in eastern Long Island, New York. One of the benefits of this conservation is that it creates aesthetically pleasing environmental conditions that attract visitors and support tourism, hospitality, and restaurant industries, which form a significant part of contemporary rural economics.

Perhaps what is most perplexing about developing a theory of rural spatial organization is the reality that many rural communities suffer from a planning deficit. Local governments are typically operated by individuals working part-time with few resources. Most rural communities do not oversee their emergency services, for instance, relying on county or state agencies to fulfill the need. Infrastructure, such as wastewater and sewage treatment and drinking water purification services, are pushed down to the household level as septic tanks and groundwater wells. In the United States, a rural electrification project was put in place by President Franklin Delano

**Figure 6.5. Aerial View of Mt. Vision, New York.**
*Source*: Microsoft Bing.

Roosevelt in the 1930s to ensure the power grid reached everyone in the countryside. However, no parallel program has been offered to ensure rural areas are connected by mobile phone towers or cables that ensure internet access—now widely viewed as an essential service. This became clear during the COVID-19 pandemic when rural children were asked to attend school virtually, revealing the extent of disparate access (Galbin 2021). Roads and bridges in rural areas are often neglected to disrepair. Zoning is generally limited or nonexistent in rural communities so that houses may be located next to heavy industry or other unwanted land uses.

As an anecdote, we brought a group of visiting scholars from China on a tour of Upstate New York. As we drove through the rural areas surrounding us, looks of bewilderment began to appear on the faces of our guests. They began asking several questions about the logic of the settlement and the development patterns they were seeing. We were somewhat unprepared for these questions but began to grasp a cultural difference. Rural areas are more carefully organized and managed by the state in China. The best we could explain the patterns in our area was that the state has few rules or regulations, leaving it up to individuals to decide how they would like to use the land. The exchange was informative for all of us as we began to consider the implications of living within a planning vacuum in many US rural communities.

Not all rural communities are a wild frontier where individual whims produce random and chaotic settlement outcomes that defy attempts to construct theories of spatial organization. If rural communities are interested in being successful tourist destinations, they need to maintain a higher level of social organization and planning. It is helpful to think of rural communities as having frontstage and backstage spaces. The backstage is devoted to residents or insiders and more concerned with function than appearance—a hardware store on Main Street may not be as quaint as a craft store, but residents need a place to buy tools. The front stage caters to outsiders or visitors and must be concerned with appearance and functionality. It is the front stage space that contains the power to attract visitors. Tourist communities, however, usually have elements both front and backstage and thus are tasked with balancing the functional needs of residents against the aesthetic pleasures of visitors.

There is a dynamic in which the community intentionally seeks to project a certain kind of image or experience. Often, the space devoted to outsiders is prioritized over the needs of local insiders. The entire community may become more concerned with projecting an image than pleasing the residents. In this context, we are likely to find the phenomena Thomas and colleagues (2011) refer to as rural simulacra.

Rural simulacra are simulations of rural life. What is odd about them is that they usually occur in places where there is already an authentic rural life, though it may be concealed. The simulation of rural life is highly mediated and controlled. When urbanites go on vacation to rural communities, they come with expectations of an idyll or bucolic experience. They are looking for some form of country charm. Images from literature and film fill their heads with ideas that create a rural representation—a model of an idealized rural community. An example of a rural simulacrum may be found in the aesthetics of business, located in tourist areas like Old Forge, New York, a community situated in the Adirondack region. The imagery of the store's exterior is rustic—exposed wood planks that resemble the exterior of an old barn or log cabin. The signs for the businesses feature natural rural and peaceful settings. Indeed, the stores project rusticity in order to attract visitors.

Seale and Fulkerson (2014) explained the process for creating rural simulacra. Their diagram begins at the level of mass society, where the ideology of urbanormativity generates generic rural representations that take the form of rural as simple, wild, and escape. These themes become embodied as objects, activities, and symbols. If this becomes a typical pattern for a given community, the result may be a generic, Disneyfied, rural character. In earlier discussions of community culture, identity, and legacy, we noted that rural simulacra proliferate in a cultural vacuum. To avoid a generic rustic image, rural communities must devote efforts to educating visitors about their unique history, local traditions, customs, and ways of life. This can result in a more respectful form of tourism, which honors the local community as significant, rather than ignoring its uniqueness.

Not all rural communities will succeed in winning urban visitors, but when they do, visitors often come in large numbers that can overwhelm and transform the community. Our earlier discussion of the political economy of growth machines is not an exclusively urban process. Rural communities can also suffer when tourism-based exchange values replace the use-values of residents. Success might mean that property values skyrocket, making it difficult for locals to buy a home or pay taxes. Prices may rise to a level that forces community members out—the primary mechanism underlying rural and urban gentrification. Indeed, successful tourist destinations often become hosts for extensive second home ownership, which permanently changes the local population (Fulkerson and Thomas, 2019).

What happens when rural communities fail to regulate their backstage space and "let it all hang out"? It is important to remember that rural communities exist within an urbanormative context and may come to be viewed as undesirable, dangerous, or even terrifying. This happens when urban expectations are violated, and visitors catch a glimpse of the real lives led by local people. The stereotypical "car on blocks" signifies backstage rural life.

The idea that whole places or communities can be stigmatized was first offered by Krase (1979), though Hayden (1997, 2000, 2014) further developed the concept of place stigmatization. Hayden emphasized how rural communities become marginalized and looked down upon through the lens of urbanormativity. More precisely, she suggests that small towns with a long history of consanguinity—multiple marriages within a small group of related people (Hayden 2021)—take on the stereotypes of rural degeneracy and inbred horror. Hayden builds on Shields (1991) observation that such communities are not just at the margins of geographic spaces but of cultural spaces. Far from the idyllic charm that exudes from the idyllic touristy rural towns, stigmatized rural places are chastised for daring to prioritize the needs of locals while keeping outsiders at bay. Even if permitted, urbanites would find little charm in the authentic everyday lives of people living in rural communities suffering from neglect and disinvestment. Touristy communities may also struggle economically and fiscally, while going to great lengths to conceal the suffering of locals and protect the frontstage since that is how the economy can improve. Without a tourism incentive, the suffering of rural poverty may be on full display.

According to Hayden (2014), the town of Seabrook, New Hampshire, acquired a stigmatized reputation. If someone were to call this place home, they would automatically be demoted in the cultural hierarchy and assigned the pejorative label of being a "Brooker." This label implies years of inbreeding and probably genetic defects. Brookers are deemed culturally and biologically inferior or degenerate. As Goffman (1963) noted in his theory, stigma is often associated with characteristics about which individuals have very little control—you cannot decide in which town you will be born and raised.

However, Hayden (2014) finds through her research that the community members in Seabrook often embrace the place stigma of their town. Though it may be painful to endure the stereotypes and cultural disapproval of being a Brooker, it is also a source of pride. Taking a more comprehensive view, we can see that many targets of cultural condemnation display incredible resiliency, not by rejecting labels and stereotypes but by loudly owning and proclaiming them as part of identity. The more generic rural sleight, redneck, is a label that many rural people embrace and proudly boast about as part of their identity. Someone might say they are "redneck strong," for instance.

Our discussion of urban and rural settlement spaces has alluded to an important insight. To understand what we see in the built environment, we must uncover the underlying logic that led to this outward manifestation.

## THE LOGIC OF SPATIAL ORGANIZATION

While human ecological and geographic approaches to space focus on form, shape, and function, they do not identify the underlying logic. Henri Lefebvre (1974) was one of the first scholars to suggest that an underlying logic encodes the streetscape of communities. Using a neo-Marxian perspective, he viewed the built environment as reflecting a political economic reality. Lefebvre advocated in-depth particularized historical analysis as the best way to understand this logic. He offered an analysis of Paris as an example. For instance, Lefebvre observed that Napoleon III created the famously wide boulevards of Paris after demolishing several working-class neighborhoods. He did this to facilitate the rapid movement of his military forces into and out of the city. Lefebvre's approach is highly critical of atheoretical and ahistorical spatial models and thus of many of the ideas we have thus far considered from the human ecology approach. A middle ground is somewhere between the generalized patterns proposed in human ecology and the particularized case studies proposed by Lefebvre. History matters, but some patterns occur in more than one place at a given time.

## Place-Structuration

Place-structuration theory (Molotch, Freudenburg, and Paulsen 2000) suggests that the built environment manifests an evolving local community character and tradition. The term *structuration* was coined by Giddens (1984) to suggest that what we call social structure, which sounds very rigid, is fluid. It results from people making and remaking social patterns or rules over time—it is evolving. When applied to the built environment, we begin to see physical reality as a fluid and changing response to cultural norms that reinforce old and create new traditions. When traditions become encoded into physical space, they can be described as the community's character (Molotch, Freudenburg, and Paulsen 2000). To illustrate, Molotch et al. offer a comparison of Ventura and Santa Barbara, California. In Ventura, the norms and traditions revolved around an extractive industry—oil extraction—which creates an industrial character. In the other community, Santa Barbara, the norms and traditions revolved around tourism, leading to a more appealing character to visitors. Tourist towns usually have a fully developed hospitality and food and beverage services infrastructure. Hence, Molotch et al. emphasize that cultural norms and values are vital to making the built environment. However, these norms and traditions are often closely aligned with the political economy of the community. Not everyone has equal influence over the way the built environment takes shape.

Earlier, we observed that rural communities and residents are often quick to declare that they live in the middle of nowhere—thereby creating the impression of a cultural and spatial void. How can cultural traditions become encoded into the local character of a community if traditions are poorly developed or nonexistent? Thomas's (2014) historical analysis of rural Hartwick, New York, blends the cultural and political economic logic to help us consider the case of a neglected rural settlement. Thomas points out that Hartwick's character is often criticized for appearing run-down or being poorly maintained—complaints that emerged as early as the 1880s. In some respects, Hartwick provides an unmitigated backstage area for the same population serving the front stage of Cooperstown's seasonal tourism economy. Thomas argues that the civic character of Hartwick results from county, state, and federal political neglect and disinvestment. The development of this small rural town was never considered a priority, and thus deficient funding streams have allowed the streetscape to wither. After the county adopted a 911 policy, Hartwick had to convert its Main Street into County Highway 11 and its North/South Street into State Route 205. Rural space thus faces challenges that are less common for urban spaces, resulting from urbanormative marginalization. The consequence can lead to the destruction of local identity and significance, or worse, to stigma.

## Patterns of Social Interaction and Viable Space

We have thus far thought about the physical space of communities in an objective manner—their outward manifestation of underlying processes. We should also consider the subjective interpretation and meaning that people assign to the built environment and how this creates patterns of social interaction in physical space. To this end, it is helpful to consider the distinction between settlement space, as the entirety of the objective physical space of a community, and viable space, which refers to how particular inhabitants subjectively experience space (Thomas 1998; Fulkerson and Thomas 2019). An array of viable spaces within a particular settlement will be unique to each individual. Thomas (1998, 20) suggests that viable space is "experienced at regular and frequent intervals and is familiar and comfortable." Each individual in a community will develop a particular routine with a spatial outline. We may go to the same stores, visit the same friends, go through the motions of moving between home and work or school, or visit different parts of the settlement for reasons of leisure or recreation. This everyday form of viable space is uniquely experienced by individuals and implies that parts of the settlement space will lie outside of everyday experience. For instance, this has important implications for social class, as more privileged members of a community may experience space in a radically different way from the individuals living on the other side of the proverbial tracks.

The key to understanding patterns of viable space and social interaction is the concept of "attractor points" (Fulkerson and Thomas 2019). An attractor point is a physical site that draws large numbers of individuals together for social interaction. For instance, schools draw people together for interaction based on teaching and learning. Churches, synagogues, and mosques draw people together for religious worship. Sports bars draw people together for sociability and viewing sporting events, as do arenas and sports fields. Shopping malls emerged in the 1970s and '80s in the United States as attractor points designed to promote retail and commercial activity. Shifts to online shopping, preference for strip malls, and convenient parking arrangements have contributed to the demise of shopping malls. Some malls have tried to repurpose themselves as sites that promote recreation and leisure. In place of department stores are large trampoline and bounce house businesses or aquariums, cinemas, laser tag, and mini-golf courses. The newly reimagined mall is a recreation and leisure as much as a shopping attractor point.

In his analysis of Anamat, Trinidad, Freilich (1963) identified "centers" as places where people interact to share information—a similar concept to attractor points. He operationalized these centers mathematically with a formula that estimates the relative popularity of each. The popularity of the center (PC) is based on the frequency (f), duration (d), and the number of people (n) involved in the interactions: $PC=\Sigma fdn$. This approach remains useful for operationalizing attractor points.

Rural people are more likely to exit their settlement space than their urban counterparts (Fulkerson and Thomas, 2019). This is because rural people typically need to enter a nearby urban or suburban space to meet requirements that the rural settlement space cannot provide, such as visiting a health provider or commuting to work. Meanwhile, urbanites can live most of their lives without ever leaving the urban settlement space. Urban spaces are functionally more diverse and complete than rural settlements, offering more shopping and dining experiences, a more extensive and diversified labor market, and a greater variety of educational, health, and religious services. These observations bring us to the issue of infrastructure and related urban–rural disparities.

## COMMUNITY INFRASTRUCTURE

While the importance of infrastructure is not usually a point of contention, ideas about what to include and how to create and deliver infrastructure are hotly contested. The dominant trend in the western world, embraced widely in the United States, is neoliberal policies that promote private ownership and access while reducing public ownership and taxes. In some cases, the model seems to work well, achieving high-quality service delivery by limiting access to paying customers. The model does not work well in other cases, mainly where access should remain universal or when the intended services do not lend themselves to a for-profit model. It is essential to bear in mind that services, such as wastewater treatment are critical to the daily functioning of the community. However, it is hard to imagine how a community would continue to function if wastewater activities were held to a for-profit standard—would the service be canceled if it was not generating revenue? If so, what would happen to the waste? Would raw sewage be allowed to enter local waterways as they did in the nineteenth century, thereby becoming a significant source of disease spread? Would there be a directive to homeowners to install septic systems in their homes, pushing the costs downward?

The push to privatize has played out with solid waste services, once widely offered as a municipal service. Instead of a municipal service paid for by taxes, a private company sends a bill for their waste removal services to the consumer. If the consumer cannot pay for waste removal services, they must turn to their own devices to be rid of waste. Often, this means midnight dumping—disposing of waste in illegal ways, such as pouring trash along roadways. This can create an unsightly outcome for the community, which may, in turn, need to pay for cleanup services.

Part of the infrastructure problem is political economic since local governments are constantly under pressure to keep taxes at their lowest levels while also providing several expected services. Under intense fiscal pressure, local governments often find it desirable to shed services by turning them over to private companies. Such companies operating in a global corporate capitalist system need to earn a profit. If their business model is unprofitable, they may cease providing the services or raise costs to customers. Since local governments have no requirement to maintain profit, they can operate at a loss or break even. This ensures rates will not be raised to higher than necessary levels. Critics suggest that the government's lack of a profit motive leads to waste and inefficiencies, which may be the case in resource-rich communities. However, more often than not, budgetary limits force intense scrutiny of spending and services, disallowing the luxury of inefficiencies. While public infrastructure may be inefficient, it guarantees access, which is the main weakness of privatizing infrastructure. For example, Samra et al. (2011) found that privatized water in India made affordability the most significant barrier to access, which further widened the urban–rural divide. Some consider water a human right, so denying access can be framed as a crime against humanity. Some believe food should be thought of in the same light.

Access becomes a community concern when private infrastructure hinders growth and development. Roberts and Townsend (2016) point out that the lack of internet infrastructure prevents the rural creative class from having an urban market. Public investment in infrastructure can thus be crucial to supporting economic growth, and this is usually an area that local government and businesses prioritize.

One of the greatest sources of inefficiency in the delivery of infrastructure services lies in the spatial organization of the community. In general, dense settlement patterns, such as we see in the nucleated settlement style, or to a lesser degree in the linear pattern, will allow more people in the community to be served with fewer resources. Consider the amount of pipe required to deliver tap water to spread out households, following the isolated or dispersed settlement styles. If houses sit on five- to ten-acre parcels, there will be miles of pipe required to serve a small number of households and occupants. A single apartment building could house the same number of residents and require far less physical piping to deliver water services. The initial cost of infrastructure can be prohibitive to the construction of rural water districts (Samra et al. 2011). Next, consider public bus services. Ideally, a bus route would be able to serve the bulk of the population by making a small number of strategic stops. If the population is distributed in small numbers over a vast space, it is nearly impossible to be efficient, as the bus would need to stop at nearly every house to serve the population. This is why bus service is not usually available in rural areas. Consider the costs associated with maintaining paved roads and bridges. Once again, with the isolated or dispersed settlement patterns, miles of road are required to support private transportation. Since most residents expect paved roads, and since road services do not lend themselves to a subscriber model, as with household water or solid waste removal, municipalities have to spend large sums of money building and maintaining roads. If the funds are insufficient, the road goes into disrepair and can create hazardous conditions leading to vehicular accidents. Few businesses will want to operate in these conditions.

The desire to achieve efficiency of services is something most conscientious consumers and taxpayers want to achieve. However, sometimes this wish runs counter to a cultural preference for living in a dispersed or isolated settlement pattern. For people who move to the country for vast space, the thought of dense development is unattractive. At the same time, if large amounts of land are required for rural production activities, such as farming, forestry, or mining, then an isolated or dispersed pattern may be required. Many rural communities were founded and evolved around such production activities. However, when these activities cease, there is usually no concerted effort aimed at spatial consolidation. Shifting to a nucleated or linear pattern would allow people in a rural community to better achieve efficiency goals.

## PLANNING CONSIDERATIONS

As seen in this chapter, one of the community's most intriguing and overlooked components is spatial organization and the built environment. Theorizing and understanding spatial organization, settlement structures, their underlying logic, and how to best deliver infrastructure pose complex challenges for communities. The challenge has been met with ideas going back to Plato's ideal model—the Greek Polis—over two thousand years ago. Subsequent ideas have been proposed by scholars such as von Thünen, Geographers studying settlement patterns, the Chicago School investigating urban space, and scholars attempting to understand the complexities of rural spatial organization and function. Their insights provide us with a way of understanding the logic of spatial organization as the product of community culture, political economy, environmental demography, and history encoded in the settlement space's physical landscape. They also point to some essential planning considerations.

From the examination of urban–rural systems, going back to von Thünen, we gain an understanding of what regional autonomy looks like. The goal of energy balance is what guides environmental demography, ensuring that the population's demand does not outstrip the ability of the environment to supply resources. As communities embrace the shift to localism, there is an implied desire to become regionally self-sufficient to a greater degree, if not entirely. With its focus on a diet of locally grown food, the locavore movement requires planning that may resemble some variation of von Thünen's rings. To be a self-sufficient community, the local environment needs to be harvested for resources. If they are to be turned into more complex goods, rural products must be transported to an urban market area with industrial activities. Notably, there are limits on what a localized urban–rural system can provide—some of the complex goods people rely upon are only possible because of complex global connections—the subject of our next chapter. Rare minerals, for instance, only occur in a few places on Earth, so no amount of local mining can produce a substitute.

Part of the planning process should consider the shape of the settlement pattern and consider ways to optimize the use of space. As we discussed, unrestricted development can lead to sprawl that erases natural areas by carving them up into linear corridors that eventually widen into an expanding nucleus. Land use conservation strategies should be considered, including creating preserves or parks that prohibit development. However, if the goal is to create a localized urban-rural system, the need for rural production, such as farming, will necessitate some sparse or even isolated development patterns. If the region has sensitive environmental features, such as threatened or endangered species, then conservation over rural production may be the best course. These are questions for local communities to consider. Concerns for infrastructural efficiency should lead to a denser, less extensive form of development—either nucleated or linear. This will ensure that fewer resources are necessary to support the infrastructure systems. Thus, sprawl is not only a problem for the environment but also the fiscal health of communities.

In thinking about the internal organization of urban spaces, one of the most crucial planning considerations should be to decide the extent to which foot traffic is a priority compared to pressures to create convenience and access for automobiles. Dense development favors pedestrians but is a nightmare for heavy automobile traffic. Alternatively, sprawling road systems lined with vast parking lots may enable smooth driving but render a space hostile to pedestrian foot traffic. We noted that the current trend is an urban development approach that favors cars and sprawl, but there is nothing that seals this fate—it is a planning decision. Urban planners can as easily decide to emphasize people and density. Oddly, people lament a downtown with few people walking around on sidewalks when the space is a sprawling mixture of parking lots and empty spaces. Poor urban design is at least partly to blame for "dead" downtowns. The discussion of viable and settlement space pointed to the notion of attractor points. Planning spatial organization should take inventory of existing and potential attractor points, as these may be areas in which dense, pedestrian-focused designs are ideal.

There are several issues to consider for rural spaces, and much of them have to do with the extent to which rural production is present. While many rural communities have been founded as farming or mining communities, these forms of production have waned in many locales, altering the need for dispersed or isolated settlement patterns. Once again, if the goal is regional autonomy and energy balance, at least some effort should be devoted to restarting and protecting rural production that is locally oriented. If rural communities move into the business of tourism, as is often the case, issues of balancing the back and front stage need to be considered. How does the community prioritize insiders versus outsiders? What safeguards are in place to ensure the local history, tradition, and culture will not be ignored? What measures are in place to stave off a wave of gentrification that an influx of second homeowners might initiate? The answers to these questions will hopefully point to socially responsible forms of tourism if that is the industry pursued. Local people, customs, history, and tradition need not be ignored or whitewashed out of existence to create a pleasant rural experience for visitors.

Our discussion of the logic of organization pointed to the roles of political economy, culture, and environmental demography in shaping the built environment. Community planners should think about how political decisions are helping or hurting the community's goals. What are the funding streams available to support local infrastructure? How does local economic activity benefit from the current spatial organization, and what might be improved? In terms of culture, how are locally unique histories being represented in the built environment? What is the community's character—is it aligned with the intended image the community wishes to project? How does the built environment contribute to the goal of energy balance at a local level? Is the community reliant on extensive global networks, or are there enough local sources of resources available to sustain the population? Our next chapter will explore the connections between urban and rural areas in more depth, from local to global connections.

# Chapter 7

# Community Connections

Before the widespread growth of large cities in the preindustrial era, it was possible to think of communities as isolated and at least relatively independent. Changes in environmental demography, political economy, and culture (including technological changes) have nearly erased independent and self-sufficient communities or regions. Over half a century ago, scholars like Roland Warren (1963) described rampant industrialization and urbanization as forces that would overwhelm the local community and render them an artifact of a bygone era. Shils (1972) claimed that social life was in the process of being reoriented to the national level of mass society—adding that this was something to be welcomed as a positive development. Such scholars created the impression that the local community is becoming obsolete, while national identity and global cosmopolitanism are relevant. It is premature to suggest that local community history and legacy are parochial, archaic, obsolete, or unimportant or that everything meaningful happens in megacities at the apex of global trade. Indeed, global cities would not exist without the resources that rural communities worldwide provide. One of the most significant flaws in contemporary thought is the neglect of rural importance and urban dependency.

The growth and strength of external linkages can present challenges for communities, but they are not insurmountable. Community resiliency in the age of globalization requires a firm understanding of how urban–rural systems work at a regional, national, and global scale. We will explore how urban–rural systems lost their geographic integrity, becoming detached. As detached systems, in which trade occurs over greater distances, we can observe a reorganization into an integrated world urban–rural system. The implications of this reorganization will also be considered.

## REGIONAL URBAN–RURAL SYSTEMS: CENTRAL PLACE FUNCTIONS AND THE HIERARCHY OF PLACE

In the last chapter, we learned about von Thünen's isolated state, a self-contained urban–rural system surrounded by areas of vast wilderness. While this may have been more common in the early nineteenth century, it is exceedingly rare to find isolated states in the contemporary world. Unfortunately, the global wilderness has dramatically diminished since von Thünen's time. By the early twentieth century, it became necessary to conceptualize regions with adjacent urban-rural systems growing, expanding, and merging together. In this context, Christaller (1933) developed a pioneering way to conceptualize development through central place theory.

Like von Thünen, Christaller understood the importance of market functions—the exchange of goods and services—which have urban and rural components. However, Christaller went beyond the market to theorize central place functions in transportation and administration. Central transportation functions include hubs such as railroad stations or airports (by today's standards), while central administrative functions refer to political entities, such as a courthouse or town hall. Sometimes communities enjoy a high level of centrality in all three categories, which is most likely to occur in larger metropolises with superior regional influence. Small rural villages and hamlets may claim only a single store for their market activity, while the only administrative function may be a post office. It is possible that a small rural community could host a transportation stop but unlikely to host the central hub, which is almost universally located in cities. Even large cities may be deficient in central place functions due to their proximity to other cities in the region. To use a contemporary example, since both Syracuse and Albany have international airports, Utica, New York, does not offer commercial passenger air service. This is surprising since Utica hosts a population large enough to rank as an average-sized American city. However, the size of the city is less important than its relative location when it comes to sorting out central place functions. If we were to transplant Utica to somewhere more remote, such as rural Wyoming or Idaho, it would probably acquire more central place functions, including an international airport, state government buildings, and robust market activity.

Central place theory maintains that population size determines thresholds for the variety of goods or services that can be supported within a given market. The distance between communities is influenced by the range people are willing to travel to access different goods and services. Christaller posited that threshold and range work together to create a regional hexagonal development pattern, as illustrated in figure 7.1. This pattern assumes that

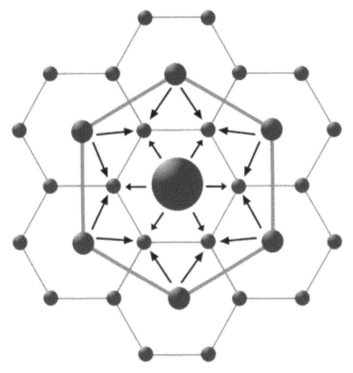

**Figure 7.1. Hexagonal Pattern and Hierarchy of Place.**
*Source*: (Wikimedia Commons, 2011).

each settlement contains its rural hinterland, which can provide the primary resources needed by the urban market. In the absence of wilderness areas, the only buffers between communities are bands of rural land. The figure contains a three-level hierarchy, beginning with the town, market town, and village levels. Higher-order places serve a broader geographic area, while lower-order places serve a smaller region. Though not in the figure, Christaller also suggested higher levels for the city and metropolis—a significantly larger city with international or global influence. He also identified a level below the village, which he referred to as the hamlet. The terms are somewhat arbitrary, but the notion of hierarchy remains relevant.

Leaving terms aside, it may be helpful to think of hierarchy as orders of magnitude, following Thomas and Fulkerson (2021). The metropolis is a first-order city that enjoys the most globalized central place functions, including, for instance, international airports, world-class art museums, and shops that sell scarce products. Next are second-order cities with central place functions that are national or regional but not global. These are followed by third-order cities that have more localized regional influence. From there, we move into the rural part of the hierarchy. Fourth-order centers are typically described as rural villages or hamlets with few central place functions that serve the immediate local population. Fifth-order centers have very few central place functions, while sixth-order centers may have a single central place function, such as a lone post office or gas station. These sixth-order centers are often unincorporated, lacking the political status of being a place. Of course, entirely rural areas have no central place functions and resemble the dispersed or isolated settlement patterns described in the last chapter. Central places usually have a nucleated development pattern with a central business district or several different centers as in the multiple nuclei model. A sixth-order hierarchical model usually captures the totality of settlements, from the most global and influential cities down to very remote or isolated rural hamlets. Some parts of the world can be characterized with fewer levels, but the general idea of hierarchy is key.

Since Christaller, like von Thünen, could not imagine cities without hinterlands, he could not anticipate the process of coalescence, in which urban settlements grow into one other, thus forming a larger urban area. This is only possible if we remove the bands of rural hinterland that traditionally enveloped urban nucleated settlements. It is challenging to identify the boundary between settlements without a rural buffer zone.

## URBAN COALESCENCE

Advances in transportation and storage, such as in our example of Chicago in the previous chapter, meant that rural production was no longer locally required by cities. Urban–rural systems have become elongated, increasing the distance between urban markets and rural production sources. We can describe the resulting arrangement as detached urban–rural systems since urban–rural geographic proximity has been removed. Without proximate rural hinterlands, the regional pattern of communities becomes transformed away from Christaller's hexagonal pattern. As a result, the boundaries between urban settlements become hazy until it is impossible to distinguish one urban settlement from another—this is the process of coalescence (Thomas and Fulkerson 2021). This pattern is illustrated in figure 7.2 below. As the population grows, thresholds expand outward. What were previously separate nucleated settlements at first become connected with dense linear development forming along transportation routes, and continued expansion results in coalesced nucleated settlements. The previous connections become absorbed as part of the internal road system.

Today, when we visit large cities, we might notice that different parts of the city have named districts. In some cases, these districts are what is left of

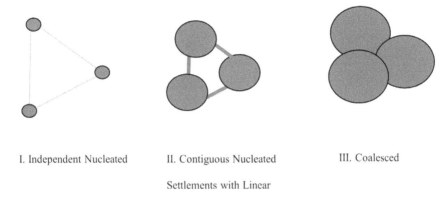

I. Independent Nucleated    II. Contiguous Nucleated    III. Coalesced

Settlements with Linear

**Figure 7.2. Coalescence from Independent Urban Settlements.**
*Source*: Created by the author.

once separate and independent communities. For instance, one of the districts in Albany, New York, is called Beverwyck. The original Dutch settlers, who were involved in the beaver (Bever-) trade, established this town (-wyck) that was not considered part of Fort Orange (predecessor to Albany). As the population in surrounding communities—West Hill and Lancaster—grew into one another, they were eventually absorbed into the Albany metropolis. It makes little sense to remain politically and economically independent when coalescence creates a more extensive combined nucleated system. The exception is when suburbs wield significant political power to retain some level of independence, typically to maintain control over infrastructure.

Perhaps one of the world's most active sites of coalescence may be found on Long Island, New York (see figure 7.3 below). The western end of the island includes portions of New York City—the boroughs of Brooklyn and Queens—and is thus part of a dense global city. Moving eastward, contiguous development continues through suburban towns and communities that are virtually indistinguishable. The only indicators are welcome signs that announce passage from one place to another. Continuing further east, the buffer zone between communities becomes more pronounced. Large natural preserves or parks prevent further development and coalescence on the far eastern end of Long Island. The island's northeastern side has widespread agricultural activity, including many vineyards. On the southeastern side, less dense development continues along the southern side of the Montauk Highway until the end of the island, where several parks combine to create a sizable natural area.

Coalescence swallows up intervening land, but this unmitigated and unrestricted growth pattern is not inevitable. Through careful planning, growth can be controlled and contained. Coalescence would not be possible if there were a concerted effort to retain rural production functions in the local

**Figure 7.3. Road map of Long Island, New York.**
*Source*: (Kobbé, 2022).

region. Since there has been a widespread abandonment of farming in rural communities in the United States and elsewhere, the vacant farmland stands vulnerable to residential or commercial development. Without a policy to preserve farmland or limit expansion, the development will likely proceed. Unfortunately, returning the land to a natural state for rural production purposes or wilderness once developed becomes complicated. When rural production is no longer local, the region loses its environmental demographic capacity for energy balance, losing sight of population pressures relative to environmental resources. Urban dependency does not disappear simply because rural connections become more ambiguous and challenging to comprehend. This precarious situation begs the question—where has all the rural production gone? Indeed, the decision to forgo regional energy balance and autonomy is to be a full participant in volatile and unpredictable national and global markets. To understand these connections, we turn to a discussion of national urban–rural systems.

## NATIONAL URBAN–RURAL SYSTEMS

The shift from local to national urban–rural systems was feared and welcomed in the mid-twentieth century. While creating a national urban-rural system varies for each nation, in the United States, it began in the early nineteenth century. For most of its colonial history, the nation was predominantly rural, and communities were reasonably self-sufficient. For the few who could afford it, long-distance trade was limited to rare urban products, such as clothing, kitchenware, and furniture. Following independence, the United States began to organize nationally. We can observe a shift in the geography of rural production that followed the Louisiana Purchase, which added what are now midwestern states with an extraordinary capacity for agricultural production. All that was needed was a supply line from the Midwest to the eastern seaboard. This was accomplished with the opening of the Erie Canal in 1821, allowing the populous urban seaboard to receive rural products— agriculture, metal ores, energy supplies—from locations far down the Great Lakes corridor, stretching past Buffalo, Detroit, and Cleveland to Chicago and Duluth.

Further, the canal enabled sea trade with inner Canadian provinces, open- ing massive supply lines to global markets—at least in theory. Most of the traffic was more regional or national. As trade in the Great Lakes, St. Lawrence, and Erie Canals flourished, rural production proximate to Eastern cities began to wane and recede. Rural populations living in New York, Pennsylvania, and other eastern states found themselves on the losing end of the competition with the Midwest. Comparatively small northeastern farms operating in a more difficult mountainous terrain could not achieve the same levels of output found on the vast flat plains of the Midwest. Disadvantages widened as railroad networks expanded, becoming transcontinental in 1869. Now rural products of landlocked midwestern states, such as Iowa, Nebraska, Kansas, the Dakotas, and Missouri, could tie into the Erie–Great Lakes ship- ping lane, further growing the rural base for consumption in the eastern urban agglomeration. Rural products could travel over 1,000 miles before reaching their final urban destination. In this respect, the Midwest was part of the New York City urban–rural system. As the supply of rural products grew, urban centers, including those located alongside shipping ports and rail hubs, saw their industries explode. Food became increasingly sold through grocery stores with canned and packaged foods that took advantage of the large agri- cultural surplus of a nationalized system. Surging populations demanded vast quantities of energy in oil, coal, and gas. The rise of the automobile caused a massive demand for steel while nearly erasing the demand for horses— another rural production activity of the northeast that became obsolete (Rhodes 2018). The highway system, greatly improved and expanded in the 1950s, further nationalizing trade networks.

The flooded supply of rural products would ultimately lead to lower prices that would undermine the economies of rural production communities while benefitting urban industries. In agriculture, a long decline in farming culmi- nated in the farm crisis of the 1980s, when international competition led many family-owned and operated farms to bankruptcy. Some of the vacated farms were bought by neighbors, leading to consolidation. Some were converted into corporate holdings, while others were sold for residential, commercial, and retail development. National policy providing support for small farms, which were part of the recovery from the Great Depression in the 1930s–1950s, began losing ground. By the 1980s, the national policy had shifted entirely to supporting corporate interests, particularly agrifood companies interested in buying the cheapest possible agricultural inputs. Price guarantees that once allowed farmers to estimate their return on investment made farming a more tenable and predictable occupation. Removing these guarantees allowed commodity prices to plummet to rock bottom levels, creating a buying bonanza for food companies and a nightmare for farmers who could not recoup their investments (Lobao and Meyer 2001).

For instance, rural communities throughout the Catskill Mountains, adjacent to the New York Metropolitan area that once provided food for New York City, could no longer capitalize on their locational advantage. While farming has not vanished from the region, it has been dramatically reduced and consolidated. The countryside is now dotted with an array of old abandoned barns. Formerly agricultural communities that were not abandoned have had to find alternative economic strategies, including manufacturing and tourism. Because of proximity, there was already strong history of tourism in the Catskills long before the decline of agriculture. However, the same improvements in transportation that expanded the range of trade also undermined the locational advantages of this once robust tourism economy, leaving behind vacant stately theaters and hotels. The Catskill economy was a casualty of the shift from regional to national urban–rural systems. There remains some potential for niche farming, like growing hops for local breweries. In this case, proximity remains as important as was conceived by von Thünen's thinking about luxury crops. By the 1990s, advances in telecommunications centered on the emerging internet spurred global trade as never before. While nationalized transportation systems helped elongate urban-rural market activity, the internet altered the logistics of markets on both the production and consumer sides. The result can only be described as a globalized or world urban–rural system.

## THE WORLD URBAN–RURAL SYSTEM

Frank and Gills (1996) once posed an apt question: is the world system 500—corresponding to the age of colonialism—or 5,000 years old, roughly corresponding to the first cities? When urban–rural systems first emerged in the ancient world, the bulk of trade occurred on a regional level between the urban market and rural hinterland—in isolated states. There were no nation-states—only nascent city-states and budding empires. However, long-distance trade did occur and could be interpreted as global. Nevertheless, this trade was part of a gift economy that was not a central feature of political economy or environmental demography. For instance, in the Fertile Crescent, home of modern Iraq and Syria, archaeologists have discovered precious jewels that traveled from Afghanistan and Persian Gulf states (Thomas 2010). However, transportation was slow and inefficient and could not be relied on for daily needs and wants, such as food, clothing, or building material. Trade was down the line rather than organized through the elaborate networks we find today (Chase-Dunn and Hall 1997).

By the colonial era, various empires and kingdoms began to resemble the world of nation-states we see today. World trade was conducted between colonial powers and colonies and was imperialistic and exploitative. Most colonies were exclusively involved in coerced rural production and often relied on slave labor. Colonial powers monopolized urban production processes, where value was added to rural products imported from various colonies worldwide. Rural colonial populations were forced to purchase urban products from their colonial masters, paying vastly more for urban products. The intolerable treatment of colonies led to countless rebellions and revolutions, often encouraged by rival colonial powers. The American Revolution would not have succeeded in defeating the British without the naval support, arms, and resources of the French.

After the end of colonialism, which took two world wars, followed by a prolonged Cold War, a singular global economy began to form. Globalization, which corresponds to the notion of a world system, is one of the most complex in the lexicon of modern social science, acquiring several often-competing definitions (Al-Rodhan and Stoudman 2006). We focus mainly on the global political economic integration of urban–rural systems. On this point, we should distinguish between international and global trade. International trade occurs between nations where urban–rural systems remain primarily within national borders. For example, after it nationalized its economy, the United States was engaged in trade with other nations, primarily for finished products. Long-distance trade is thousands of years in the making, achieving an impressive level of coordination that linked all corners of the world by the year 1000 CE (Hansen 2020). However, global trade includes urban–rural systems that transcend national boundaries.

Global commodity chains are broken into different subtasks assigned to different nations. Rural communities in one nation might export resources to a domestic urban market or to urban markets in other nations. These urban markets export finished or semi-finished products to other nations to complete the manufacturing process—the manufacturing complexity results in more circuits of urban-to-urban trade between nations. Based on global commodity chains, we may thus think of globalization as a relatively new phenomenon of the twentieth century. It is the latest stage in scaling up urban–rural systems from local, regional, and national to an integrated world urban–rural system (Thomas and Fulkerson 2021).

Figure 7.4 illustrates a multinational commodity chain with a fourth-order place hierarchy. The size of the nodes represents the level of place, with the largest and most central being a large metropolis—a global city. It is connected by three second-order cities and lower, third-order places. At the bottom are fourth-order rural communities. The eleven numbered boxes represent nations. The first-order city is in the same nation (2) as one of the second- and third-order cities. None of the rural communities are in the same nation as the first-order city. At the bottom of the diagram are nations with only rural communities—entirely rural nations (4, 5, 6, 8, 11). Nations 7 and 10 correspond to the notion of semi-peripheral but lack rural production. Nation 9 has rural production and a domestic urban market that exports to nations 3 and 2. Nation 1 has higher-order urban functions but still lacks a first-order global city, so it trades with country 2.

Though figure 7.4 is an imperfect way to conceptualize the relationship between the geography of communities, regions, and nations connected by global commodity chains, it reveals the complexity of detached urban–rural systems. Many of the nations involved in trade lack rural production (1, 2, 3, 7, 10), while many rural nations have no urban markets (4, 5, 6, 8, 11). As a result, urban–rural interdependency creates international interdependency. Recalling the notion of urban dependency, we might recount that the rural nations engaged in international trade retain the option of shifting strategies and becoming more self-reliant. Urban nations assume a steady flow of rural products but may be left in a vulnerable state if the flow slows or stops.

The globalization project, defined by expanding global commodity chains (McMichael 2004), is organized primarily by multinational corporations (MNCs). These corporations operate globally and, therefore, simultaneously have to answer to several nations while being held accountable to none. Encompassing branches and functions that span an array of nations, MNCs can simultaneously engage in internal and international trade through foreign

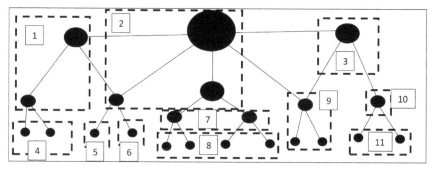

**Figure 7.4. Global Commodity Chain Showing Place Hierarchy and National Boundaries.**
*Source*: Created by the author.

direct investment (FDI). MNCs have to operate within the parameters of international trade agreements. These include the World Trade Organization and regional agreements on free trade (USMCA (formerly NAFTA), ASEAN, AU, EU). These trade agreements ensure unobstructed operations that seamlessly empower MNCs to build and coordinate commodity chains across international boundaries.

The world urban–rural system encompasses multinational corporations controlled by global cities, which sit atop a global hierarchy of places as first-order cities. These global cities and their corporations coordinate where and how global trade is conducted, which has implications for which specific countries, lower-order cities, and, eventually, rural communities will be involved. Global cities control markets that dictate the pricing of commodities. For example, the New York Mercantile Exchange (NYMEX) is where commodity futures are traded, which sets a global price standard. When rural coffee farmers in Kenya try to sell their beans, they must heed the current price established in such commodity markets as found in London and New York.

## THE CONSEQUENCES OF DETACHED
## URBAN–RURAL SYSTEMS

The vast physical, social, and epistemological distance created by world urban–rural systems causes many challenges, including a moral indifference that permeates the top of the hierarchy, as explored in the last chapter. It is easier to exploit the nameless and faceless rural workers living thousands of miles away in unknown locations than to exploit rural workers in a neighboring community. Moreover, those at the top of the hierarchy can labor under the illusion of limitless resources. There are no visual reminders of environmental limits without a visible rural hinterland. If an urban community is consuming an inordinate amount of forest products, there is no visible deforestation that reminds them of the consequences of their actions. The people living in von Thünen's isolated state would have been keenly aware of finite rural resources because they could see limits for themselves. Culturally, detached rural hinterland communities are not valued for their contributions to urban life, making them vulnerable to having their needs ignored and badly exploited. The reality of urban dependency is easy to ignore if there is never interaction with rural producers. The history and legacy of rural communities remain unseen, and the sacrifices of rural workers remain unappreciated. Thus, the worst forms of poverty, environmental problems, and cultural erasure globally are found in the most remote corners of predominantly rural nations.

While adjacent urban and rural communities have become detached, it is possible to estimate the amount of rural land required to serve urban demand. The caloric well (Fulkerson and Thomas 2021), introduced earlier, is a method used for calculating the energy demands of a population relative to the amount of land required to generate enough supply. Based on population size, we can estimate how much of the surrounding hinterland would be required to rebuild a geographically intact urban–rural system. In some cases, the size of the population is so great that the prospect of localizing urban–rural trade is impossible.

Just as urban demand can be estimated on a per capita basis, using the caloric well method, so too can the environmental supply of the hinterland be estimated on a calorie per unit of land (e.g., the acre or hectare) (Fulkerson and Thomas 2021). Using this technique to estimate the land required to support a large urban population may lead to the realization that it is impractical to support the current population. In some cases, the entire area of a state is insufficient to feed one city, as we found in New York City's metro area (Fulkerson and Thomas 2021). In such cases, the Franklin solution of exporting population, from chapter 2, may be worth pursuing. If environmental resources are insufficient, energy balance can only be achieved by altering the population part of the equation. Here we run into the challenge of setting population goals that require potentially unpopular policies. Population policies that seek stability or decreases can focus on limiting fertility or boosting outmigration. Large cities owe their size mainly to migration patterns rather than high fertility rates since fertility tends to be very low in urban settings. Curbing additional growth means limiting the number of people moving to the city while providing incentives to leave.

## POLICY CONSIDERATIONS

This chapter has sought to develop a better understanding of how communities are connected through urban–rural systems on a regional, national, and global scale. Geographically intact urban–rural systems offer locally complete and resilient regions that link urban and rural communities with clear and direct exchange networks. Predictable development patterns emerge when urban–rural systems are regional, as we find outlined by central place theory. The built-in buffer zones of rural hinterlands, even in the absence of natural wilderness areas, ensure a limit to the expansion of urban communities. Using local environmental resources reminds populations about the reality of the energy economy and the limits to growth and consumption imposed by environmental constraints. Culturally, urban and rural communities can more easily grasp and understand their mutual interdependence and shared historical legacy.

Given this background, communities should consider examining how they are connected to other communities and how they participate in broader urban–rural systems. The first step will be to identify where the community falls within the hierarchy of place: first-, second-, third-, fourth-, fifth-, or sixth-order. Next is considering how the community connects to urban–rural systems. While this may seem a complex task, a few questions can make a beginning. How and from whom do people in the community access the goods and services they want and need? How far do people travel for these goods and services? Where do people work—is it with local employers, or is it a community of commuters? How much rural production—the energy economy—happens in the community and proximate region? How much direct urban–rural exchange takes place in the immediate region? What are the central place functions of the community in terms of economy, politics, culture, and transportation? Are there linkages to networks outside of the community?

Based on the answers to these questions, communities should discuss whether the goal of creating an intact urban–rural system is feasible. To help explore this, it may help to review the community's recent history, identifying any challenges or problems that have arisen from the current arrangement of physical space. Have there been occasional or ongoing problems for community members getting where they want or need to go? Have national and global linkages served the community well?

It is important to note that state and federal policies often take precedence over local community ordinances, which can serve to either help or hinder local efforts. Usually, there is at least some ability to control zoning and related land-use policies, which can go a long way in planning spatial organization. Given what we have discussed about coalescence and threats to surrounding rural land uses, communities should consider policies that constrain growth and expansion that leads to coalescence. What measures have been taken already—are there protected areas? Where are there development pressures in the community and region? Is it expanding or stable?

One of the most useful philosophical approaches for thinking through these issues is bioregionalism, which seeks to promote sustainable regional planning and development (McGinnis 1999). Rather than starting with arbitrary political boundaries, bioregions are based on natural zones, such as watersheds. However, even watersheds can be massive in size, so a more limited natural boundary might be desirable, based perhaps on bodies of water or the topography of large hills or mountains. There are no definitive rules about what counts as a natural boundary since local conditions are unique. Generally, bioregionalism emphasizes aligning political boundaries with natural contours while encouraging local food systems, local material consumption, and working with native species.

Aligning the energy economy with local environmental conditions can maximize efficiency while minimizing negative impacts on the population. Developing a familiarity with the local hydrology, for instance, can point the way toward harnessing the power of water. While water mills are often considered quaint obsolete features, they remain a viable tool for generating local power. Watermills were the lone tool used to spark the industrial revolution in the United States, long before the use of coal and other fossil fuels. So important were water mills in Utica, New York, that many town names continue to include the word, such as Washington Mills, Clark Mills, and New York Mills. Bodies of water, including rivers, streams, and lakes, should thus be considered when planning the built environment and general spatial organization around the environmental demography of the community.

Moreover, advances in solar power mean that local communities can invest in their ability to capture sunlight to power homes, businesses, and other consumers. Windmills may also be viable but are more dependent on local wind conditions. If the local capacity for energy production is high, it may be worth considering making these resources publicly accessible as part of the infrastructure portfolio. Low-cost, locally produced energy would probably be very attractive to potential businesses and would be welcome by homeowners. However, if the ability to provision resources for the local population is limited, the community should consider the issue of population size. It is not unreasonable to think about and plan for an ideal population size based on the infrastructure, built environment, and natural environmental limits.

Once local energy production is afoot, the local economy can grow in a way that is truly from the ground up and less dependent on extra-community linkages—some of which span the globe. Global energy dependence has long been a problem, leading to international conflicts and war—avoiding participation in these systems has benefits on many levels. Our earlier discussion of civic capitalism, local economics, and associated local political organization is thus consistent with the goals of bioregionalism. Though often underappreciated, economic value has its foundation in energy (Fulkerson and Thomas 2021). Local economic activity can use locally available resources, such as forest products, though the goal should be to harvest these resources sustainably. Some environmental philosophies would frown on this, emphasizing the value of maintaining pristine environmental conditions to the fullest extent possible. However, as long as a local population consumes resources, refusing to harvest them locally only means displacing the burden for other communities to bear. We should consider whether planning efforts will lower the environmental impacts or simply move them elsewhere.

The bioregional approach incorporates humans' social and cultural worlds into the local bioregion, which is consistent with our earlier suggestions of developing a coherent cultural narrative and legacy. This will take work and may include investigating indigenous populations and learning how they lived with the land. This knowledge can be obtained through oral histories, or local archives may hold clues. This cultural knowledge can inform strategies for improving the local environmental demography and political economy. It also means aligning social interaction and spatial organization with the natural features of the bioregion. The attractor points we noted earlier might have more popularity if they emphasize and take advantage of areas with natural beauty—including scenic vistas or spots that overlook bodies of water.

There is no one-size-fits-all strategy for applying the principles of bioregionalism. As a philosophy, it can guide planning, and the brief discussion above should lay a foundation for starting meaningful conversations. Communities can use bioregionalism to instill sustainable planning in their decisions to make investments in the various capitals of the community. Communities may benefit from joining the bioregional movement, though this is not necessary to benefit from its philosophical ideas. The value of this regional focus will lie in creating a protective layer of resiliency, protecting the community from national and global market shifts.

*Chapter 8*

# Community Planning and Development

At this stage, we have explored the most critical aspects of urban and rural communities, developing a deeper understanding of how they work and how they are connected regionally, nationally, and globally. We focused on environmental demography, political economy, and sociocultural dimensions. We considered policy issues and solutions relevant to each as we examined these concepts. We now look toward developing an informed course of action to address these policy concerns to improve community life. There are two ways this can be accomplished. The first involves a community acting independently to implement a change process, referred to as community agency. We will explore how this might happen, associated with having the right mixture of robust social interaction and sound leadership. However, not all communities have the capacity for agency or to implement a practical and reflexive change process that is sustainable. This brings us to the second strategy, which involves community development (CD). By definition, the process of community development is initiated when a community development specialist (CDS), or change agent, is intentionally hired to make improvements and interventions in the community. According to Robinson and Green (2011, 4), community development "can be considered a positive science, focusing on identifying the most effective ways to promote development in communities. This view of community development sees the importance of basing local programs on empirical evidence and not just on the desires and preferences of residents." This definition reminds us that the guiding paradigm in science is applied to improve the community. The main approaches include self-help, conflict, and technical assistance (Christensen and Robinson 1989). Each community has unique conditions, and each approach offers value specific to certain conditions.

Garkovich (1989) clarifies an essential distinction between the development *of* the community and development *in* the community. The former

143

refers to efforts geared toward the process of planning and development and is focused on improving social interaction and the community field; the latter aims to improve economic, political, cultural, and environmental conditions or outcomes relevant to community well-being.

According to Robinson and Green (2011), CD has roots in the Progressive Era, which emerged at the beginning of the twentieth century. Progressives were eager to solve various social problems, including crime, deviance, and delinquency. These were caused by disruptive social changes associated with urbanization and industrialization. The period leading to the First World War was marked by activism that sought the prohibition of alcohol, women's suffrage, corporate regulations, and anti-trust laws. Sociologists, such as Jane Addams, were working as scholar-activists. Addams's Hull House was established to aid new European immigrants, resembling the protagonists mentioned above in Upton Sinclair's *The Jungle*, as they attempted to settle in Chicago.

After the Progressive Era, the 1960s were the next intense period of social activism to ignite community development efforts, confronting widespread social inequalities related to sex, race, class, and age while tackling problems related to the environment, war, and poverty. The War on Poverty helped launch community development as we know it today by providing new funding streams. Initially focused on issues of housing, job training, and social services, it later expanded to include education, health care, and environmental concerns—broadly part of social development and sustainability efforts. Because it is concerned with improving local economic conditions, CD is often confused or equated with economic development. While there is overlap, economic development has a narrower focus, which may at times lead to actions that undermine broader social development, the environment, and sustainability. CD tends to take a more holistic view instead of a narrow economic focus.

If communities lack agency and decide not to pursue CD, what then? As the saying goes—the only thing constant is change. Whether communities wish to take a proactive approach to change is optional. However, it is hard to imagine local improvements resulting from unreflective haphazard change that produces damaging mistakes. As astutely noted by Christensen, Fendley, and Robinson (1989), "People have the opportunity to effect change or be affected by it." Just as individuals can benefit from careful reflection on their lives, coupled with planning and visioning of the future, so can communities. Whether a community wants to have any say in its future, it is better to prevent a void in community planning and development, as special interests usually fill such voids.

## COMMUNITY AGENCY, INTERACTION, AND LEADERSHIP

As discussed in our chapter on social interaction, communities differ in their ability to practice agency by engaging the community field. The strength of the community field suffers when there is a dearth of social interaction, and there are many challenges that may act as a barrier. We see a decline in public attractor points, including third places, resulting in fewer opportunities for interaction. There may be a growing cultural preference for individualism and privacy—with people preferring the comforts of their own home—over mutualism and public community life. These feelings may be rooted in distrust and fear or the absence of social capital. It could be a community with high levels of factionalism when subgroups have strong internal ties but weak bridging ties, undermining the general community field.

A community may be able to overcome these obstacles and practice agency, but it is often a significant challenge. In community development (CD), much effort is devoted to fostering social interaction and building bridging and strong ties in communities. A community development specialist (CDS) is trained to facilitate social interaction and foster the creation of social ties. For this to be successful, the CDS needs to conduct an initial assessment of the community field while watching for instances of clientelism (too many weak ties), factionalism (too many strong ties), or individualism (too few ties of any type). These three conditions pose different sets of challenges.

Suppose a community is fortunate enough to have a high capacity for agency. In that case, the planning and development processes may already be part of the fabric of the community field. In this case, the community may not require the assistance of a CDS to facilitate and provide support for the development process. Such an expert would have little to do in a community where residents are already holding public discussions about what they want to see in their community while identifying strategies to reach goals collectively. A community with entrepreneurial social infrastructure is poised to act (Flora and Flora 2015).

If there is factionalism, the solution will generally be the creation of a representative and general council through which to build the community field. If all subgroups and relevant stakeholders in the community are identified, then members of each should be invited to serve as representatives. If any group is excluded from the planning and development process, it will not likely succeed. If there is clientelism, the solution may be to promote participation in local groups. It may be that such groups need to be created first. Our earlier example suggested that commuter communities often lack local ties since residents have more bridging than bonding ties. If individualism runs amok, bonding and bridging ties will need to be developed, perhaps by creating local groups in which members can participate, coupled with efforts to create a representative council. Each community will need a tailored approach since one-size-fits-all policies generally do not work.

Another essential part of building social interaction and community agency is identifying and fostering appropriate leadership styles. As noted by Weber, a leader may refer to a formal role (rational-legal), an inherited set of privileges (traditional), or someone with personal qualities that inspire others (charisma). There are three basic styles of leadership. An autocratic leader embodies and embraces their authority, issues directives to those under their control, and claims responsibility for any successful outcomes. A laissez-faire leader will identify goals for the planning and development process but will play a hands-off role in managing the process. The democratic leader will actively engage and facilitate discussions and listen to all members while trying to allow objectives and processes to emerge from the collectivity. A democratic leader is usually very hands-on but resists issuing directives.

A creative study was devised by Lewin (1939) in the 1930s to test the effectiveness of these three basic leadership styles. He arranged three experimental groups with an adult leader and a small number of ten-year-old participants, each asked to complete the same group task. The three groups correspond to the autocratic, laissez-faire, and democratic styles. He found that while participants in the autocratic group worked the hardest in the presence of their leader, they ceased working when the authority was no longer present. They did not feel a sense of ownership over the project and resented being ordered around. They were also the most likely to behave aggressively toward one another. The laissez-faire leader was the least effective of the groups, as the participants were not engaged in the activity and became easily distracted. Rather than becoming aggressive, the members of this group were mainly aloof. The democratic leadership group worked at a high level both in the presence and absence of the leader since the group members felt a personal sense of ownership over the activity. The group members were supportive of one another and were not aggressive or aloof about their activity. The findings of this research are insightful for what they say about political systems and, for our purposes, how they inform the most effective ways to engage in community planning and development. Members of the community should thus strive to be democratic leaders. They should try to develop this approach with other leaders in the community by discouraging autocratic or laissez-faire approaches. The planning and development process will be more successful in local communities if community leaders and members feel a sense of ownership of the process.

Stovall, Robinson, Nylander, and Brown (2011) compare what they refer to as the developmental, directive, and permissive leadership styles, which roughly correspond to the democratic, autocratic, and laissez-faire forms examined by Lewin. However, Stovall et al. explain these leadership styles in organizational settings. Stovall et al. suggest that in directive organizations, people are viewed as lazy, dependent, irresponsible, hostile, lacking in imagination and creativity, while lacking in forethought or vision. Directive leaders address these shortcomings by finding ways to motivate action, provide direction, and maintain close supervision while generally mistrusting and opposing subordinates' ideas and issuing and enforcing a top-down outline and plan of action. An excellent example of this style may be found in the military.

In contrast, the developmental organization has leaders who view individuals as dynamic and self-motivated, independent, responsible, allies, creative, and imaginative with vision. The developmental leader thus focuses on providing guidance and guidelines while allowing self-direction, instilling trust, encouraging cooperation and collaboration, creating conditions that foster creativity, and allowing members to help generate their plans of action. Companies in the technology sector, such as Google, have a reputation for conducting business.

Shifting from the organizational to the community level, we can further extend the logic of leadership styles. The developmental community is one in which a democratic leader works with community members collaboratively and helpfully. The leader assumes that community members bring valuable ideas and knowledge to the table, encourages members to provide input and shape the general direction of community planning and development without imposing string rules or guidelines. The resulting context will be one in which creativity and self-direction are encouraged and supported. Alternatively, the directive community is one in which the leader views members as having little to contribute in terms of ideas. The leader will assume community members need incentives in the form of sticks and carrots to motivate action. The community members will be issued the plan of action and ordered to perform the required tasks to meet the leader's objectives. As we will see, the three main approaches to community development correspond with leadership styles. If a community has sufficient agency, its leaders will create a sustainable process for planning while meeting benchmarks based on defined development objectives. If it is difficult to achieve, then a community might seek the aid of a CDS.

# TECHNICAL ASSISTANCE AND
# DIRECTIVE LEADERSHIP

When the thought of soliciting the help of a community development specialist arises, the expectation is often that by hiring an expert, the community is
identifying someone to tell them what to do to improve the community. The
analogy is like hiring a doctor to diagnose an illness and prescribe a course of
action, which may include medication or a lifestyle change. The problem with
applying this logic to community development is that the residents probably
know more about the strengths and weaknesses of their home than an outside
expert. Matters of improvement are primarily subjective, so outsiders have
no right to impose their tastes and preferences. Further, community members
must live with the results of the planning and development process. At the
same time, a hired specialist probably resides elsewhere and maintains no
long-term connection to the community. Therefore, it would be questionable
to give an expert directive leadership power allowing them to define objectives and issue orders. This is the crux of the technical assistance approach.
The community is the patient, and the CDS is the doctor. The problems are
diagnosed and then treated with a prescription. Technical assistance is most
appropriate when a technical problem needs to be addressed.

The folly of subscribing to a pure technical assistance approach was
revealed in the 1950s and '60s during the Green Revolution—an agricultural
movement that involved the adoption and diffusion of new agricultural technologies throughout the third world. The objectives of the Green Revolution
were to increase farming yields to overcome hunger and malnutrition.
Norman Borlaug a key figure who received the 1970 Nobel Peace Prize for
his contributions. Green Revolution technologies included new seed varieties
bred to maximize yields (high-yield varieties), pesticides, fertilizers, mechanized irrigation methods, and various innovations related to plowing, planting, and harvesting crops. In our chapter on culture, we noted that technology
is inherently cultural. With these innovations came a package of values,
beliefs, and norms that privilege modern scientific farming methods over
local and traditional methods. At the base of these cultural beliefs was a sense
that traditional farming methods were archaic. The broader ideology of modernization drove many initiatives, and when it visited the countryside, it was
manifested as the Green Revolution. Modernization embraces industrialization and urbanization while viewing rural life as an obstacle to be overcome.

The problem with the Green Revolution was not with the overall goals to
defeat hunger but with the process of how the objectives were met, sometimes
leading to uncertainties, uneven outcomes, or failure. The top-down process
used to expand the adoption and diffusion of technologies ignored significant

concerns and warnings of local people. Since culturally, there was immense faith in modern science, there was distrust in local populations, despite their experience farming the land for generations. Their techniques were viewed as backward and obsolete. By convincing local farmers that they knew nothing about agriculture—a key indicator of directive leadership—it became possible to encourage them to adopt the new modern technologies.

The intended objective was met in some cases, and yields began to increase. However, in other cases, the results were catastrophic. The introduction of fertilizers causes damage when an abundance of nitrogen accumulates in local waterways, giving rise to algal blooms that suck the oxygen out of aquatic ecosystems—the process of eutrophication—this negatively impacted population relying on fish and other aquatic species as part of their diet. In addition, pesticides, while helpful for fighting off unwanted pests, also hold the potential to kill indiscriminately, undermining terrestrial and aquatic wildlife. For instance, populations of seabirds began to plummet when nesting mothers crushed weakened eggshells—a direct result of eating fish contaminated with DDT. Humans are also vulnerable to health problems by consuming contaminated fish and wildlife. Mechanized irrigation pumps may have effectively improved the watering of crops. However, reliance on fuel for the pumps made the irrigation system dependent on continual access to costly diesel, thereby weakening the profitability of farming. Traditional irrigation methods were often effective and avoided such cost and dependence. Finally, even with the application of innovations, overall yields were not always improved, revealing that there may have been greater wisdom in the local farming knowledge previously ignored by the scientific experts. Suppose the technologies of the Green Revolution were offered as an option to indigenous farmers, assuming they held the necessary knowledge about how to farm in their communities. In that case, a developmental approach in place of a directive approach may have been utilized to a more significant effect. The potential gains in yields could have been carefully weighed against potential risks to the environment and population.

More responsible use of technical assistance is to think twice before seeking expertise and solutions. This is better than uncritically adopting whatever seems the best fix (Robinson and Fear 2011). When offered in a developmental rather than directive setting, expertise can be kept in check and scrutinized. With this in mind, there are times when technical input is helpful. If a community deems it necessary to build a bridge over a river, hiring an engineer to design the bridge is better than amateurs constructing a bridge of questionable integrity. That does not preclude the engineer from presenting several options to the community for consideration, which would allow input, deliberation, and ownership by the community. The key is monitoring the power structure (Fear, Gamm, and Fisher 1989). Ceding all power to experts creates a technocratic power structure, a variation of directive leadership. It is possible to maintain a democratic and developmental power structure while hiring experts to work in service of the community's wishes.

## SELF-HELP AND DEVELOPMENTAL LEADERSHIP

The central idea of the self-help approach is that communities should be self-directed, taking responsibility for their planning, problem-solving, deliberation, and decision-making (Littrell and Hobbs 1989; Green 2011). In other words, the goal is to build agency. A twist on the self-help approach, created by Kretzman and McKnight (1993), is referred to as asset-based community development (ABCD). Instead of starting with a list of problems to solve, it begins with a list of assets to enhance.

Whether focused on assets or problems, the self-help approach presumes that communities have the freedom to act of their own accord. Implied is a context that is compatible with western democratic pluralism. It is unlikely in autocratic nations, where directive top decisions are made. Unlike the technical assistance approach, the self-help approach does not develop a reliance on an outside expert, who receives blame or credit for failures and successes. Successful self-help is usually indicated when the CDS is no longer required and community agency prevails. While technical assistance is focused on development *in* the community, self-help focuses on the development *of* the community—the outcomes are less important than the process. The ideal process will be democratic and pluralistic, including representatives from all community segments. The role of the community development specialist is to initiate the process through empowerment and facilitation—the hallmarks of a developmental leader.

Historically, self-help was introduced by change agents working for the United Nations, the US Agency for International Development (USAID), and the US Cooperative Extension Service as part of a national development agenda. It was a response to the shortcomings of technical assistance but initially struggled to differentiate as an approach due to pressures to expedite the development process (Littrell and Hobbs 1989). The experience of CDSs was challenging as they encountered fatalistic attitudes or conflicting local and national goals. Rather than invest time to facilitate self-help through developmental leadership, the CDS was more likely to revert to directive leadership and technical assistance due to external constraints. CDSs became gatekeepers for outside resources, encouraged by their agencies to promote the adoption and diffusion of technologies, including those associated with the Green Revolution. It needs to move beyond adoption and diffusion toward broader national and regional grassroots development goals and build on horizontal partnerships for self-help to work. This history reminds us of the vital need for a supportive organizational framework. If self-help is going to be pursued, it takes time to develop. Organizations need to give the CDS and the community time to engage and grow the community interaction field.

While self-help is generally viewed as an ideal approach to community development, it is challenging to initiate since it is the most democratic and inclusive. Widespread participation is not possible unless members of the community are motivated, interested, and willing to participate—conditions that are not always met. Further, there may be structural challenges to full participation. Communities do not fully control their destiny. When communities face complex technical problems, the need for expertise becomes great, making technical assistance appealing. The answer to overcoming some of these challenges is to incorporate a measure of technical assistance, which can break complex issues down into manageable choices that the public can debate and consider. Providing external resources and funding can supplement and enhance a community's ability to act when resources are deficient. It may cause more damage if the self-help ideology is strictly enforced to become a pull-yourself-up-by-your-bootstraps strategy. Employing a broad and participatory decision-making process does not necessarily preclude the use of external resources, provided that a total reliance is not fostered. Perpetual reliance is not consistent with a long-term agency.

Green (2011) lays the general outline for productively initiating self-help, which he states begins with creating a local advisory committee and preliminary discussion of the expected outcomes of the development process, resources, and time frame. Next, the advisory council must determine how the group will meet its objectives—how decisions will be made, and who will be consulted. Once these preliminary steps are complete, the next phase is action planning. This will involve a visioning process and possibly creating a strategic plan that helps prioritize specific projects and plans. Once planning is underway, it is crucial to maintain momentum by keeping everyone engaged and motivated. Finally, monitoring and evaluating the process is essential for concluding progress toward meeting benchmarks. We will return to the process of evaluation.

A final concern for the self-help approach is based on the internal power dynamics of the community, which may privilege some groups over others along factional lines. Such lines may include ethnicity, race, age, sex, gender, religion, social class dimensions, or other cultural, linguistic, or political differences. These differences may not pose a challenge, but when factions intersect with structures of power and privilege, problems emerge. Groups that have traditionally been in power may be happy to retain control, ignoring the input and participation of rival factions. It may be the case that there are groups actively oppressing or excluding other groups in the community or broader region. The response to this situation will depend on the agency's expectations of employing the CDS—government, university, foundation, or other community groups—and their level of commitment to diversity, equity, and inclusion. A skilled CDS, a developmental leader, will learn to identify divisions and devise strategies for overcoming inequities. This may require a shift to the conflict approach.

## CONFLICT, FACTIONS, AND INEQUALITY

As the discussion of self-help reveals, conditions in a community may not be appropriate for broad, representative, and inclusive forms of planning and development. When there are gross abuses of power, deliberate efforts at discrimination and exclusion, and the differential treatment of minority groups of any type, power dynamics must be addressed if meaningful planning and development occur. If left unaddressed, planning and development efforts will be hijacked and geared toward specific interest groups rather than the entire community. In some cases, ideological impasses lead to perpetual conflict, which will require a detailed response.

The inventor of the conflict approach is generally recognized as Saul Alinsky, who wrote persuasive books with instructions on how the oppressed can take back power and demand justice. Alinsky's *Rules for Radicals* (1971) is often cited as his magnum opus. According to Horwitt (1989), Alinsky began his studies as a sociology student of Park and Burgess at the University of Chicago and was thus instructed in human ecology and social disorganization. Alinsky would reject this training as it failed to explain the inequalities and power dynamics that he saw as pervasive. Later, the field of sociology would agree and shift to a conflict paradigm. He was ahead of his time in this regard. Alinsky was less interested in scholarship and more interested in the act of intervening to create change—he was an applied scholar in the tradition of Jane Addams. Alinsky first actively organized industrial workers in Chicago through the Industrial Areas Foundation. By 1946, he rallied Chicago Stockyard meatpackers—the object of Upton Sinclair's novel—to walk out on their jobs to demand better working conditions. Alinsky also won these workers concessions from landlords and local government. Following these successes, he applied the same methods in other communities. He intervened in Rochester, New York, where Kodak was thought to be exploiting African American workers. A controversial figure, Alinsky had his share of critics, including his conservative foe, William F. Buckley, who acknowledged that Alinsky was an organizational genius, even if he disagreed with his ideas. Thus, in the tradition of Alinsky, the heart of the conflict approach is the act of organizing and empowering a minority group.

Broadly, a conflict arises whenever a behavior threat is rooted in a community's incompatible values, beliefs, and goals (Robinson 1989). The role of the CDS is less neutral than in the self-help approach, though both are variations on the developmental leader. A conflict approach demands that a CDS take sides with the group under duress, becoming an ally and an advocate. How this role is performed can vary. Alinsky was confrontational and often viewed as an instigator or agitator. Other community organizers perform the role more cooperatively. Former President Barack Obama worked as a community organizer, emphasizing advocacy but refraining from confrontation.

Using the conflict approach requires a particular orientation toward conflict itself. Rather than viewing it as something averse, conflict must be viewed positively. If a genuinely democratic process is functioning, there will be disagreements. Ignoring differences and feigning agreement or consensus is not genuinely democratic—it is poor conflict resolution. Learning to manage conflict can make parties feel heard and validated, making the process appear as legitimate. Robinson (1989) points out that conflict can work out dissatisfactions, lead to new norms, reveal existing power structures, determine boundaries between groups, create the opportunity for group bonding and solidarity, and reduce stagnation. Alternatively, conflicts can lead to bitterness, destruction and violence, intergroup tension, disrupt cooperation, and become a diversion from group objectives. Because of the potential negative consequences, many CDSs are reluctant to adopt the conflict approach.

Dr. Robert Moxley, emeritus professor of North Carolina State University, used the analogy of sports teams. Many teams develop bitter rivalries but relish the opportunity to compete with one another, creating intense cohesion for the competing teams' fans. While competition can turn negative, the overall experience is something that everyone wants to continue. The individual athletes learn to be team members, mitigate conflict, and defuse tense situations. Another context in which conflict is normalized is based on an adversarial model in the criminal justice system. While most crimes result in plea agreements, based on a consensus approach, when needed, litigants can have their day in court.

Robinson (1989) identifies a process for using conflict, which begins with an appraisal of local leaders and the overall power structure of the community. Next is an analysis of the situation and territory under threat. Then, dissidents are encouraged to voice their grievances, which can have therapeutic benefits. A definite problem will emerge from discussions of grievances—something singular and clearly stated that can be addressed. At this stage, coming up with a solution begins with organization. This may be informal, or it may be a formal organization with rules and business meetings. Once organized, an exercise of the group's power should be demonstrated in a small but meaningful way. As words of advice, he suggests avoiding a head-on confrontation of the power structure and a willingness to compromise. Finally, to make the change lasting, it is essential to formalize the group's organization, perhaps by becoming a registered nonprofit or nongovernmental organization. Once a formal organization is created, tackling additional projects becomes more manageable.

While the above suggestions may be helpful, there is no one way to proceed with the conflict approach. Suppose a compromise cannot be reached; there are many possible outcomes to consider. Robinson and Smutko (2011) identify five possible outcomes based on the intersection of concern shown for one's interests and those of the opposing party. A compromise is not ideal because it results from a medium concern for oneself and the other party. If a concern is high for oneself and others, the result is a collaboration or a win-win situation. This is better than a partial lose–partial lose compromise. Avoidance results from low concern for self and others and is a lose-lose outcome. In between these extremes are accommodation, which is low concern for self and high concern for the other, and competition, which is a high concern for self and low concern for the other. While ideal, it is not practical for all conflicts to end in a win-win collaboration. Sometimes issues should be avoided until a later time. Sometimes conflict with nefarious groups should remain in competition—how can there be a compromise or collaboration with a hate group, for instance?

Conflict resolution can result in negotiation, mediation, arbitration, and litigation, ranging from informal and loose to most formal and binding outcomes (Robinson and Smutko 2011). The informal and loose nature of negotiation and mediation can result in collaborative outcomes, while arbitration and litigation result in win-lose outcomes. The hope is thus to resolve conflicts through informal private negotiation or mediation. If an agreement cannot be reached, it may escalate to arbitration, which is formal and private. Litigation is public, formal, and binding, though decisions can be appealed.

## OBJECTIVES, BENCHMARKS, AND EVALUATION

Each of the three approaches to community development is interested in developing its objectives for the community, so it is crucial to track progress toward meeting them. The objectives can range from mission-critical to luxury wishes and desires. As we have studied community, the environmental demography, political economy, culture, social interaction, and the built environment have been highlighted as the core of community life. These roughly circumscribe the significant issues to consider when defining objectives. Ensuring that the community population has access to food at the bare minimum is a fundamental environmental demographic objective. Meeting the objective may mean going outside the usual channels we now associate with restaurants and grocery stores. We discussed the possibilities for locally oriented agrarian or peasant farming in rural areas, which can go a long way toward feeding the entire community. In urban areas, reclaiming parks and other natural areas for urban gardens can provide a supplement, but there is no getting around the risks of urban dependency. Assessing and removing food deserts should be considered mission-critical.

In terms of political economy, we discussed options communities have for enhancing local economic activity, drawing on the civic capitalism perspective and using community resources. Ensuring a pluralist power structure is vital for any community, and as we noted in this chapter, the community should consider a conflict approach when this is not the case. A great deal of social science research shows how the power structure is related to the economy's structure. When there is a strong foundation of independent local businesses in a community, the power structure tends to be more equitable. When global corporations are the leading employers, politics tend to be concentrated and dominated by the employer's interests. Communities should consider it mission-critical to protect themselves from the powerful grip of large companies by investing in a foundation of locally owned and operated independent businesses.

When it comes to the local culture, local communities hold the primary responsibility for telling their narrative of who they are and whence they came. Most people have some knowledge about national and world history, but there is less emphasis on learning about the local, leaving residents to lack a sense of place significance. It may seem like a superfluous luxury to develop local histories. However, the future of a community may hinge on how people are willing to view it as a meaningful place to live. Leveraging local histories for other purposes, such as enhancing tourism, can factor into the local economy but may not be as critical to the community's survival. However, rural tourism without a well-defined local history can have a negative impact. Communities should consider work related to building a local narrative as an essential objective while devising methods to do so democratically.

Objectives related to social interaction should strive toward balancing strong and weak ties or bridging and bonding social capital. Defining specific steps to promote public interaction can be tied to assessing attractor points, combined with efforts to increase the number and ease of access for these attractor points. Supporting a local library, park, recreational center, or community center can be a municipal goal. Private interests can support interaction through third places like cafés, bars, and restaurants. These objectives will be linked to those surrounding the built environment. Communities should assess their spatial layout and be on the lookout for careless sprawl, seeking ways to promote dense development—particularly in rural areas where it is tempting to allow or even encourage sprawl. The protection of natural areas and productive rural lands are both important considerations.

Regardless of which approach is taken, the process of community development is a scientific one, which means it involves collecting and analyzing data. Ideally, data collection and analysis will begin early once benchmarks for various objectives have been identified. How data are collected always depends on the kind of information sought. More objective data, such as population size, are available through such sources as the US Census. So too are data on employment, education, and commuting patterns. However, if we measure something subjective, such as local attitudes about the significance of a place, we will need to turn to survey research methods or qualitative interviews.

Evaluation research should include collecting and analyzing data related to the community's objectives, as this is the only way to know if progress is being made toward meeting the objectives. If an intervention is attempted—a job training program is started to increase employment, for example—then the data collection can be treated as an experiment. The community members going through the program can be compared to those not going through the program (control group). If those in the program were having more success finding gainful employment, we could conclude that the program was effective.

What we evaluate is also critical. We are seeking to find out if objectives are being effectively met. However, we are also considering issues like time and money invested in the development process—a cost-benefit analysis may be informative in this respect. We might also wish to evaluate the process, asking the extent to which the community was fairly represented as a cross-section of the population. Process evaluation is critical for those using the self-help and conflict approaches especially, while cost-benefit analyses or cost-effectiveness strategies are central to technical assistance.

The path to planning and development for a community may be unlike anything happening in other communities—each one is unique. Hopefully, every community will discover a way to either exercise community agency or else opt to enlist the help of a community development specialist to aid in the process. Any kind of planning and development is better than nothing, even if it is a flop. We can always learn from mistakes, but only if we take the time to reflect and try again. Hopefully, we have also learned that what may ostensibly seem like a successful outcome is a failure because the process behind the outcomes was unfair, unequal, or even oppressive.

# Conclusion

## TOWARD SUSTAINABILITY AND JUSTICE

We have reached the end of our tour, reflecting on the overall value of studying and understanding the community. Hopefully, the discussion has led to a deeper understanding of urban and rural communities and their connections to regional, national, and global urban–rural systems. We identified central concepts related to environmental demography, political economy, culture, social interaction, and the built environment. We reflected on planning insights in each chapter before considering how to implement changes through community agency or the formal process of community development. In this conclusion, we will revisit some of these critical ideas and consider how they align with broader systemwide community sustainability and justice goals.

## RECAP OF KEY IDEAS

In the introduction, we reflected on the multifaceted meaning of community while considering how community profoundly affects our experiences as individuals. Our identity is the product of a complex socialization process in our community or communities. As much as we like to think of ourselves as unique individuals, we often find we have a great deal in common with someone growing up in the same community because we share many of the same experiences. This is true for urban and rural communities, leading to urbane and rustic identities. Since the community is vital for shaping who we are, we must carefully consider the place we want to call home. It is a big commitment and one with significant consequences. The decision to move from one place to another can feel scary when we know how much is at stake.

As should be clear, it is crucial to grasp urban–rural dynamics when studying community. To grasp these dynamics, we must first understand the rich meaning of urban and rural. While generally thought of in purely demographic terms based on high (urban) or low (rural) population density, we cannot ignore the political economy, or we will miss how communities are interconnected. The concept of the urban–rural system helps us grasp these interconnections by focusing on the exchange of urban and rural products. We also must pay attention to the sociocultural dimension since a worldwide cultural hierarchy elevates urban over rural status while perpetuating an ideology of urbanormativity—the belief in the superiority of urban over rural life. For individuals, urban and rural status factors into personal identity construction, with some people identifying as more rustic or urbane, though they may not use those terms. How urban and rural become embedded in individual identity reminds us of the significant role community plays in our daily lives. The uneven political economic exchange between urban and rural areas is legitimized by the sociocultural acceptance of urban superiority and the corresponding view of rural backwardness or primitiveness. The terms of trade benefit urban populations, who are viewed as deserving. The environmental demographic dimension, which involves population and environmental considerations, results from the political economic and sociocultural since favorable urban trade and cultural status support large urban populations and shrinking rural populations, enabled by transferring rural resources to urban consumers.

Taking a distant view of urban–rural systems reminds us that other environmental demographic systems have come before. If the story of human existence were a book, urban–rural systems would be the last one or two chapters, following three or four chapters of agrarian settlement and pastoral nomadism. The first ten chapters or more would be on nomadic foraging. Modern humans and prehuman hominids long survived by directly engaging in the energy economy, consuming what was needed immediately, allowing little wealth or social inequality accumulation. Primitive communism, as defined by Marx and Engels, created a sense of mutuality among nomadic foragers, while mechanical solidarity, described by Durkheim, ensured strong social bonds. Through cooperation and collaboration, groups of humans could overcome many challenges. Foremost among them was the constant challenge of finding enough resources to support the population.

The carrying capacity limited population size, while overshoot led to Malthusian corrections. As humans settled into agrarian villages, innovations unlocked more environmental resources that would support growing populations. The development of urban–rural systems meant that fewer people were needed for cultivation, and more could become freehands. Rural communities would specialize in cultivation, and their products could be traded for more complex urban products. This agreement has been eroding as rural producers find it increasingly difficult to survive on the wages received for their work. Many of the world's rural populations have fled to cities, searching for more livable wages. The urban–rural environmental demography has thus become unsustainable, with a level of urban dependency never before seen. As urban and rural trade spans greater distances, the immediate effect of urban consumption on rural communities becomes less direct, visible, and concrete. However, the social and environmental consequences are vast. The caloric well was introduced as a method for estimating the amount of land and resources required to support a given urban population. This information can be used to inform environmental demographic planning. Urban communities can invest in their local regions by supporting local rural production efforts; rural communities can invest in the production of rural resources, both for consumption and trade with nearby urban populations. In terms of farming, this will require a strategy shift from the commodity model that pervades much of the countryside to a more sustainable form of agriculture geared toward local consumption. These efforts will ensure that communities invest in and leverage their available natural capital.

Approaching community from the perspective of local regions can restore viable intact urban–rural systems, which can be more resilient than nationalized or globalized systems. The question then becomes how to carve out a locally oriented political economy. One of the risks of local politics is the development of a power elite, who may steer the community toward initiatives that serve private interests over the general public welfare. Growth machines result when private exchange-values are given priority over public use-values. A narrow economic approach to development is partly to blame, but the local political structure is too. Creating mechanisms that ensure public input and participation in the development of their community can promote democratic pluralism. The economic logic of civic capitalism should be applied where possible to create a strong foundation of local businesses, which lessen vulnerability to shifts in national or global markets. Both urban and rural communities with a dependence on global corporations have felt the pain of a factory closure or other major economic shocks. While large companies can boost the local economy in the short term, there should be ongoing consideration of the long-term future. Supporting local sources of economic development that invest in community ties and improvements will serve the community better than temporary sources of economic growth. The social and environmental consequences of growth machines are well documented in the political economy literature. They suggest that local businesses are less likely than national or global firms to alienate and exploit workers or pollute the environment. Building a local political economy does not necessarily equate to isolationism since external national and global linkages can

be beneficial. The goal is to shield the community from the painful consequences of decision-makers residing far outside the community, ceding local
control. These efforts constitute investments and leveraging of both political
and economic capital.

Locally oriented development has an advantage over national or global initiatives—it can capitalize on the community's unique historical and cultural
legacy within the broader region. Finding ways to invest and profit from this
legacy is leveraging cultural capital. Tourism and the wider hospitality sector benefit from marketing local uniqueness by enticing visitors to come to
the community and experience what it offers. Careful planning can accommodate meaningful experiences for visitors that preserve the integrity of the
community without allowing it to be commodified or rendered generic. Rural
communities should prevent the emergence of rural simulacra that create a
generic rural experience without dignifying the legacy of the community.
Ignoring the value embedded in local historical legacy also opens the door
to gentrification efforts. Communities will want to have ongoing conversations about local identity, local culture, and local reputation. As noted earlier,
some communities become stigmatized for deviating from outsiders' expectations. The concept of a community brand may help inspire these discussions.
Research can help communities learn who they are and what puts them on the
map, while gauging their general reputation. Planning efforts should consider
historical identification and preservation high priorities since they are efforts
to invest in cultural capital.

Perhaps most vital to a community is social capital, the health of which
can be measured by social interaction through bridging and bonding ties. The
emergence of the community field depends on it. Without the community
field, there can be no planning or development efforts. So, investment and
leveraging social capital is, in some ways, the most important investment a
community can make. As long as the community engages in social interaction, there is hope for improvement even if there are widespread problems
and challenges. Investing in social capital requires planning. Communities
should research and identify the attractor points in the community, including
an inventory of third spaces. Investment should be made to ensure adequate
spaces for community members to engage in public dialogue. In addition,
planning should also be directed to mapping and reinforcing the local organizational structure. What organizations exist that promote public interaction?
If there is a deficit here, then efforts might be directed toward creating or
attracting new organizations that serve the social needs of the local community. Private businesses, such as restaurants, cafes, bookstores, and shops, can
contribute spaces for social interaction. Communities with a large commuting
class or culture of individualism will face some of the biggest challenges in
convincing residents of the value of participating in local social interaction.

The goal is to support or create a culture of being joiners, as described by Putnam (1995, 1996, 2021).

As noted, social interaction is connected to the spatial organization of the community's built environment. The built environment can be examined internally by studying the layout of the community itself. It can be examined externally to understand how the community is connected to the broader region, nation, and world. Internally, communities can focus on development patterns and consider the benefits of density as found in the nucleated pattern. To protect environmental resources for rural production or conservation, even rural communities, typically characterized by linear or dispersed settlement, should look for ways to promote nucleated development. Density is also helpful for optimizing infrastructural efficiencies. It is difficult to impossible to deliver infrastructure to a community that is sprawling.

Studying the built environment externally means focusing on community connections, spanning from regional to national and global connections. Central place functions serve as the primary mechanism for creating a hierarchy of settlements. Understanding this hierarchy can help a community comprehend how it fits the broader context. For urban communities, the process of coalescence should be monitored and managed. In the absence of natural or rural barriers between urban settlements, expanding pressures may lead to unmitigated growth and development that consumes the local environmental resources, thus undermining environmental demographic goals. Creating protected areas for farmland or natural parks can create boundaries that limit outward expansion.

## SYSTEMS-ORIENTED DEVELOPMENT VS. PROJECT-ORIENTED DEVELOPMENT

Having reviewed the systems that drive a community, we should pause to reflect on two paradigms that can govern development efforts. Unfortunately, most of what communities wind up focusing on is part of project-oriented development (POD), which is based on individual projects borne out of a narrow set of concerns (Thomas 2020). Alternatively, system-oriented development (SOD) is based on long-term trajectories in community evolution. While SOD is more likely to be successful, the nature of extra-local political economic organizations tends to favor POD. When a community approaches development from a holistic systems perspective, such as provided by the capitals framework, while considering regional urban–rural systems, then there is a greater chance of success.

When we engage in development with a system focus (SOD), we attempt to introduce changes that alter the current trajectory, hopefully achieving the intended results, but knowing there are always unexpected factors in complex systems. Small changes can lead to long-term benefits. A careful examination should follow if development fails to produce the intended outcomes. The cause may lie outside the locus of personal or community control. The key is to work toward system improvements and look warily upon isolated projects (POD) that have little bearing on systemwide goals. The next question is what principles should guide systemwide development. We will consider two goals of community sustainability and justice.

## COMMUNITY SUSTAINABILITY

The first guiding systemwide principle to consider is sustainability. The term sustainability is as multifaceted as the word community—it is widely used, though there is much disagreement about it. One of the best discussions of sustainability is offered by Edwards (2005), who approaches it from the standpoint of a social movement—the *Sustainability Revolution*. For Edwards, the concept implies a balancing act between the three "Es" of environment, economy, and equity. Lester Brown was one of the first to popularize the concept when he brought it to the United Nations in 1992. Now, the concept forms the skeleton of the Millennial Development Goals, which guide the global development efforts of the United Nations.

Community scholars have relied on the community capitals framework to inform a balanced approach to development, and it is highly compatible with a sustainability framework, which includes financial, political, natural, built, cultural, social, and human capital (Flora and Flora 2015). Indeed, these capitals were addressed throughout this book, but now proposes a new way to conceptualize them as a sustainability pyramid, as shown in figure C.1.

The capitals are arranged in a pyramid to reveal the hierarchical nature of community needs, similar to Maslow's (1943) hierarchy of needs for individuals. For Maslow, individual needs start at a basic physiological level with food, water, and rest, followed by needs for safety and security. Once these are met, higher psychological needs of belonging and esteem emerge. At the peak is self-fulfillment as self-actualization. Maslow's hierarchy shows that it takes a lot more than food and water to make a complete human being— but the higher-order needs cannot be addressed until the lower-order needs are fulfilled. The same is true for communities. The logic of the SCP begins with the basic needs of the community, which must be met before moving into higher-order needs. The peak includes human, cultural, and social capital required to make a complete community. Failing to develop a community or individual fully means they are merely existing.

# Sustainable Capitals Pyramid

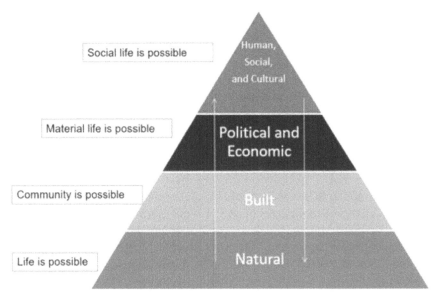

Figure C.1. The Sustainable Capitals Pyramid.
*Source*: Created by the author.

Interpreting the SCP more precisely, starting at the bottom, is natural capital associated with environmental demography. It is the foundation of any community to find a balance between population and environment. This includes an essential requirement for the local environment to be suitable for life. There must be safe drinking water sources, breathable air, and land to build and derive resources. Some natural capital can be imported, as is often the case for food, but some forms of natural capital must be regionally accessible, like freshwater. This is especially the case for farm communities that rely on water for irrigation purposes. While bottled water provides a way to import drinking water, most freshwater is used in irrigation. The sheer quantity of water used in irrigation makes importation a logistic improbability if not an impossibility. This can be avoided through the import of virtual water. When food is imported, the irrigation water used to produce it is also imported since it is embedded as virtual water. The need for environmental support is one of the most important reasons for adopting a regional approach to community planning and development. It should also sound an alarm when development is proposed in challenging environmental conditions, such as desert or tundra climatic zones.

The next layer in the SCP includes built capital. Sometimes perceived as the physical community—the buildings, roads, houses, and other built environment infrastructure are necessary to make community life possible. The necessity of built capital often becomes most visible in the wake of a disaster that temporarily or permanently destroys infrastructure. A historical review of cities in the Middle Ages would reveal the horrors of urban life without adequate built capital, where human sewage would be found in drinking water sources, where transportation routes were muddied and unsafe, and where fires were frequently found destroying homes and businesses. Higher-order rural communities may have similar vulnerabilities, but lower-order rural communities usually have very little built capital. This is one of the reasons businesses may be reluctant to locate in remote rural areas since vital supports are missing, not the least of which are internet access, paved roads, and water/ sewage treatment.

Moving up the SCP, we find political and economic capital. As we noted in our discussion of political economy, it is complicated to separate these two forms of capital. In this model, we see that communities require some kind of political organization and leadership structure, combined with economic activity that accounts for the production, distribution, and consumption of resources. Political economy is necessary to manage the built and natural capital of the community while translating them into a form that is usable for members of the population. A community may have a freshwater source (natural capital), but to turn that into water that flows to homes and businesses, and infrastructure of pipes must be planned (political capital) and funded (economic capital). While water infrastructure is a common feature in communities, we might also wonder to what extent the local political economy can manage agriculture and food production. While it may be unusual, the local political economy is responsible for ensuring that the population can obtain the means for what they need, which usually means jobs that provide income and the ability to provide input on critical political decisions.

For many communities, having a functioning political economy is the extent of planning. However, as we see in the SCP, there is still another layer associated with human, social, and cultural capital. The political economy creates a physical community, but the peak is where the heart and soul of the community may be found. As we have observed throughout the book, social interaction is the lifeblood of a community. When community development specialists focus on improvements, this entails creating more opportunities for social interaction between and within groups. Building social capital is investing in the development of the community. However, social interaction benefits greatly from safe, healthy, and educated individuals—the essence of human capital. There are specific infrastructures to support human capital, including schools, health care facilities, and public safety. Social interaction cannot flourish in a population of individuals who are fearful of leaving their homes because of crime or health threats. Education ensures that social interaction is informed, leading to improvements in all of the other capitals. Finally, cultural capital is the community's identity, history, legacy, and reputation. Preserving cultural capital in a community is like preserving the sense of self in an individual—one can survive without it but will find less meaning or purpose in life. Instead of an individual asking, "who am I?" the community asks, "who are we?"

## COMMUNITY JUSTICE

In addition to sustainability, a second worthy systemwide goal is community justice. We can think of justice as internal dynamics between groups and as external dynamics between communities within the urban–rural system. First, we must consider the meaning of justice. Rather than provide a complete review here, the reader is referred to Fulkerson and Thomas (2019), where the utilitarian approach is considered relative to Rawlsian justice and the perspective of Amartya Sen (2000) and his notion of "development as freedom." Sen's notion of justice revolves around the principle of maximizing capabilities. Poverty, for Sen, is defined as capability deprivation—when one cannot realize their capabilities to achieve the things in life they desire. Built into Sen's justice is equity since the goal is to maximize capabilities for all, not just the majority, as we would find in a utilitarian approach. While utilitarian philosophy tolerates the denial of a minority group for the greater good, development as freedom does not. We can thus apply Sen's approach to both the inner workings of the community and the external connections between communities.

Internally, as urban–rural scholars have observed, heterogeneity and diversity can vary substantially from one community to another. While many equate rural communities with homogeneous populations, the reality on the ground is far more complex. While there are such rural communities that match the ideal type considered by Tönnies and Durkheim for their gemeinschaft and mechanical solidarity, rural communities are incredibly diverse, particularly when they welcome new immigrant groups. Such communities will also vary in how bridging ties come to be formed between existing groups and new arrivals. Urbanormative stereotypes generally expect intolerance and hostility to emerge in such encounters, and some communities may fit the stereotype, but other rural communities do not. This is the problem with stereotypes—even if they possess a grain of truth, they overgeneralize.

In her documentary case study of Fleishmann's, New York, Jessica Vecchione (2009) found a depressed and largely abandoned rural community reinvigorated by new Mexican immigrants' energy and enterprising spirit. A previously boarded-up business district saw the opening of a new restaurant (La Cabaña) and store or tienda (Mi Lupita). Older residents were generally thrilled to see the downtown coming back to life. While there was conflict, with youth being teased for cultural differences, the overall level of acceptance led to a balance of bonding and bridging ties. When disaster struck, and a fire destroyed the new restaurant, community members turned out to help rebuild it. This level of community agency is only possible when the right balance of entrepreneurial social infrastructure (ESI) is in place and there is a robust and inclusive community field.

Urban communities are often lauded as bastions of diversity, which is often well-deserved. Nevertheless, just as rural communities vary in efforts to forge bridging ties between groups, so too do urban communities. Diversity alone does not lead to inclusion or equity. Many urban communities are balkanized, with separate disconnected groups residing in different spatial sectors of the city, with few to no bridging ties. In some cases, as we witnessed in the 1950s and '60s, several cities watched as white populations fled to the exclusionary suburbs, creating intensified racial and ethnic divides. Residential segregation led to inequities, from access to recreational facilities to disparate public schools. In *The Sum of Us*, author Heather McGhee (2021) relays a story about a swimming pool in the Baltimore area that was shut down because white residents refused to share the pool with black children—a pattern repeated in several towns throughout the United States following desegregation. McGhee aptly points out that in closing the pool, the white residents were also denying themselves an amenity as much as their black neighbors. It was a lose-lose outcome. The painfulness of this result lies in how it could have been avoided—if, instead of reinforcing factionalism, efforts were made to develop bridging ties, then it could have effortlessly become a win-win.

However, not all injustices occur within communities—we must also look at the space between. When we examined urban–rural systems, we moved from isolated regions to situations with several intact regional urban–rural systems. We wound up with nonregional detached urban–rural systems. The world urban–rural system is comprised of this latter network of detached rural communities producing natural resources, which are sold and exported to urban communities for processing or consumption on the global market. Global commodity chains often coordinate the activities of multiple urban and rural communities, which reside across a range of nations—global production has become truly multinational. In the current arrangement, the distance between communities contributes to the indifference that is often shown for the world's rural populations. The global ideology of urbanormativity combines with epistemic distance to create moral indifference toward the hardships of rural communities (Fulkerson and Thomas 2019). Whether working as independent farmers, growing commodities to be compensated through fair trade, or working as farmworkers for giant corporate plantations, rural people have been subjected to the most challenging and dangerous conditions with the lowest pay. For instance, many of the metals used in smartphone batteries, such as cobalt, are mined by women with small children, who lower themselves into dark, unsupported holes in the ground, constantly at risk of mine collapse and radiation exposure. Banana plantation farmworkers must routinely apply pesticides to maximize yields but are often pressured to produce more quickly and therefore do not protect against contamination from the known carcinogens found in pesticides. Even the independent farmer, who avoids the horrors of corporate plantation work, must negotiate the sale of their harvest, leaving them exposed and vulnerable to market exploitation. The poverty-rate prices for global rural commodities result in an unsustainable situation for the farmer, who may ironically be under or malnourished despite bringing millions of calories worth of energy into the world economy.

Working to resolve injustices between urban and rural communities will be a complex task. However, returning to regionalized urban–rural systems decreases distance and moral indifference. It allows members of one community to see how members of neighboring communities are faring and draw connections. The urban–rural systems of von Thünen's and Christaller's times were proximate and functional. They continue to offer a workable model.

## CONCLUDING REMARKS

Thinking of urban and rural communities as complex adaptive systems that are part of broader systems—regional, national, and world systems—opens the door to studying the underlying logic. In the CAS framework, each system level has emergent qualities, so we need to avoid committing the ecological fallacy (generalizing from a high level to a lower level) or the reductionist fallacy (generalizing from a lower level to a higher level). We are mainly focused on the community level but cannot avoid thinking about the region in which communities are situated. While we can talk about different levels of systems, they are not discrete realities. They are connected in a continuous fashion. Working toward community sustainability and justice is inseparable from promoting regional sustainability and justice. The challenge is more significant if community connections are remote and abstract rather than immediate and concrete. From environmental demographics, the community's environmental needs—the energy resources it consumes—will approach sustainability only when rural production is localized regionally. Ensuring just relations between urban and rural communities will be more direct and measurable in a regional context. Building a regional urban–rural system requires the creation of bridging ties. For instance, if an urban restaurant needs particular food items, they can contract with a local farmer in a rural community to grow the requested items. This contract can be arranged before any production has begun, guaranteeing a price and quantity, which can help the restaurant estimate how much it can provide and let the farmer estimate the cost-benefit analysis of the production request. If a builder requires lumber, they can place an order with a local forester, who might send raw timber to a mill in another local community to fulfill the order. These kinds of arrangements are pragmatic and often cost-effective. In this manner, bridging ties can be forged one at a time, building a functional regional urban–rural system. In this context, individual communities will gain a level of local control and resiliency.

Notably, the goal of creating or restoring regional integrity is not predicated on severing ties to the outside world. Regions can become important national or global actors once they are capable of more significant local political economic activity. Ties between regions can be forged, which is crucial in support of tourism and hospitality and can infuse a region with external funding and resources. The danger is when external linkages dominate or erase internal linkages. Developing the sociocultural resources of communities and regions will be vital to making the region competitive as a destination. Investing in historical research can help a community and region learn about itself, providing content and form to local identity. As we observed in the Sustainability Capitals Pyramid, much of what happens in communities' social, human, and cultural aspects requires a foundation in environmental demographic and political economic systems. Hence, planning and development priorities should consider this hierarchy of community needs. At the same time, decisions about environmental demography and political economy can be reshaped by the sociocultural direction of local values, attitudes, and beliefs. Communities can and do change over time, while the dominant values of one generation may be supplanted by the different values of the next generation. Recall the process of place-structuration in which traditions become encoded in the built environment as the character. The character of a community will have consequences for political economy and environmental demography. In the end, investing in our communities will enhance our lives. Too much emphasis on individualism has undermined community. Improvements, however, are well within reach. They start at the ground level, with one person talking to another. From this beginning, others can be invited to join the conversation. Working together, neighbors can create the world they want to inhabit in their shared community.

# References

Abdullahi, A. A. & Salawu, B. "Ibn Khaldun: A Forgotten Sociologist?" *South African Review of Sociology* 43, no. 3 (2012): 24–40.

Abu-Lughod, J. L. *Before European Hegemony: The World System A.D. 1250–1350.* New York: Oxford University Press, 1991.

Alderson, A. S., and J. Beckfield. "Power and Position in the World City System." *American Journal of Sociology* 109, no. 4 (2004): 811–51.

Algaze, G. The End of Prehistory and the Uruk Period. In *The Sumerian World*, edited by Harriet Crawford, 68–95. London: Routledge, 2013.

Alinsky, S. *Rules for Radicals: A Pragmatic Primer for Realistic Radicals.* New York: Random House, 1971.

Al-Rodhan, N. R. F., and G. Stoudmann. "Definitions of Globalization: A Comprehensive Overview and a Proposed Definition." *Program on the Geopolitical Implications of Globalization and Transnational Security*. Geneva Centre for Security Policy, 2006.

Anderson, B. *Imagined Communities*. New York: Verso, 1983.

Anthony, D. W. (2010). The horse, the wheel, and language: How bronze-age riders from the Eurasian steppes shaped the modern world. Princeton University Press.

Ashwood, L., J. Canfield, M. Fairbairn, and K. De Master. "What Owns the Land: The Corporate Organization of Farmland Investment." *The Journal of Peasant Studies* 49, no. 2 (2020): 233–62.

Bauer, V. *Predictive Policing in Germany. Opportunities and Challenges of Data-Analytical Forecasting Technology in Order to Prevent Crime*. Master's thesis, 2019. http://dx.doi.org/10.13140/RG.2.2.35642.95688

Bell, C., and H. Newby. *Community Studies: An Introduction to the Sociological Study of Local Community.* London: George Allen and Lundwin, 1971.

Bellah, R. N., R. Madsen, W. M. Sullivan, S. Tipton, and A. Swidler. *The Good Ssociety*. New York: Knopf, 1991.

Bellah, R. N., R. Madsen, W. M. Sullivan, A. Swidler, and S. M. Tipton. *Habits of the Heart: Individualism and Commitment in American Life*. Berkeley: University of California Press, 1985.

Besser, T. L., Recker, N., and Agnitsch, K. (2008). The impact of economic shocks on quality of life and social capital in small towns. *Rural Sociology*, 73, 4, 580–604.

Blanchard, T., and T. L. Matthews. "The Configuration of Local Economic Power and Civic Participation in the Global Economy." *Social Forces* 84 (2006): 2241–58.

Bourdieu, P. "The Forms of Capital" (1986). *Cultural Theory: An Anthology* 1 (2011): 81–93.

———. *Distinction: A Social Critique of the Judgement of Taste.* Routledge, 2019.

Bradshaw, T. K. "The Post-Place Community: Contributions to the Debate about the Definition of Community." *Community Development* 39 (2008): 5–16.

Brehm, J., and W. Rahn. "Individual-Level Evidence for the Causes and Consequences of Social Capital." *American Journal of Political Science* 41, no. 3 (1997): 999–1023.

Brehm, J. M., B. W Eisenhauer, and R. S. Krannich. "Dimensions of Community Attachment and Their Relationship to Well-Being in the Amenity-Rich Rural West." *Rural Sociology* 69, no. 3 (2004): 405–29.

Brook, E., and D. Finn. "Working Class Images of Society and Community Studies." In *On Ideology*, Centre for Contemporary Cultural Studies. London: Hutchinson, 1978.

Brown, L. R. *Plan B 3.0: Mobilizing to Save Civilization (Substantially Revised).* W. W. Norton & Company, 2008.

Bruhn, J. G. *The Sociology of Community Connections.* (2nd edition). New York: Springer, 2011.

Bullard, R. D. *Dumping in Dixie: Race, Class, and Environmental Quality.* New York: Routledge, 2018.

Burt, R. S. *Structural Holes.* Harvard University Press, 1992.

Carolan, M. *The Sociology of Food and Agriculture.* New York: Routledge, 2016.

Carr, P. J., and M. J. Kefalas. *Hollowing Out the Middle: The Rural Brain Drain and What It Means for America.* Beacon Press, 2009.

Castells, M. *The Urban Question: A Marxist Approach.* London: Edward Arnold, 1977.

Catton Jr., W. R., and R. E. Dunlap. "A New Ecological Paradigm for Post-Exuberant Sociology." *American Behavioral Scientist* 24, no. 1 (1980): 15–47.

Catton, W. R. (1982). Overshoot: The ecological basis of revolutionary change. University of Illinois Press.

Cernenko, E. V. *The Scythians 700–300 BC.* Bloomsbury Publishing, 2012.

Chase-Dunn, C., and T. D. Hall. *Rise & Demise: Comparing World Systems.* Boulder, CO: Westview, 1997.

Ching, B. (2016). The cow college and critical rural knowledge. Pp. 111-122 in (eds., Fulkerson, G.M. & Thomas, A.R.) *Reimagining rural: Urbanormative portrayals of rural life.* Lanham, MD: Lexington Books.

Christaller, W. *Die zentralen orte in Süddeutschland (The Central Places in Southern Germany).* Gustav Fischer, Jena, 1933.

Christensen, J. A., K. Fendley, K., and J. W. Robinson, Jr. Community Development. In *Community Development in Perspective*, edited by J. A. Christensen and J. W. Robinson, Jr. (3–25). Ames, IA: Iowa State University Press, 1989.

Christensen, J. A., and J. W. Robinson, Jr. *Community Development in Perspective.* Ames, IA: Iowa State University Press, 1989.

Clements, F. E. *Plant Succession: An Analysis of the Development of Vegetation.* Carnegie Institute of Washington Publication, No. 242. Washington, DC: Carnegie Institution, 1916.

Cohen, A. P. Epilogue. In *British Subjects: An Anthropology of Britain*, edited by N. Rapport. Oxford: Berg, 2002.

Coleman, J. S. "Social Capital in the Creation of Human Capital." *American Journal of Sociology* 94 (1988): S95–S120.

Cooley, C. H. "The Theory of Transportation." *Publications of the American Economic Association* 9, no. 3 (1894): 13–148.

Dahl, R. A. *A Preface to Democratic Theory* (Expanded ed.). Chicago: University of Chicago Press, 2006.

Day, G. *Community and Everyday Life*. New York: Routledge, 2006.

Dewey, J., and Rogers, M. L. (2012). The public and its problems: An essay in political inquiry. Penn State Press.

Du Bois, W. E. B. "The Negroes of Farmville, Virginia: A Social Study." *Bulletin of the Department of Labor No 14* (January 1898): 1–38.

———. *The Philadelphia Negro: A Social Study*. University of Pennsylvania Press, 1899.

Durkheim, E. *The Division of Labor in Society*. Routledge, 2019.

Edwards, A. R. (2005). The sustainability revolution: Portrait of a paradigm shift. New Society Publishers.

Emory, M., and C. Flora. Spiraling Up: Mapping Community Transformations with Community Capitals Framework. *Community Development: Journal of the Community Development Society* 37, no. 1 (2006): 19–35.

Fear, F. A., L. Gamm, and F. Fisher, F. "The Technical Assistance Approach." In *Community Development in Perspective*, edited by J. A. Christensen and J. W. Robinson Jr. (69–88). Ames, IA: Iowa State University Press, 1989.

Flora, C. B., and J. L. Flora. *Rural Community: Legacy + Change* (5th ed.). Routledge, 2015.

Florida, R. *The Rise of the Creative Class*. Basic Books, 2019.

Foster, J. B. "Marx's Theory of Metabolic Rift: Classical Foundations for Environmental Sociology." *American Journal of Sociology* 105, no. 2 (1999): 366–405.

Frank, A. G. *The Development of Underdevelopment*. Monthly Review Press, 1966.

———. *Capitalism and Underdevelopment in Latin America*. Monthly Review Press, 1967.

Frank, A. G., and B. K. Gills. *The World System: Five Hundred Years or Five Thousand?* Routledge, 1996.

Frazer, E. (1999). The problems of communitarian politics: Unity and conflict. Oxford University Press.

Freilich, M. "Toward an Operational Definition of Community." *Rural Sociology* 28, no. 2 (1963): 117–27.

Friedmann, J. "The World City Hypothesis." *Development & Change* 17 (1986): 69–83.

Fulkerson, G.M. and Lowe, B.M. (2016). Representations of rural in popular North American television. Pp. 9–34 in (eds., Fulkerson, G.M. & Thomas, A.R.) *Reimagining rural: Urbanormative portrayals of rural life.* Lanham, MD: Lexington Books.

Fulkerson, G. M., and A. R. Thomas. *Studies in Urbanormativity: Rural Community in Urban Society.* Studies in Urban-Rural Dynamics Book Series. Lanham, MD: Lexington Books/Rowman & Littlefield, 2014.

———. *Reimagining Rural: Urbanormative Portrayals of Rural Life.* Studies in Urban–Rural Dynamics Book Series. Lanham, MD: Lexington Books/Rowman & Littlefield, 2016.

———. *Urbanormativity: Reality, Representation, and Everyday Life.* Studies in Urban–Rural Dynamics Book Series. Lanham, MD: Lexington Books/Rowman & Littlefield, 2019.

———. *Urban Dependency: The Inescapable Reality of the Energy Economy.* Studies in Urban–Rural Dynamics Book Series. Lanham, MD: Lexington Books/Rowman & Littlefield, 2021.

Fulkerson, G. M., and G. H. Thompson. "The Evolution of a Contested Concept: A Meta-Analysis of Social Capital Definitions and Trends, 1988–2006." *Sociological Inquiry* 78 (2008): 536–57.

Galbin, A. "Children's Participation in Online School: Perspectives of Children from Rural Areas." *Revista de Asistenţ* XX, no. 2 (2021): 49–56.

Galpin, C. J. *Rural Life.* New York: The Century Company, 1918.

Garkovich, L. E. "Local Organizations and Leadership in Community Development." In *Community Development in Perspective*, edited by J. A. Christensen and J. W. Robinson Jr. (196–218). Ames, IA: Iowa State University Press, 1989.

Gasteyer, S., J. Carrera. (2013). "The Coal-Corn Divide: Colliding Treadmills in Rural Community Energy Development." *Rural Sociology* 78, no. 3 (2013): 290–317.

Giddens, A. *The Constitution of Society: Outline of the Theory of Structuration.* Cambridge: Polity Press, 1984.

Gillin, J. L., and J. P. Gillin. *Cultural Sociology.* New York: MacMillan, 1948.

Gini, A. *My Job, My Self: Work and the Creation of the Modern Individual.* Routledge, 2013.

Glynn, T. J. "Psychological Sense of Community: Measurement and Application." *Human Relations* 34 (1981): 780–818.

Goffman, E. *Stigma: Notes on the Management of Spoiled Identity.* New York: Touchstone, 1963.

Granovetter, M. "The Strength of Weak Ties." *American Journal of Sociology* 78, no. 6 (1973): 1360–80.

Green, G. P. "The Self Help Approach to Community Development." In *Introduction to Community Development: Theory, Practice, and Service-Learning*, edited by J. W. Robinson Jr. and G. P. Green (71–83). Thousand Oaks, CA: Sage, 2011.

Guiffre, K. *Communities and Networks.* Malden, MA: Polity, 2013.

Hansen, V. *The Year 1,000: When Explorers Connected the World—and Globalization Began.* New York: Scribner, 2020.

Harris, C.D., and E. L. Ullman. "The Nature of Cities." *The Annals of the American Academy of Political and Social Science* 242 (1945): 7–17.

Harvey, D. *The Urban Experience*. Oxford: Blackwell, 1989.

Hawley, A. H. *Human Ecology: A Theory of Community Structure*. New York: The Ronald Press Company, 1950.

Hayden, K. *A Wonderful, Barbarous State in the Midst of Civilization: An Exploration of the Mythology of a Pariah Community*. PhD Dissertation: Northeastern University, 1997.

———. "Stigma and Place: Space, Community and the Politics of Reputation." *Studies in Symbolic Interaction* 23 (2000): 219–39.

———. "Stigma, Reputation, and Place Structuration in a Coastal New England Town." In *Studies in Urbanormativity: Rural Community in Urban Society*, edited by G. M. Fulkerson and A. R. Thomas (67–85). Lanham, MD: Lexington Books/Rowman & Littlefield, 2014.

———. *The Rural Primitive in American Popular Culture: All Too Familiar*. Studies in Urban–Rural Dynamics Book Series. Lanham, MD: Lexington Books/Rowman & Littlefield, 2021.

Hillery, G. A. "Definitions of Community: Areas of Agreement." *Rural Sociology* 20, no 2 (1955).

Horwitt, Sanford D. *Let Them Call Me Rebel: Saul Alinsky, His Life and Legacy*. New York: Alfred A. Knopf, 1989.

Hoyt, H. (1939). The structure and growth of residential neighborhoods in American cities. US Government Printing Office.

Hunter, F. *Community Power Structure: A Study of Decision Makers*. UNC Press Books, 2017.

Jamal, H. "Chrystaller Central Place Theory—Definition and Principles." (2017). Retrieved 6/1/2022 from https://aboutcivil.org/Chrystaller-Central-Place-Theory.

Jicha, K. A. (2016). Portrayals of rural people and places in reality television programming: How popular American cable series misrepresent rural realities. Pp. 35-58 in (eds., Fulkerson, G.M. & Thomas, A.R.) *Reimagining rural: Urbanormative portrayals of rural life*. Lanham, MD: Lexington Books.

Kasarda, J. D., and M. Janowitz. "Community Attachment in Mass Society." *American Sociological Review* (1974): 328–39.

Kay, J. S., Shane, J., and Heckhausen, J. (2016). High-school predictors of university achievement: Youths' self-reported relationships with parents, beliefs about success, and university aspirations. *Journal of Adolescence*, 53, 95–106.

Keller, S. *Community: Pursuing the Dream, Living the Reality*. Princeton, NJ: Princeton University Press, 2003.

Kemper, M. *Community Matters: An Exploration of Theory and Practice*. Chicago: Burnham Inc. Publishing, 2002.

Klein, B.R., Allison, K., and Harris, C.T. (2017). Immigration and violence in rural versus urban counties, 1990–2010. *The Sociological Quarterly*, 58, 2, 229–253.

Kobbé, G. Road Map of Long Island. Public Domain. (2022). Retrieved 6/1/2022 from https://mapcollections.brooklynhistory.org/map/road-map-of-long-island-published-by-gustav-kobbe/.

Krase, J. Stigmatized Places, Stigmatized People. In *Brooklyn, USA: The Fourth Largest City in America*, edited by Miller, R.S. (251–62). New York: Brooklyn College Press, 1979.

Kretzman, J., and J. McKnight. *Building Communities from the Inside Out: A Path toward Finding a Mobilizing Community's Assets*. Evanston, IL: Center for Urban Affairs and Policy Research, Northwestern University, 1993.

Kubrin, C. E. "Social Disorganization Theory: Then, Now, and in the Future." *Handbooks of Sociology and Social Research* (2009): 225–36. https://doi.org/10.1007/978-1-4419-0245-0_12.

Kuhn, T. S. *The Structure of Scientific Revolutions*. University of Chicago Press, 2012.

Lansing, J. S. "Complex Adaptive Systems." *Annual Review of Anthropology* 32 (2003): 183–204.

Laycock, K. E., and W. Caldwell. "Exploring Community Cohesion in Rural Canada Post-Extreme Weather: Planning Ahead for Unknown Stresses." *Social Indicators Research* 139, no. 1 (2018): 77–97.

Lefebvre, H. *La production de l'espace (The Production of Space)*. Paris: Anthropos, 1974.

Lenin, V. *Imperialism, the Highest Stage of Capitalism*. London: Lawrence and Wishart, 1948 (1916 original).

Lewin, K. (1939). Field theory and experiment in social psychology: Concepts and methods. *American Journal of Sociology*, 44(6), 868–896.

Lipton, M. *Transfer of Resources from Agriculture to Non-Agricultural Activities: The Case of India*. Communication 109, Institute of Development Studies, University of Sussex, 1973.

———. *Why Poor People Stay Poor: A Study of Urban Bias in World Development*. Cambridge: Harvard University Press, 1977.

_____. "Urban Bias Revisited." *Journal of Development Studies* 20, no. 3 (1984): 139–66.

Littrell, D. W., and D. Hobbs, D. "The Self-Help Approach." In *Community Development in Perspective*, edited by J. A. Christensen and J .W. Robinson Jr. (48–68). Ames, IA: Iowa State University Press, 1989.

Lobao, L., and K. Meyer. "The Great Agricultural Transition: Crisis, Change, and Social Consequences of Twentieth Century US Farming." *Annual Review of Sociology* 27, no. 1 (2001): 103–124.

Logan, J., and H. Molotch. *Urban Fortunes: The Political Economy of Place*. Berkeley, CA: University of California Press, 1987.

Luloff, A. E., and J. Bridger. "Community Agency and Local Development." *Challenges for Rural America in the Twenty-First Century* (2003): 203–213.

Lynd, R., and H. Lynd. *Middletown: A Study of American Culture*. New York: Harcourt Brace, 1929.

Lyon, L., and R. Driskell. *The Community in Urban Society*. (2nd ed.). Long Grove, IL: Waveland Press, 2012.

Lyson, T. *Civic Agriculture: Reconnecting Farm, Food and Community*. Medford, MA: Tufts University Press, 2004.

———. "Big Business and Community Welfare: Revisiting a Classic Study by C. Wright Mills and Melville Ulmer." *American Journal of Economics and Sociology* 65, no. 5 (2006): 1001–24.

Mantu, C-M. "Cucuteni–Tripolye Cultural Complex: Relations and Synchronisms with Other Contemporaneous Cultures from the Black Sea Area." *Studia Antiqua et Archaeologica*. Iași, Romania: Iași University. VII (2000): 267.

Marx, Karl. Capital, Volume III, Electric Book Company, 2000. ProQuest Ebook Central, https://ebookcentral.proquest.com/lib/oneonta/detail.action?docID=3008517.

Marx, K., and F. Engels. *The Communist Manifesto*. Trans. Samuel Moore. London: Penguin, 1967.

———. *The Economic and Philosophic Manuscripts of 1844 and the Communist Manifesto*. Prometheus Books, 2009.

Maslow, A. H.. "A Theory of Human Motivation." *Psychological Review* 50, no. 4 (1943): 370–96.

McGhee, H. *The Sum of Us: What Racism Costs Everyone and How We Can Prosper Together*. New York: One World, 2021.

McGinnis, M. V. *Bioregionalism*. New York: Routledge, 1999.

McMichael, P. *Development and Social Change*. Thousand Oaks, CA: Pine Forge Press, 2004.

McMillan, D. W., and D. M. Chavis.. "Sense of Community: A Definition and Theory." *Journal of Community Psychology* 14, no. 1 (1986): 6–23.

Michels, Robert. *Political Parties: A Sociological Study of the Oligarchical Tendencies of Modern Democracy.* Translated into English by Eden Paul and Cedar Paul. New York: The Free Press, 1915 (1911, original German source).

Mills, C. W. *The Power Elite*. New York, 1981 (1956).

Mills, C. W., and Ulmer, M. "Small Business and Civic Welfare: Report of the Smaller War Plants Corporation to the Special Committee to Study Problems of American Small Business." Document 135. US Senate, 79th Congress, 2nd Session, Feb. 13. Washington, DC: U.S. Government Printing Office, 1946.

Molotch, H. "The City as a Growth Machine: Toward a Political Economy of Place." *American Journal of Sociology* 82, no. 2 (1976): 309–32.

Molotch, H., Freudenberg, W., & Paulsen, K.E. (2000). History repeats itself, but how? City character, urban tradition, and the accomplishment of place. *American Sociological Review*, 65, 6, 791–823.

Moore, M. D., and Recker, N. L. (2017). Social capital groups and crime in urban counties. *Deviant behavior*, 38, 6, 655–667.

Nurick, R., and S. Hak. "Transnational Migration and the Involuntary Return of Undocumented Migrants across the Cambodian–Thai Border." *Journal of Ethnic and Migration Studies* 45, no. 16 (2019): 3123–40.

O'Connor, J. "Capitalism, Nature, Socialism: A Theoretical Introduction." *Capitalism, Nature, Socialism* 1, no. 1 (1988): 11–38.

Odum, E. *Fundamentals of Ecology.* Philadelphia, PA: W.B. Saunders Co., 1953.

Office of Management and Budget (OMB). 2020 Standards for Delineating Core Based Statistical Areas. (2021). Retrieved 1/10/2022 from https://www.federalregister.gov/documents/2021/07/16/2021-15159/2020-standards-for-delineating-core-based

-statistical-areas#:~:text=The%202020%20standards%2C%20which%20reflect
%20modest%20revisions%20to,and%20Micropolitan%20Statistical%20Areas
%2C%20supersede%20the%202010%20standards.

Oldenburg, R. *The Great Good Place: Cafes, Coffee Shops, Community Centers, Beauty Parlors, General Stores, Bars, Hangouts, and How They Get You through the Day.* New York: Paragon House, 1991.

Pahl, R. "The Rural Urban Continuum." *Sociologia Ruralis* 6 (1966): 299–329.

Park, R., Burgess, E. W., and McKenzie, R. D. *The City.* Chicago: University of Chicago Press, 1925.

Parsons, T. *The Social System.* Glencoe, IL: Free Press, 1951.

Prebisch, R. *The Economic Development of Latin America and Its Principal Problems.* New York: United Nations, 1950.

Putnam, R. D. "Bowling Alone: America's Declining Social Capital." *Journal of Democracy* 6, no. 1 (1995): 65–78.

———. "The Strange Disappearance of Civic America." *American Prospect* 7, no. 24 (1996): 34–48.

———. *Bowling Alone: The Collapse and Revival of American Community.* Simon and Schuster, 2000.

———. *The Upswing: How America Came Ttogether a Century Ago and How We Can Do It Again.* Simon & Schuster, 2021.

Putnam, R. D., R. Leonardi, and R. Y. Nanetti. *Making Democracy Work.* Princeton University Press, 1993.

Ratcliffe, M., C. Burd, K. Holder, and A. Fields. "Defining Rural and the U.S. Census Bureau." (2016). ACSGEO-1, U.S. Census Bureau, Washington, DC. Retrieved 1/10/2022 from https://www.census.gov/library/publications/2016/acs/acsgeo-1 .html.

Recker, N. (2013). Bonds, bridges and quality of life in small towns. *Applied research in quality of life,* 8, 1, 63–75.

Rees, W. E. "Revisiting Carrying Capacity: Area-Based Indicators of Sustainability." *Population and Environment* 17, no. 3 (1996): 195–215.

Rhodes, R. *Energy: A Human History.* Simon and Schuster, 2018.

Ritzer, G. *Classical Sociological Theory.* 2nd ed. New York, NY: The McGraw Hill Companies, Inc, 1996.

Roberts, E., and L. Townsend. "The Contribution of the Creative Economy to the Resilience of Rural Communities: Exploring Cultural and Digital Capital." *Sociologia Ruralis* 56, no. 2 (2016): 197–219. https://doi-org.oneonta.idm.oclc.org /10.1111/soru.12075

Robinson, Jr., J. W. "The Conflict Approach." In *Community Development in Perspective,* edited by J. A. Christensen and J. W. Robinson Jr. (89–116). Ames, IA: Iowa State University Press, 1989.

Robinson, Jr., J. W., and F. A. Fear. "The Technical Assistance Approach." In *Introduction to Community Development: Theory, Practice, and Service-Learning,* edited by J. W. Robinson Jr. and G. P. Green (55–70). Thousand Oaks, CA: Sage, 2011.

Robinson, Jr., J. W., and G. P. Green. *Introduction to Community Development: Theory, Practice, and Service-Learning.* Thousand Oaks, CA: Sage, 2011.

Robinson, Jr., J. W., and L. S. Smutko. "The Role of Conflict in Community Development." In *Introduction to Community Development: Theory, Practice, and Service-Learning*, edited by J. W. Robinson Jr. and G. P. Green (101–18). Thousand Oaks, CA: Sage, 2011.

Ross, M. L. "The Political Economy of the Resource Curse." *World Politics* 51, no. 2 (1999): 297–322.

Sachs, J., and A. Warner. "Natural Resource Abundance and Economic Growth." *NBER Working Paper* (5398) (1995). doi:10.3386/w5398

Samra, S., J. Crowley, and M. C. S. Fawzi. "The Right to Water in Rural Punjab: Assessing Equitable Access to Water through the Punjab Rural Water Supply and Sanitation Project." *Health and Human Rights* 13, no. 2 (2011): 1–14.

Schnaiberg, A. *The Environment: From Surplus to Scarcity.* New York: Oxford University Press, 1980.

Schwartz, G. M., and S. E. Falconer. "Rural Approaches to Social Complexity." In *Archaeological Views from the Countryside: Village Communities in Early Complex Societies.* Smithsonian Institution Press, 1994, 1–9.

Seale, E. K. and G. M. Fulkerson. "Critical Concepts for Studying Communities and Their Built Environments." In *Studies in Urbanormativity: Rural Community in Urban Society*, edited by G. M. Fulkerson and A. R. Thomas (31–42). Lanham, MD: Lexington/Rowman & Littlefield, 2014.

Seale, E. K., and C. M. Mallinson. *Rural Voices.* Studies in Urban–Rural Dynamics Book Series. Lanham, MD: Lexington Books/Rowman & Littlefield, 2018.

Sen, A. (1999). *Development as freedom.* New York: Anchor Books.

Sharp, E. H., J. Seaman, C. J. Tucker, K. T. Van Gundy, and C. J. Rebellon. "Adolescents' Future Aspirations and Expectations in the Context of a Shifting Rural Economy." *Journal of Youth & Adolescence* 49, no. 2 (2020): 534–48.

Shaw, C. R., and H. D. McKay. *Social Factors in Juvenile Delinquency: A Study of the Community, the Family, and the Gang in Relation to Delinquent Behavior, for the National Commission on Law Observance and Enforcement.* US Government Printing Office, 1931.

———. *Juvenile Delinquency and Urban Areas.* Chicago: University of Chicago Press, 1942.

Shields, R. *Places on the Margin: Alternative Geographies of Modernity.* New York: Routledge, 1991.

Shils, E. *The Intellectuals and the Powers, and Other Essays.* Chicago: University of Chicago Press, 1972.

Simmel, G. "The Metropolis and Mental Life." In *The Sociology of Georg Simmel*, edited by K. H. Wolff (404–24). New York: The Free Press, 1950.

Smith, A. *The Wealth of Nations.* New York: Modern Library, 1937 (1776).

Smith, P.J. (2014). Return to Ridgefield Corners: Cultural continuity and change in a rural community. Pp. 163-180 in (eds., Fulkerson, G.M. & Thomas, A.R.) *Studies in urbanormativity: Rural community in urban society.* Lanham, MD: Lexington Books.

Sorokin, P. *Contemporary Sociological Theories.* New York: Harper & Brothers, 1928.

Sorokin, P. A., and C. Zimmerman. *Principles of Rural-Urban Sociology.* New York: Henry Holt & Co., 1929.

Sorokin, P. A., C. Zimmerman, and C. J. Galpin. *A Systematic Sourcebook in Rural Sociology.* Minneapolis: University of Minnesota Press, 1930.

Steuart, J. "What Are the Principles Which Regulate the Distribution of Inhabitants into Farms, Hamlets, Villages, Towns, and City?" In *An Inquiry in the Principles of Political Economy, Book I,* 1767. Retrieved from: https://www.marxists.org/reference/subject/economics/steuart/book1_09.htm#ch09.

Stovall, J., J. W. Robinson Jr, A. Nylander, and R. B. Brown. "The Role of Leadership Behaviors and Structures in Community Development." In *Introduction to Community Development: Theory, Practice, and Service-Learning,* edited by J. W. Robinson Jr. and G. P. Green (141–54). Thousand Oaks, CA: Sage, 2011.

Ternes, B. *Groundwater Citizenship.* Studies in Urban–Rural Dynamics Book Series. Lanham, MD: Lexington Books/Rowman & Littlefield, 2021.

Theodori, G. (2003). The community activeness consciousness matrix. Journal of Extension, 41, 5, 1–3.

Thomas, A. R. (1998). Economic and social restructuring in a rural community. PhD Dissertation: Northeastern University.

Thomas, A. R. *Gilboa: New York's Quest for Water and the estruction of a small Town.* New York: University Press of America, 2005.

———. *The Evolution of the Ancient City: Urban Theory and the Archaeology of the Fertile Crescent.* Lanham, MD: Lexington/Rowman & Littlefield, 2010.

———. "Urbanization before Cities: Lessons for Social Theory from the Evolution of Cities." *Journal of World Systems Research* 18, no. 2 (2012): 211–35.

———. "Historic Hartwick: Reading Civic Character in a Living Landscape." In *Studies in Urbanormativity: Rural Community in Urban Society,* edited by G. M. Fulkerson and A. R. Thomas (43–66). Lanham, MD: Lexington/Rowman & Littlefield, 2014.

———. "Social Systems and Community Development: Cooperstown, New York, and Its Imitators." *Community Development* 51, no. 2 (2020): 107–22.

Thomas, A.R., Lowe, B.M., Fulkerson, G.M., & Smith P.J. (2011) *Critical Rural Theory: Structure, Space, Culture.* Lanham, MD: Lexington Books.

Thomas, A. R., and G. M. Fulkerson. *Reinventing Rural: New Realities in an Urbanizing World.* Studies in Urban–Rural Dynamics Book Series. Lanham, MD: Lexington Books/Rowman & Littlefield, 2016.

———. "What Makes Urban Life Possible? On the Historical Evolution of Urban–Rural Systems." *Comparative Sociology* 18 (2019): 595–619.

———. *City and Country: The Historical Evolution of Urban–Rural Systems.* Studies in Urban–Rural Dynamics Book Series. Lanham, MD: Lexington Books/Rowman & Littlefield, 2021.

de Tocqueville, A. *Alexis de Tocqueville on Democracy, Revolution, and Society.* University of Chicago Press, 1982.

Tolbert, C., III, M. Irwin, T. A. Lyson, and A. Nucci. "Civic Community in Small Town USA." *Rural Sociology* 67 (2002): 90–113.

Tolbert, C., III, T. A. Lyson, and M. Irwin. "Local Capitalism, Civic Engagement, and Socioeconomic Welfare." *Social Forces* 77 (1998): 401–27.

Tolnay, S. E. "The African American 'Great Migration' and Beyond." *Annual Review of Sociology* 29 (2003): 209–32.

Tönnies, F. *Community and Society (Gemeinschaft und Gesellschaft).* Translated and edited by Loomis, C. P. East Lansing: Michigan State University Press, 1957

Trinidad, J.E. (2019). Will it matter who I'm in school with? Differential influence of collective expectations on urban and rural US schools. *International Studies in Sociology of Education*, https://doi.org/10.1080/09620214.2019.1673791.

Turkle, S. *Alone Together: Why We Expect More from Technology and Less from Each Other.* Basic Books, 2017.

US Census. "Urban Areas for the 2020 Census—Proposed Criteria." (2020). Retrieved 1/10/2022 from https://www.federalregister.gov/documents/2021/02/19/2021-03412/urban-areas-for-the-2020-census-proposed-criteria.

———. "Calculating Migration Expectancy Using ACS Data." (2021). Retrieved 3/31/2022 from: https://www.census.gov/topics/population/migration/guidance/calculating-migration-expectancy.html

US Department of Agriculture (USDA). "Documentation." Economic Research Service. (2013). Retrieved 1/11/2022 from https://www.ers.usda.gov/webdocs/DataFiles/53251/ruralurbancodes2013.xls?v=2765.2.

———. "Rural–Urban Continuum Codes." Economic Research Service. (2020). Retrieved 1/10/2022 from https://www.ers.usda.gov/data-products/rural-urban-continuum-codes.aspx.

———. "Food Security and Nutrition Assistance." Economic Research Service. (2022). Retrieved 1/27/2022 from https://www.ers.usda.gov/data-products/ag-and-food-statistics-charting-the-essentials/food-security-and-nutrition-assistance/.

Vecchione, J. *Welcome to Fleishmann's (Bienvenido a Fleischmann's).* Vecc Videography, 2009.

Vidich, A., and J. Bensman. *Small Town in Mass Society: Class, Power, and Religion in a Rural Community.* Princeton University Press, 1958.

von Thünen, J.H. (1966 [1826]). *Von Thunen's isolated state: an English edition of Der isolierte Staat.* Translated by Wartenberg, C.M. & Hall, P. Oxford: Pergamon Pr.

Wackernagel, M. "Ecological Footprint and Appropriated Carrying Capacity: A Tool for Planning toward Sustainability." PhD thesis, School of Community and Regional Planning, The University of British Columbia, OCLC 41839429. Vancouver, Canada, 1994.

Wackernagel, M., and W. Rees. *Our Ecological Footprint: Reducing Human Impact on the Earth* (Vol. 9). New Society Publishers, 1998.

Wacquant, L. *Territorial Stigmatization in the Age of Advanced Marginality.* Thesis Eleven 91 (2007): 66–77.

———. *Urban Outcasts.* Cambridge, MA: Polity Press, 2008.

Walter, B. F. *How Civil Wars Start: And How to Stop Them.* Crown, 2022.

Warner, W. L., and P. S. Lunt. The Social Life of a Modern Community. Yale University Press, 1941.

Warren, R. L. *The Community in America*. Chicago: Rand McNally, 1963.

Weber, Max. *From Max Weber* (translated and edited by Gerth and Mills). New York: Free Press, 1946.

———. (1947). *Theory of social and economic organization*. Translated by A. M. Henderson and Talcott Parsons. Glencoe, IL: The Free Press.

———. *Economy and Society*. Berkeley, CA: University of California Press, 1978.

Wikimedia Commons. "Burgess Model." (2006). This file is made available under the Creative Commons CC0 1.0 Universal Public Domain Dedication. Retrieved 6/1/2022 from https://commons.m.wikimedia.org/wiki/File:Burgess_model.svg.

———. "Christaller Model 1." (2011). This file is made available under the Creative Commons CC0 1.0 Universal Public Domain Dedication. Retrieved 6/1/2022 from https://commons.m.wikimedia.org/wiki/File:Christaller_model_1.svg.

———. "The Von Thunen Model." (2014). This file is made available under the Creative Commons CC0 1.0 Universal Public Domain Dedication. Retrieved 6/1/2022 from https://commons.m.wikimedia.org/wiki/File:Von_Thunen_Model .svg.

Wilkinson, K. *The Community in Rural America*. Dog-Eared Publications (Subsidiary: Social Ecology Press), 1991.

Wilson, J. Q., and G. L. Kelling. "Broken Windows." *Atlantic Monthly* 249, no. 3 (1982): 29–38.

Wimberly, R. C., and Morris, L. V. "The Regionalization of Poverty: Assistance for the Black Belt South?" *Journal of Rural Social Sciences* 18, no. 1 (2002): 11.

Winders, B. *The Politics of Food Supply*. Yale University Press, 2009.

Wirth, L. (1938). Urbanism as a Way of Life. *American Journal of Sociology*, 44(1), 1–24.

Zukin, S. *Landscapes of Power: From Detroit to Disney World*. Berkeley, CA: University of California Press, 1993.

# Index

absolute advantage, 65–66, 76
Addams, Jane, 144, 152
Africa, 36, 42, 44, 63–64, 88, 152
agrarianism, 16, 21, 30, 33–36, 39,
    48–49, 51, 54, 60–63, 66, 94, 99,
    101, 155, 158
agriculture, 6, 26, 34–35, 46, 50–52,
    66–67, 70, 72, 100–1, 113, 133–34,
    149, 159, 164. *See also* agrarianism.
    *See also* horticulture. *See also*
    pastoralism.
alienation, 17, 58, 65–66; forms of, 66
Alinsky, Saul, 152–53
American Sociological Association
    (formerly, Society), 13
Amish, 51, 79
anomie, 5, 17, 93, 102–3
ASA/ASS. *See* American Sociological
    Association
attractor point, 121–22, 126, 141,
    145, 155, 160
authority: and environmental
    demography, 61–64; and political
    systems, 59–60; traditional, 58–61,
    64; rational–legal, 58–60, 64–65,
    146; charismatic, 58–60, 62,
    146; urban, 27

Bellah, Robert, 2, 12

bioregionalism, 139–41
blasé attitude, 80–81
Bolshevik Revolution, 59, 75
Borlaug, Norman, 46–47, 148
Bourdieu, Pierre, 7, 89
brain drain, 3
Britain, 36, 42, 63–64, 112, 135
built capital, 8–9, 39, 164. *See also* built
    environment

caloric well, 6, 16, 26, 49–50, 54, 138
carrying capacity, 16, 41, 43, 158
CAS. *See* complex adaptive systems
Castells, Manual, 12
Çatalhöyük, 34
Catton, William, R., Jr., 16, 47
central place theory, 15, 18, 128–130,
    138–39, 161
China, 36–37, 46, 62, 79, 117
Chicago School, 10, 109, 112–14, 124,
    130, 133, 144, 152
Christaller, Walter, 128–30
City and Country, 14–15
civic capitalism, 17, 58, 75–76, 78, 140,
    155, 159. *See also* economic systems
climate change, 47, 55, 109
coalescence, 18, 114, 130–31, 139, 161
Coleman, James, 7
collective framework, 5

# About the Author

**Gregory Fulkerson, PhD,** is professor and chair of Sociology at the State University of New York at Oneonta. He received his PhD from North Carolina State University with expertise in global social change and development and rural and community sociology. He is co-editor of the Studies in Urban-Rural Dynamics book series with Lexington/Rowman & Littlefield and has co-authored (with Dr. Alexander Thomas) three recent books for the series—*Urbanormativity* (2019), *Urban Dependency* (2021), and *City and Country* (2021). Each of these works incorporate ideas, theories, and analyses to help better understand and explain urban–rural systems and the interactions of population, environment, culture, and the environment. He is currently part of a multipartner regional consortium investigating the COVID-19 outbreak in central New York State.